Philosophical Perspectives on Gender in Sport and Physical Activity

There are a broad variety of sex and gender resonances in sport, from the clash of traditional ideas of femininity and athleticism represented by female athletes, to the culture of homophobia in mainstream male sport. Despite the many sociological and cultural volumes addressing these subjects, this collection is the first to focus on the philosophical writings that they have inspired. The editors have selected twelve of the most thought-provoking philosophical articles on these subjects from the past 30 years, to create a valuable and much needed resource.

Written by established experts from all over the world, the essays in this collection cover four major themes:

- Sport and the construction of the female
- Objectification and the sexualisation of sport
- Homophobia
- Sex boundaries: construction, naturalisation and opposition

The book gathers a broad range of philosophical viewpoints on gender in sport into one unique source, subjecting the philosophical origins and characteristics of some of the most controversial topics in sport to rigorous scrutiny. With a balance of male and female contributors from both sides of the Atlantic, and a comprehensive introduction and postscript to contextualise the source material, *Philosophical Perspectives on Gender in Sport and Physical Activity* is essential reading for all students of the philosophy of sport, sport and gender, and feminist philosophy.

Paul Davis is a Teaching Fellow at the University of Abertay, Dundee. He has had numerous articles published in the *Journal of the Philosophy of Sport*, as well as having written an introductory text on metaethics. His background is in philosophy, including the philosophy of sport.

Charlene Weaving is an Assistant Professor in the Human Kinetics Department at St. Francis Xavier University, Nova Scotia. She teaches gender and sport, Canadian sport history, qualitative research methods and an advanced Olympic Games course. Her current research interests include philosophical analysis of gender, sport, an

Philosophical Perspectives on Gender in Sport and Physical Activity

Edited by Paul Davis
and Charlene Weaving

Routledge
Taylor & Francis Group

LONDON AND NEW YORK

First published 2010
by Routledge
2 Park Square, Milton Park, Abingdon, Oxon, OX14 4RN

Simultaneously published in the USA and Canada
by Routledge
270 Madison Avenue, New York, NY 10016

Routledge is an imprint of the Taylor & Francis Group, an Informa business

Typeset in Sabon and Gill Sans
by Keystroke, Tettenhall, Wolverhampton
Printed and bound in Great Britain
by TJ International Ltd, Padstow, Cornwall

British Library Cataloguing in Publication Data
A catalogue record for this book is available from the British Library

Library of Congress Cataloging-in-Publication Data
Philosophical perspectives on gender in sports / edited by Paul Davis and
Charlene Weaving.
p. cm.
1. Sports for women. 2. Sports for women--Philosophy. 3. Sports for
women—Social aspects. 4. Sports for women—Cross-cultural studies.
5. Gender identity. I. Davis, Paul. II. Weaving, Charlene.
GV709.P45 2010
796.082–dc22
2009017151

ISBN 10: 0–415–47661–5 (hbk)
ISBN 10: 0–415–47662–3 (pbk)

ISBN 13: 978–0–415–47661–4 (hbk)
ISBN 13: 978–0–415–47662–1 (pbk)

We dedicate this anthology to Jane English (1947–1978), philosopher and sport adventurer who strived to stimulate philosophical argumentation on gender and sport.

Contents

Preface

There is a voluminous body of literature on the fascinating set of philosophical questions connected to sex and gender in sport. We felt, however, that there was a gap to be filled by an anthology such as this one. There is no comparable Anglo-American anthology. Nor is there any obviously comparable text that is not about specifically men or women. This anthology does not privilege either men or women (for instance, the fourth section, on homophobia, considers phobic attitudes towards gay men and lesbians).

We hope that the book will have several benefits. We imagine that it will function as a text for students who wish for some feel of the landscape. We envisage, too, that it will be welcome to some that already have some knowledge of the landscape and would like a text providing thematised sets of stimulating essays. And we hope it will be welcomed by a broader public receptive to the issues.

We don't pretend that discipline boundaries are not fuzzy, and we acknowledge that some contributions come from what is, formally, sport sociology. However, we believe that one ground of the book's uniqueness is its philosophical flavour. First, many of the contributors are or were practising sport philosophers, and one – Iris Marion Young – is a luminary of feminist theory. And second, contributions from, for instance, sociology of sport, are there only because of their philosophical purchase within the sections they inhabit, a purchase not fully appreciable without reading the other essays in their respective sections.

Sport's ever-expanding scale as a cultural phenomenon allows it to luminously showcase major anxieties and controversies of the era. It might be, as we have been counselled for some time now, that old and once serviceable social paradigms of (for instance) sex, gender, sexuality, agency, humanity, and even sport itself are being tested to breaking point. If so, then the topics of this anthology are liable to ring increasingly urgent, making sport's well-documented political and ideological evasiveness unsustainable.

We trust that this anthology not only articulates some tricky challenges, but also offers some tools with which to meet them.

Paul Davis
University of Abertay, Dundee
Scotland

Charlene Weaving
St. Francis Xavier University
Antigonish
Nova Scotia
Canada

Acknowledgements

The articles collected here have been published already, with the exception of Chapter 6, and Chapter 3 is slightly revised.

We thank Bill Morgan for kindly allowing us to reprint Chapter 1; *Feminist Studies* for the reprint of Chapters 2 and 10; Routledge for allowing us to reprint Chapter 3; Human Kinetics for allowing us to reprint Chapters 4 and 7; Carolyn McLeod and the *Canadian Journal of Philosophy* to reprint Chapter 5; Rebecca Ann Lock for the reprint of Chapter 8; Andrew Fiala, editor of *Philosophy in the Contemporary World,* for allowing us to reprint Chapter 9; Brian Pronger for the reprint of Chapter 11, and Eric Anderson for allowing us to reprint Chapter 12.

We would like to thank Simon Whitmore, Samantha Grant, Brian Guerin and Mike McNamee, all of whom provided important guidance and encouragement. And we would also like to thank Maggie Lindsey-Jones, Graham Bradbury, and Emma Wood for their invaluable work in the production of this book.

Introduction

Paul Davis and Charlene Weaving

Feminism is a potent influence on the current intellectual, social, and cultural landscape, and the most identifiable contributor to the hotchpotch of conceptual, sociological, and normative questions concerning sex, gender, and sexuality. Yet it has had remarkably little to say about sport. Feminist philosophers and sociologists of sport have thought this a blind spot of considerable significance, for at least three (overlapping) reasons. First, sport is a site for the reproduction of masculine character qualities esteemed in patriarchal society and critiqued in feminism. These qualities include aggression, competition, instrumental (goal-directed) rationality, the repression of pain, and the repression of emotion. Success in sport is success at masculinity. If feminism's critique of masculinist culture is to approach completion, then it needs to reckon with a massive social practice that celebrates masculine character qualities. Second, as Young argues in the first essay of this anthology, the historical exclusion of women from sport has considerable conceptual and existential ramifications. Sport celebrates the human as body-subject, therefore its historical exclusion of women reinforces the female human as body-*object*. Third, sport is, perhaps by historical accident, a site for the reinforcement of social attitudes challenged by feminists and others. These include notions of what it is to be an authentic man or woman, and related hostility towards gays and lesbians. Gay men are lesser men, girlish and therefore trespassers upon sport. Lesbians are lesser women, mannish and perhaps fit for sport, but not fit to be women.

The preceding qualities and consequences of sport allow it to showcase debates within feminism. What, if any, is the proper feminist vision? Is it, for instance, sameness or difference, humanist or gynocentric? And what are its consequences for sport? Are masculine norms fine, except for the fact that women are excluded or impeded from what these norms promote? If so, then the vision for sport might be one in which women are granted full and equal participation in a practice that otherwise is unchanged. Or it might in fact be one in which sport is unchanged except for the fact that women and men generally compete alongside and against each other in 'sex-blind' competition? Or is some version of the 'Different but Equal' doctrine correct? If so, then women and men might legitimately seek different but equally prestigious goods within sporting practice. This might manifest itself in doing different sports, or in doing the same sports with (say) different attitudes or priorities. Or is the species of bodily subjectivity and attendant character qualities elevated in sport misplaced through and through? For instance, is the emphasis on speed, strength, and power, and perhaps the attitudes that typically accompany these, in need of overhaul? If so, then *both* women and men should be doing sport very differently from how the dominant paradigm prescribes. Do we need a new gender paradigm that detaches biological maleness and femaleness from the respective cultural pressures of masculinity and femininity? Should we *abolish* gender altogether? What would be the consequences for sport? And biological sex: does it yield an innocuous distinction? What exactly is it and what is its significance, in life in general and in sport in particular?

Despite feminism's general neglect of sport, philosophers and sociologists of sport have generated a formidable body of literature on topics such as those above. This anthology seeks, not to adjudicate between the myriad feminisms, but to provide an appetising set of readings from the philosophy and sociology of sport in the area of sex and gender.

The first section is a diffuse discussion that reflects how women and participation in sport have been conceptually, existentially, and culturally antithetical. Women's historical exclusion from sport in turn reinforces the antithesis, providing a potent illustration of the mutual reinforcement of ideology and practice. The first essay, by Iris Marion Young, takes off from the notion that sport is a celebration of the body-subject. Since sport features the application of bodily capacities to contrived problems, it celebrates human bodily capacities for their own sake. Masculinist culture, however, defines women as the body-*object*, that is, sexy, passive flesh sunk in upon itself. The sense of incompatibility between women and sport is therefore a conceptual and symbolic necessity. Women frequently take up their identities as body-objects, regarding their bodies as 'mannequins to be pruned, shaped, dressed, and painted.' This makes women in turn less enthusiastic body-subjects, and therefore less inclined to challenge their bodies in sport. Young believes that such differential access to physical power contributes significantly to the social power men have over women. Furthermore, since sport symbolises human freedom through its non-instrumental ('autotelic') transformation of nature, the exclusion of women from sport implies their exclusion from the idea of human freedom, providing a rare instance in which the equation of humanity with masculinity is explicit. This equation is tacitly and potently reinforced in the fact that the most popular and prestigious sports centralise qualities, such as speed and power, in which men generally excel over women, and in the fact that they tend to be conducted with hypermasculine doses of aggression, competitiveness, and pressure.

Young's vision of a redeemed sport is, like her broader feminist vision, gynocentric. The present ethos of sport not only diminishes women, but also distorts sport and men. Young invokes Duquin's humanising prescription of androgyny, which involves the practical and symbolic incorporation into sport of feminine virtues such as expressiveness and grace, alongside a cessation of sport's pathological masculine excesses. This requires new sports and a liberalisation of the concept of sport.

Part 1's second essay, by Elizabeth Spelman, does not deal explicitly with sport. But it provides important thematic continuities with the first and third essays. Spelman queries the disparagement of women characteristic of Western philosophy since Plato. She accounts for it in terms of three assumptions. The first is mind/body dualism. Mind and body are irreducibly different. No mind is physical and no body is mental. The second is the epistemological, ontological, moral, and aesthetic primacy of the mental. The body is an unreliable inlet of knowledge, less real than the mind, liable to morally corrupt the mind (or 'soul'), and liable to distort one's aesthetic judgement. For Spelman, Plato's soul/body distinction is effectively a distinction between the rational and irrational (although she recognises that Plato attributes an irrational *part* to the soul). The third assumption is the identification of women with the body. Spelman concludes that misogyny results from Plato's belief that women's lives are essentially *body-directed*. For Plato, women exemplify the dysfunctional soul/body relationship, in (for instance) hysterical fear of death, boasts, conceits, grief, lamentations, and vulgar love.

There is a good deal more to Spelman's essay, naturally. But it suffices to note here that the fearsome legacy of the Platonic outlook extends far beyond philosophy, and further accounts for the historical exclusion of women from sport. Sport features, as Young says, the body-*subject par excellence*. It is the unity of the rational and corporeal, a disciplining of the body by a freedom that transcends the bodily needs and perturbations that allegedly define the female. (For Plato, the point of doing sport is the health of the soul.) As creatures allegedly deficient in the transcendence required for sport, females do not make convincing participants.

A feminist dilemma might, again, arise. Do women accept the terms of the game and try to show that they have the mental qualities historically withheld from them? Or do they propose a new paradigm that rejects the Platonic mind/body dualism and accompanying disparagement of the body? Spelman sees feminist luminaries De Beauvoir and Friedan as exponents of the former approach, but aligns herself with the latter. She invokes Rich in suggesting, for instance, that 'the point of "natural childbirth" should be thought of not as enduring pain, but as having an active physical experience – a distinction we recognize as crucial for understanding, for example, the pleasure in athletics'.

The section's final essay, by Angela Schneider, swiftly notes that it has been thought, from the time of the ancient Olympics, that sport is incompatible with what women are or should be. Ideals of sport and women underlie the constellation of discussions about women's involvement in sport.

Schneider observes, first, that the desirable characteristics of a woman's body at the time of the ancient Olympics are softness, grace, weakness, and beauty, desiredata which have not disappeared. Second, the desirable female qualities in the same period are, largely, beauty, chastity, modesty, obedience, discretion, and being a good wife and mother. The traditional ideal athlete is very close to the ideal man, converging upon the role of *warrior*. These antithetical ideals – illustrated in the history of female competitive body-building – underlie what Schneider sees as the morally troubling paternalism to which women in sport have been subject. Women have often been excluded from sport on the ground that participation would be bad for them. Schneider argues that, even if true, women should, as competent adults, be allowed to choose. She also shows, relatedly, that the ideology of female reproductive processes makes it very difficult for women in the sport milieu to 'win', ideologically.

Schneider notes the putative limitations in the application of a sameness/difference discourse to sport, and proposes that the key conundrum here might be the gender-independent one of two conflicting *ideals of sport*. However, she regards Tannsjo's radical proposal of sex-blind competition insupportable in the world we inhabit.

Separate women's events means, in turn, gender verification, begging the question of what makes a woman a woman. There is, Schneider concludes, no non-contingent answer, and no obvious reason why one criterion should decide.

Schneider's vision for women in sport adapts Tong's bioethics methodology, characterised by the rejection of ideologically spun 'facts', female consciousness-raising, and a form of discourse ethics.

The first section offers some explanation of the historical belief that serious sport and real women are incompatible. The solution might seem obvious: greater numbers of women who visibly impress in the prestigious, masculine sports. The second section illustrates the inadequacy of this solution. The ideology of female as body-object is sufficiently potent to inscribe such oppositional moments tacitly from within. Even successful female participation in masculine sports admits of ideological reconfiguration that reinforces women's status as body-objects. The most obvious device is the presentational and discursive eclipse of athletic status by sexual appeal. This section goes deeper into the notion and practice of objectification from within the discourse and imagery of sport. The first piece in Part 2, Davis's 'Sexualization and sexuality in sport', examines the difference between sexualisation and sexuality and the connection with women athletes, providing an important theoretical step in the examination of sexualisation. Davis holds that there is nothing inherently wrong in perceiving women athletes as sexual beings. The problem arises when women athletes are sexualised in the media. Davis sees sexualisation in the presence of any of three properties: (i) the deliberate focus on particular, sexually significant body parts for the purpose of titillation; (ii) the attunement to bodily postures that, through freezing or emphasis, are intended to be sexually titillating; and (iii) in the case of photographs in either of the preceding categories, an accompanying, frequently punned caption that confirms the moment as one of sexualised comic relief (page 57). Davis's argument is illustrated in the case of women's beach volleyball (not Davis's example). In the 2000 (Sydney) Olympics, North American newspaper coverage typically depicted the Olympians in highly sexualising positions. For example, the main focus of the image was often the player's backside or crotch area. The captions below signified the sexual meaning of the scene; for example, 'buns of gold, silver and bronze'.

In the second article, McLeod takes a different approach from Davis. She acknowledges the full range of objectification in the lives of women and argues that we need a theory showing how objectification can come in degrees. For McLeod, we need to be able to say that women can be both bosom and legitimate job candidate. The parallel in our subject area is the facility to see women as both bosom and legitimate athlete. There are cases where one desires to be viewed as not just a tennis player. Conversely, there are cases when one's tennis ability should be the sole focus of attention, in competition for example.

McLeod's arguments reverberate within the discussion over the increasing trend of women athletes to pose nude. For instance, can an elite Olympian pose nude in *Playboy*, and the following month compete and be admired and respected for her athletic ability? Or does our hypersexualised view of the female body prevent us from perceiving women athletes as athletes first and bosoms second? In a culture that historically reduces the female to sexual object, does nude female posing doom the poser to a totalising sexual objectification, regardless of her other modes of public presentation? If not, what contextual backdrop would distinguish the totally sexually objectified nude poser from she who is not so completely objectified (and who can therefore be defined in another context as something else, e.g. athlete)? McLeod leans on the work of Martha Nussbaum and offers an auto-biographical demonstration that women can be sexually objectified *and* powerful. As a teenager, she took part in a tennis competition. A picture from her performance appeared next day in a local newspaper. It was a crotch shot, which some males taped up in the locker room of the local factory plant.

In the final essay of Part 2, Charlene Weaving argues that discursive interdependencies between sport and heterosexual sex sponsor the mas-culinist subordination of women in sport and in the rest of life. She adduces examples from sport hunting, mountaineering, and the promotion of a women's squash tournament, alongside recognition of the 'male pussy' and of descriptions of heterosexual sex typically used by males. The messages inscribed within these cases are that women are passive, weak, harm-apt, and totalised within their (hetero) sexuality, and that the female position in heterosexual sex is one of passivity, manipulation, deception, and *harm*. This conception of the female is singularly incompatible with the female athlete. Therefore, ideological tension is inscribed within the concept of the female athlete.

One of the most explicit sites, historically, for the reinforcement of the preceding masculinist discourses is that of male rugby culture. Weaving provides some acknowledgement and illustration, before considering the putatively oppositional subculture of female rugby. She finally rejects its oppositional credentials, on the ground that its counter-orthodox inversions replicate the sex-harm logic of masculinist culture. Genuine female empowerment, she concludes, resides in the cessation of the sex-harm discourse. This would, in turn, weaken the ideological conflict of the female athlete, and the broader sexism in which this conflict figures.

We noted that Schneider's essay, in Part 1, acknowledges the tricky question of what it is to be female. Part 3 goes deeper into this and adjacent territory. Many studies of bodybuilding argue that it either challenges or reinforces gender and sexual norms. Saltman's 'Men with breasts' argues that it is not wholly on either side. Saltman acknowledges that it reinforces these norms, alongside, more broadly, patriarchy (and capitalism). Yet he stresses bodybuilding's transformative dimensions. In bodybuilding, men become 'real' men, true. But they also become women. They develop conspicuous breasts, and they engage in feminine disciplinary regimes in preparation for pageantry; for example, preening and primping. The bodies of female bodybuilders, similarly, become hard to distinguish from men's. Bodybuilding demonstrates that the 'real man' and 'real woman' are artifices that can be attached and dismantled like prostheses. Indeed, at the hyper-masculine limit, a new, asexual gender, available to both male and female bodybuilders, is created. Yet female bodybuilding also reconfigures the feminine as dominant and self-sufficient, yielding new forms of identification and sexual desire. Saltman proposes, indeed, that objectification admits of emancipatory effects for the female bodybuilder. Whether Saltman has a sufficiently clear, discriminate, or persuasive conception of sexual objectification is not obvious, however. It might be conceptually helpful to recognise emancipatory possibilities in female bodybuilding, but resist their attachment to objectification.

In the section's second essay, Rebecca Lock proposes a partial critique of the popular distaste of doping. She acknowledges that a plurality of narratives and values is relevant. However, she finds the normative power of Butler's (1990) 'heterosexual matrix' particularly worthy of recognition. She believes, moreover, that a key element of it has not been adequately recognised in the literature to date. The heterosexual matrix is the tacit ontological aggregation of sex, gender, heterosexual femininity, and appearance. Lock believes that it is the heterosexual imperative that has not been adequately recognised hitherto. Being female (itself a socially constructed category) is causally connected, through acculturation, to the performance of femininity. The less feminine woman is the less authentic woman. However, heterosexuality is, in turn, constitutive of femininity. To be feminine is to be heterosexual. The lesbian or bisexual is *ipso facto* less feminine, and therefore less of a woman. And the identifying marker, socially, of heterosexuality, is appearance. The more heterosexually attractive one is, the better is one's performance at (heterosexual) femininity, and therefore the more convincing is one's pitch at being a woman.

The root social crime of the typical female doper, argues Lock, is her poor performance at heterosexual femininity. The typical female doper is untypically muscular, and is liable to (for instance) facial hair. These qualities are regarded heterosexually unattractive, resulting in attributions of ugliness, masculinity, and lesbianism. Lock supports her diagnosis with a broader social reflection and with illustrations from sport. The broader social reflection is that the hostility suffered by the typical female doper is continuous with that suffered by non-doping women who fail to meet the demands of heterosexual femininity. Any woman who is muscular or has facial hair, for instance, is liable to be derogated as ugly, masculine, or lesbian. Therefore, it is *this* – not doping – that is the actual crime of the typical female doper. And Lock's illustrations from sport are compelling. On the one hand, (lesbian) Martina Navratilova did not dope, but was scorned as a doper would have been, on account of her failure at heterosexual femininity. And the discourses of 'Flo Jo' (accused of doping) and Katrin Krabbe (tested positive), on the other hand, each demonstrate that heterosexual legitimacy can finally trump the fierce obloquy that is otherwise the fate of the female doper.

In the final essay of Part 3, Michael Burke echoes some of the insights of earlier contributors. However, Burke's radical offering supersedes the others in its recommendation that female athletes transgress drugs policy as a gender political démarche.

Burke details several, overlapping elements of the social psychology that inscribes sport at the level of policy and ideological practice. One is the fiction of naturally fixed sex boundaries. These must be maintained, and in turn require the appropriate sexing of bodies. And appropriate body sexing is required to sustain the belief that males are superior at sport, and in turn superior *tout court*.

This social psychology manifests itself in segregation, 'emphasised femininity', and drug laws. Most sport is played in single-sexed categories, and it is when female performance reveals gender overlap that men are most precious about segregation. Women in sport famously respond to the sport-female ideological antithesis with counterpunches such as make-up and feminine kit, and the female bodybuilder is even reconfigured so as to preserve femininity. And, finally, rigid gendering of bodies is a strong motivation for the drugs ban.

If men won't play with women, then women can radicalise their sport space to significant political effect. Key to Burke's prescription is the notion of the cyborg. Cyborg political intervention involves, in Burke's words, 'the production of counter-discourses of subversion and transformation from a variety of dissatisfied subject positions'. Cyborg feminist intervention could be particularly necessary in sport, to elevate women to positions of discursive authority. It could usefully involve the explicit refusal of emphasised femininity, and with it the patriarchal drugs ban. Patriarchal limitations on female performances and embodiments would therefore diminish, and with them some previous, broader limitations upon female horizons.

Part 4 is a set of essays on sport's homophobia. Two are focused on gay men and one on lesbian women. The much-ballyhooed shifting sexual agendas have not made much inroad into locker-room attitudes. One of the best insults to male athletes, as Weaving notes (see above), is to refer to them as female or to associate them with female sex organs. It is thus apparent that women are viewed as weaker athletes, not as capable as their male counterparts. Homosexual male athletes are considered weaker because they too are associated with the female. The first reading, Cahn's 'From the "muscle moll" to the "butch" ballplayer: mannishness, lesbianism, and homophobia in U.S. women's sports', describes the lesbian identity associated with women's sport. The article focuses on the 'mannish' lesbian athletes, and examines the lived experience of the mid-twentieth century lesbian athletes. It is argued that in sports such as softball, strategies were put in place to emphasise heterosexuality and suppress so-called 'mannishness'. Cahn sees the post-Wold War II era as heavily implicated in the creation of hostility towards mannishness, female homosexuality, and athletes suspected as lesbian. This climate meant that any woman participating in activities not believed to be ideal feminine pursuits was coined mannish and/or lesbian. Indeed, wearing one's hair short was sufficient ground for indictment. Cahn's article is a key sociohistorical account that facilitates better understanding of the current homophobic climate in sport.

Pronger's 'Outta my endzone: sport and the territorial anus' provides an analysis of postmodern, gay and queer theories. He draws parallels between the phallic penis, the territorial anus and highly competitive elite sport. It is argued that competitive sport is a social form that involves the capacity of bodies to connect. Pronger suggests that competitive sport is masculinising and believes this is why some women have been discouraged from participating. Using a Foucauldian approach, Pronger concludes that homoeroticism plays a major role in augmenting homophobic sentiments. Men's sport allows males to exclude women from certain all-male environments, permits them to play with each other's bodies and to see each other naked in the showers and in locker rooms, and to enjoy this all-male contact. Pronger argues that competitive sport surrounds itself with a construction of desire. This is, arguably, not unique to sport. It might be common to most business, academic, and sexual practice. This desire, Pronger argues, parallels phallo-centric homophobic sexual desire. Phallocentrism is considered to parallel sexism and racism, territorialising the body and organising it into parts in a concrete simulation of the phallic enterprise.

Pronger's essay is intriguing and proposes a very radical view of competitive sport for males. Yet Pronger stresses that masculine desire is not restricted to males, even though it is expected of them; females can possess masculine desire in sport, but they are discouraged from producing desire so assertively and protectively.

In the final reading of Part 4, 'Openly gay athletes: contesting hegemonic masculinity in a homophobic environment', Anderson examines the experiences of openly gay male team sport athletes. Contact sports are described as an arena where hegemonic masculinity is reproduced and defined. Here, male athletes learn what it is to be a man. And there is, Anderson emphasises, no universal experience of coming out on a team.

Anderson argues that gay male athletes are often viewed as a paradox because they comply with the gender script of masculinity through direct participation in sport, yet violate another masculine expectation because of their same-sex desires, and thus threaten sport as a prime site of hegemonic masculinity and masculine privilege. Using 'grounded theory', Anderson interviews gay athletes to examine how gender is produced in sport and how openly gay athletes negotiate gender. The interviews reveal that interviewees casually dismiss the routine anti-gay locker-room banter. They do not think that their teammates really mean anything by terms such as 'fag'. Anderson argues that the normalisation of homophobic dialogue in sport helps to subjugate the gay male identity as an inferior form of masculinity, and to marginalise gay athletes, with the result that they maintain segmented identities. Their identities as athletes are accepted but their identities as gay are not.

The primary goal of including two articles with a male-centred focus is to reinforce the critical point that the relevance of feminist studies and theories extends beyond women. In discussing women's positioning in sport, it is vital to consider males. Sport's homophobia impacts upon women and men equally, and is interconnected with our stereotypes and beliefs about how the sexes ought to act and be.

We realise, naturally, the limitations of the anthology, and the fact that it won't please everyone. It is twelve essays from a voluminous body of writing. Perhaps it has something of an Anglo-American bias too, since there are no contributions from Eastern philosophy, for instance. Again, we have not been able to give mileage to the commerce between gender discourses and discourses of race and class. Selection of material is not easy, and no doubt reflects our own intellectual predispositions and classroom experiences. We trust, however, that we have provided an anthology that will appeal and will in turn lure readers into further exploration.

Part I

Sport and the construction of the female

Chapter 1

The exclusion of women from sport

Conceptual and existential dimensions*

Iris Marion Young

Conceptual and normative issues about women's relation to sport have not been given nearly enough attention by either philosophers or feminists. Jane English began to take up these issues in her paper "Sex Equality in Sport."[1] This paper, which is dedicated to Jane's memory,[2] develops those issues further.

In Section I, I argue that insofar as our culture defines woman's body as object, the culture necessarily excludes women from its concept of sport. In Section II, I discuss the institutional and practical exclusion of women from sport in our society. Section III argues that insofar as our culture excludes women from both the idea and reality of sport, it excludes us from full participation in humanity itself. Hence inclusion of women in both the idea and institutions of sport is a fundamental condition of women's liberation. Finally, in Section IV, I argue that the cultural exclusion of women from the idea and reality of sport has given sport a masculinist bias which prevents sport itself from exhibiting its potential humanity. Hence the inclusion of women in the idea and institutions of sport is a fundamental condition for the humanization of sport.

I

The most basic aspect of woman's existence in a male dominated society, according to de Beauvoir (1974), is that the symbols and institutions of the society define woman as the Other. Masculinist culture defines woman as immanence as opposed to transcendence, determinate nature as opposed to the self-chosen subject. This symbolic elaboration of woman as the Other identifies the female body as mere body-object, as opposed to the body-subject which is the man.

* Originally published as 'The exclusion of women from sport: conceptual and existential dimensions in philosophy of sport' in *Philosophy in Context*, 1979, vol. 9, pp. 44–53. © Philosophy in Context, Cleveland State University.

> The ideal of feminine beauty is variable, but certain demands remain constant; for one thing, since woman is destined to be possessed, her body must present the inert and passive qualities of an object. Virile beauty lies in the fitness of the body for action, in strength, agility, flexibility; it is the manifestation of transcendence animating a flesh that must never sink back upon itself . . . Her body is not perceived as the radiation of a subjective personality, but as a thing, sunk deeply in its own immanence; it is not of the world, it must not be the promise of things other than itself; it must end the desires it arouses (de Beauvoir 1974: 178).

There is little question that the status of women has undergone alteration in the present century, and to a large degree it has been progressive change. There has been little weakening, however, of the masculinist identification of the feminine body as object. Indeed, I believe it can be argued that the objectification of the female body in contemporary American culture is greater than that of many cultures, but I will not make that argument here. In any case, the symbolic media of contemporary society convey an image of the female body as mere flesh. Those aspects of a woman's body most gazed at and discussed, and in terms of which she herself all too often measures her own worth, are those which least suggest action – neck, breasts, buttocks, etc. Contemporary film, advertising, popular literature and periodicals, and countless other media objectify the female body as sexy, passive flesh. They use this objectification of the female body, moreover, as a means of sensualizing other objects, thus making them desirable. Finally, while norms of dress retain much of the liberality that emerged in the sixties, in recent years there has been a revival of "feminine" styles which tend to make the female body inactive, both in appearance and reality.

Now sport is a notoriously slippery concept, and I do not wish here to enter the discussion about how it should be defined.[3] Whatever else it is or is not, however, sport is the achievement of a non-utilitarian objective through engagement of bodily capacities and/or skills. In sport, at least ideally, the body is spontaneous subject and the subject is wholly embodied. The identity of body and active subjectivity reaches its paradigm in sport; the very stance, muscles, movement and directionality of the athlete exhibit directly her or his intentions and projects. To be sure, the body-subject underlies all human activity, and many activities, such as physical labor, require skill, strength, and dexterity in the use of the body's capacities. Athletic activity, however, abstracts the body's movement and accomplishment from its natural involvement in the complex web of natural and social goals; sport calls upon the body's capacities and skills merely for the sake of determining what they can achieve.

By its nature, then, sport exhibits the essential body-subject. Masculinist culture defines women, on the other hand, as the essential body-object. Thus in a culture which defines woman as Other, sport and woman are mutually exclusive concepts. This suggests that the sense of incompatibility between women and sport which still dominates in our society is not a social accident, but a conceptual and symbolic necessity. To the degree that in our society the female body is objectified, women must be excluded from the concept of sport. It follows that if there is a particular female person participating in sport, either she is not "really" a woman, or the sport she engages in is not "really" a sport. These two interpretations of the phenomenon frequently occur in our society, often together.[4]

II

Not only have women been excluded from the idea of sport, the institutions and practices of sport to a large degree still exclude women as well. The causal relationship between the cultural symbols of sport and the institutions of sport are indeed complex, and I do not wish to develop those here. I shall merely describe aspects of the exclusion of women from sport and practice.

The degree to which young girls are discouraged from engaging in physical activity, often in very subtle ways has been noted in much recent literature.[5] To a large degree the sanction on girls' physical activity does have the effect of reducing the level of physical activity of girls, especially relative to boys. There is, however, a certain girlhood culture of resistance. Many pre-adolescent girls engage in some physically challenging play such as jumping rope, roller skating, bike racing, various bouncing ball games, hop scotch, and countless other games. Our society does not take these girls' games seriously as sport, however, and by the time we reach ten or eleven we have put them away as childish things. The sort of physical play in which girls typically engage has institutional form only in the world of the girls themselves; the girls engage in their play "spontaneously" largely without the help, notice, guidance and institutionalized resources of the larger society.

Specifically what our society largely denies girls is access to the organized and institutionalized sport which it takes for granted as an essential part of the boy's childhood and adolescent environment. Boys generally play at games institutionalized in the larger society. From an early age parents, older children, teachers and coaches provide them the opportunity to develop their athletic skill in a self-conscious way. The society encourages, recognizes, develops and rewards the physical activity and achievement of boys, at the same time it discourages and often ignores that of girls.

The absence of institutionalized sport for girls and women, coupled with the active sanction against their physical activity that girls often experience, does much to develop in us a sense of ourselves as weak, frail, sedentary. Exclusion from sport as the paradigm of physical engagement with the world is not merely something that *happens* to girls, however. We also actively choose ourselves as inactive bodies.

The female person who grows up in a society which defines the female body as object rarely escapes developing a bodily self-image in conformity with that definition. As she passes through the years of adolescence she increasingly experiences the sexually objectifying gaze of men and the measuring gaze of other women which assess her in terms of her "feminine beauty." When others look upon us in this way it is difficult not to regard ourselves from the same objectifying point of view. More often than not we actively take up our identity as body-objects. We regard our bodies as mannequins to be pruned, shaped, dressed, and painted.[6] A number of psychological studies report that women have significantly higher bodily awareness than men.[7]

This body image has a definite impact on our potential for sport. In his book on sport, Paul Weiss considers the question of why women take an interest in sport less frequently than men. He answers that each sex naturally stands in a different relation to its body. Men are more abstract and intellectual than women. While women are capable of intellectual endeavors, in general, 'a woman is less abstract than a man because her mind is persistently ordered toward bodily problems' (Weiss 1969: 217). The very process of maturing, Weiss claims, brings women into natural unity with their bodies, whereas the intellectual tendency of men sets them in tension with and separated from their bodies. Men seek to engage in sport in order to resolve this tension and achieve a unity with their bodies. Women tend to be less interested in sport, because we already have this unity.

Despite the obviously sexist and mystifying character of this metaphysical appeal to male and female natures, there is a grain of truth in Weiss' explanation of why women tend to be less interested in sport than men. The reason does lie in part in the relation in which women stand to our bodies. To the degree that we choose ourselves as body-objects, we find it difficult to become enthusiastic body-subjects and frequently do not desire to challenge our bodies in sport. The mutual exclusivity of women and sport which exists at the ideal level thus enters the experience and self-definition of women themselves.

III

The major symbols and institutions of sport in our society continue by and large to exclude women. This exclusion of women from sport implies our exclusion from full participation in humanity, at both the symbolic and practical levels. Mary E. Duquin has suggested that sport symbolizes human transcendence of nature in the establishment of culture. Following Ortner, she claims that virtually all cultures associate woman with nature and man with culture (Ortner 1974). The exclusion of women from sport, then, symbolizes the exclusion of women from humanity itself as the cultural transformation of nature (Duquin 1977).

Along similar lines, Eleanor Metheny argues that sport symbolizes human freedom. She argues that sport abstracts from the constraints and requirements of the natural and social world in which we seek to enact our particular material goals. In such everyday action one must submit to the constraints of external ends, worldly resistances and unintended consequences. In sport, on the other hand, the conditions, rules and restraints, as well as the goals, are self-chosen, and one engages one's body capacities purely for the sake of showing them at their best. In this way sport serves as a symbol of freedom.[8] If sport stands in this way as a symbol of freedom, then the exclusion of women from the idea of sport implies our exclusion from the idea of human freedom.

The dominant ideology of formal equality denies the feminist claim that our society excludes women from full participation in humanity. Our exclusion from most aspects of humanity is subtle and slippery. The explicit conceptual and symbolic exclusion of women from sport, coupled with sport's symbolization of transcendence and freedom, provide us with one of those few instances in our culture where the equation of humanity with masculinity appears explicitly.

Exclusion of women from the institutions and practices of sport, moreover, has a real effect on our opportunity to develop our human capacities. The female person who defines herself and is defined by others as fragile, weak, awkward and passive, and who receives little encouragement to engage her body in physical activity, will more often than not become weak, awkward, and physically timid. As I have developed elsewhere, feminine bodily existence under these conditions is characterized by contradictory structures of bodily comportment and spatiality. Sexist society excludes us by definition and in practice from developing ourselves as free body subjects (Young 1980).

If, as Merleau-Ponty argues, the basic structures of human existence – consciousness, intentionality, purposiveness, etc. – have their foundation in the body as acting and expressing subject (Merleau-Ponty 1962), then the inhibition of women's development of our body subjectivity implies a profound inhibition of our humanity.[9] In our society athletic activity is one of the few institutionalized opportunities a person has for developing a sense of himself or herself as a vigorous, powerful, skilful, coordinated and graceful body. In contemporary advanced industrial society laboring activity, and even to an extent military activity, rely little on physical virtues of strength, agility and coordination. Thus in our society sport has a more crucial role in the founding of body subjectivity than perhaps it has had in the past. The exclusion, including the self-exclusion, of women from participation in sport thus prevents us from realizing fundamental aspects of our humanity.

From the above considerations it follows that a fundamental condition of the liberation of women is our full inclusion in both the idea and reality of sport. For the exclusion of women from sport not only deprives us of important human opportunities, it gives a fundamental advantage to men. The same society which discourages the physical development of women actively encourages man's exercise of physical strength and skill. There can be little doubt that such differential access to physical power is a significant element in the social power men have over women, as well as the social justification of this power distribution.

From several points of view, then, the call for full inclusion of women in the symbols and institutions of sport may represent a demand more fundamental and far reaching than demands for simple justice, like equal pay for equal work or shared housework, despite the importance of these other demands.[10] If the exclusion of women from the concept of sport symbolizes our exclusion from humanity itself, and if our exclusion from the institutions of sport contributes in a basic way to a sense of weakness, body-objectification and physical timidity among women, then the inclusion of women in the symbols and institutions of sport is a basic aspect of our full participation in humanity.

IV

The exclusion of women from the symbols and institutions of sport has consequences not only for the condition of women, but for the nature of sport itself. Because sport excludes women at the same time that it serves as a foundation of masculinist privilege and ideology, the masculinist bias which permeates the symbols and institutions of sport in our culture blunts and deforms its potential human significance.

English has pointed out how the very kinds of sport which exist in our society reflect this masculinist bias. The most celebrated and most practiced sports put a premium on height, mass, strength and speed – attributes in which on the average men will tend to excel over women. The sport imagination has not even begun to tap the possibilities latent in the physical capacities in which women will tend to excel over men.[11] Most of the sports played today have their origins in male experiences in sex segregated activities, such as hunting or warfare. None have arisen from the specific activities of women or from women's specific experience.

Perhaps more importantly, in contemporary society sport appears to carry the full weight of the meanings of masculinity. Most masculinist societies contain a number of institutions in which a man can show himself a "real" man, and from which women are excluded. In contemporary society, however, sport remains one of the few institutions which explicitly serves this function, and hence it is overburdened with a masculine image. Contemporary society, moreover, provides few contexts in which physical fighting among men is socially sanctioned, yet it continues to associate masculinity with being the strongest and best fighter. In this way as well sport must bear the brunt of the associations of masculinity.

Numerous writers lament the contemporary equation of sport and masculinity as distorting both sport and men. They declaim the overly aggressive character of contemporary sport, its excessively competitive character, the typical emphasis on winning at all costs, the high pressure under which (usually male) athletes work.[12] To the degree that sport and sportsmen are under high pressure in our society to "prove" themselves, to be aggressive, and pursue winning in a highly rationalized and technologized fashion, it would seem that sport presently lacks some of the freedom which Metheny claims for it.

These undesirable features of contemporary sport practices, which many writers explicitly associate with the masculinist bias of sport, stand in marked contrast to the virtues which philosophers have attributed to sport in recent years. Philosophers analyze sport as part of the aesthetic realm; sport, they argue, embodies virtues of form, rhythm, drama, beauty and grace. Just as often they claim for sport fundamental moral qualities: justice, fairness, cooperation, sense of community and so on.[13] To the degree that these accounts fail to pose the alleged virtues of sport as what sport *should* be, rather than what it is and has been, they function as ideological justifications for the institutions of sport as they presently exist.[14]

As long as sport must carry nearly the full weight of masculinist images, it cannot also realize its potentially aesthetic and moral qualities. Inclusion of women in the symbols and institutions of sport, then, is a necessary condition for the humanization of sport. Mere inclusion of women in the existing concept and institutions of sport, however, is not sufficient. Sports programs for women today frequently model themselves on and measure themselves by the standards of sports programs which have traditionally been reserved for men. There is more justice in this situation than in the exclusion of women entirely, but the masculinist bias of sport is not thereby removed.

Duquin suggests that only when sport becomes androgynous in its symbolic meaning and real content will sport have achieved its human possibilities. Androgyny in sport means for her the encorporation of virtues typically associated with women into the symbols and practice of sport – such as expressiveness and grace – along with a corresponding decline in the present overly aggressive and instrumentalist aspects of sport which are typically associated with masculinity.[15]

The mere entrance of women in sport in greater numbers – even in masculinist sport – will, in my opinion, begin to break down the masculinist meaning of sport; perhaps this process has already begun, though it is too early to tell. Both the liberation of women and the liberation of sport, however, require in addition the invention of new sports and the inclusion in our concept of sport of physical activities presently outside or on the boundaries of sport.

Notes

1 *Philosophy and Public Affairs*, 1978, vol. 7, no. 3, pp. 269–77.
2 Jane English died in 1978 while climbing the Matterhorn. In her much too short career, Jane English contributed a great deal to the development of feminist studies in philosophy. She edited two anthologies in the area, as well as publishing several

papers. Her death came as a great shock and loss to the community of women philosophers.

3 For some examples of different approaches to this problem, see Ellen Gerber (ed.), *Sport and the Body: A Philosophical Symposium* (Philadelphia: Lea and Febiger, 1972), especially the articles in Part I, "The Nature of Sport."

4 See Jan Felshin, "The Dialectics of Woman and Sport," in Gerber, Felshin, Berlin and Wyrick, *The American Woman in Sport,* Reading, MA: Addison-Wesley Publishing Co. (1974), pp. 179–210.

5 See, for example, Lenore J. Weitzman, "Sex Role Socialization," in Freeman (ed.), *Woman: A Feminist Perspective* (Palo Alto, CA: Mayfield Publishing Co., 1975), pp. 105–44.

6 For an account of the connection of this body self-image and sexual objectification, and of the effect of both on the oppression of women, see Sandra Lee Bartky, "Psychological Oppression," in Sharon Bishop and Marjorie Weinsweig, (eds.), *Philosophy and Women* (Belmont, CA: Wadsworth Publishing Co., 1979), pp. 33–41.

7 Seymour Fisher cites a number of studies coming to this conclusion, and reports some of his own, in *Body Experience in Fantasy and Behavior* (New York: Appleton-Century-Crofts, 1970), especially pp. 525–40.

8 See Eleanor Metheny, "The Symbolic Power of Sport," in op. cit. Gerber, *Sport and the Body*, pp. 221–227.

9 Perhaps it should be pointed out here that insofar as the development of bodily expressiveness is inhibited in men, their humanity is also inhibited.

10 Francis Keenan, in "Justice and Sport," *Journal of the Philosophy of Sport,* Vol II, 1975, pp. 111–23, calls for equality for women in sport, and appears to see this call as comparable to these other demands.

11 See English, and Weiss, Chapter 13.

12 See Marc Feigen Fasteau, *The Male Machine* (New York: McGraw-Hill, 1974), Chapter 9; Harry Edwards, *Sociology of Sport* (Homewood, IL: The Dorsey Press, 1973); Arnold R. Reisser, *The Madness in Sports: Psychosocial Observations on Sports* (New York: Appleton-Century-Crofts, 1967), esp. Chapters 14 and 16.

13 See relevant sections in Gerber, *Sport and the Body;* there are numerous papers in the *Journal of the Philosophy of Sport* which develop these themes as well.

14 See Cf. Felshin, 1974.

15 See Mary E. Duquin, "The Androgynous Advantage," in Carole A. Oglesby (ed.), *Women and Sport: From Myth to Reality.*

References

De Beauvoir, S. (1974) *The Second Sex*. New York: Vintage Books.

Duquin, Mary E. (Spring 1977) 'Effects of Culture on Women's Experience in Sport,' *Sport Sociology Bulletin*, vol. 6 (1).

Merleau-Ponty, Maurice (1962) *The Phenomenology of Perception*. New York: The Humanities Press.

Ortner, Sherry B. (1974) 'Is Female to Male as Nature is to Culture?' In Rosaldo and Lamphere (eds.), *Woman, Culture, and Society*. Stanford University Press, pp. 67–88.

Weiss, Paul (1969) *Sport: A Philosophical Inquiry*. Carbondale: Southern Illinois University Press, p. 217.

Young, Iris Marion (1980) 'Throwing Like a Girl: A Phenomenology of Feminine Body Comportment, Motility and Spatiality,' *Human Studies*, vol. 3.

Chapter 2

Woman as body

Ancient and contemporary views*

Elizabeth V. Spelman

> and what
> pure happiness to know
> all our high-toned questions
> breed in a lively animal.
>
> Adrienne Rich, from "Two Songs"

What philosophers have had to say about women typically has been nasty, brutish, and short. A page or two of quotations from those considered among the great philosophers (Aristotle, Hume, and Nietzsche, for example) constitutes a veritable litany of contempt. Because philosophers have not said much about women,[1] and, when they have, it has usually been in short essays or chatty addenda which have not been considered to be part of the central body of their work,[2] it is tempting to regard their expressed views about women as asystemic: their remarks on women are unofficial asides which are unrelated to the heart of their philosophical doctrines. After all, it might be thought, how could one's views about something as unimportant as women have anything to do with one's view about something as important as the nature of knowledge, truth, reality, freedom? Moreover – and this is the philosopher's move par excellence – wouldn't it be charitable to consider those opinions about women as coming merely from the *heart*, which all too easily responds to the tenor of the times, while philosophy "proper" comes from the *mind*, which resonates not with the times but with the truth?

Part of the intellectual legacy from philosophy "proper," that is, the issues that philosophers have addressed which are thought to be the serious province of philosophy, is the soul/body and mind/body distinction (differences among the various formulations are not crucial to this essay). However, this part of the philosophy might have not merely accidental connections to attitudes about women. For when one recalls that the Western philosophical

---

* Originally published as 'Woman as body: ancient and contemporary views' in *Feminist Studies*, 1982, vol. 8, no. 1 (Spring), pp. 109–132.

tradition has not been noted for its celebrations of the body, and that women's nature and women's lives have long been associated with the body and bodily functions, then a question is suggested. What connection might there be between attitudes toward the body and attitudes toward women?

If one begins to reread philosophers with an eye to exploring in detail just how they made the mind/body distinction, it soon becomes apparent that in many cases the distinction reverberates throughout the philosopher's work. How a philosopher conceives of the distinction and relation between soul (or mind) and body has essential ties to how that philosopher talks about the nature of knowledge, the accessibility of reality, the possibility of freedom. This is perhaps what one would expect – systemic connections among the "proper" philosophical issues addressed by a given philosopher. But there is also clear evidence in the philosophical texts of the relationship between how the mind/body distinction, is drawn, on the one hand, and the scattered official and unofficial utterances about the nature of women, on the other.

In this article, I shall refer to the conceptual connections between a philosopher's views about women and his expressed metaphysical, political, and ethical views. That is, I shall refer to conceptual relations internal to the texts themselves, and not to relations between the texts and their political and historical contexts. So my task is different from that of a historian of ideas or a social historian who might look at the relation between the political, economic, and cultural conditions under which a philosopher writes, on the one hand, and the focus and force of that philosopher's writings, on the other.[3]

My focus below is on the works of Plato, to discover what connections there are between his views about women and his views about the philosophical issues for which he is regarded with such respect. His descriptions of women's nature and prescriptions for women's proper societal niche recently have been under scrutiny by feminists.[4] What I hope to show is why it is important to see the connections between what Plato says about women and other aspects of his philosophical positions. For as I shall explain in the latter part of this essay, feminist theorists frequently have wanted to reject the kinds of descriptions of women's nature found in Plato and other philosophers, and yet at the same time have in their own theorizing continued to accept uncritically other aspects of the tradition that informs those ideas about "woman's nature." In particular, by looking at the example of Plato, I want to suggest why it is important for feminists not only to question what these philosophers have said about women, but also what philosophers have had to say about the mind/body distinction.

Plato's lessons about the soul and body

Plato's dialogues are filled with lessons about knowledge, reality, and goodness, and most of the lessons carry with them strong praise for the soul and strong indictments against the body. According to Plato, the body, with its deceptive senses, keeps us from real knowledge; it rivets us in a world of material things which is far removed from the world of reality; and it tempts us away from the virtuous life. It is in and through the soul, if at all, that we shall have knowledge, be in touch with reality, and lead a life of virtue. Only the soul can truly know, for only the soul can ascend to the real world, the world of the Forms of Ideas. That world is the perfect model to which imperfect, particular things we find in matter merely approximate. It is a world which, like the soul, is invisible, unchanging, not subject to decay, eternal. To be good, one's soul must know the Good, that is, the Form of Goodness, and this is impossible while one is dragged down by the demands and temptations of bodily life. Hence, bodily death is nothing to be feared: immortality of the soul not only is possible, but greatly to be desired, because when one is released from the body one finally can get down to the real business of life, for this real business of life is the business of the soul. Indeed, Socrates describes his own commitment, while still on earth, to encouraging his fellow Athenians to pay attention to the real business of life:

> [I have spent] all my time going about trying to persuade you, young and old, to make your first and chief concern not for your bodies nor for your possessions, but for the highest welfare of your souls. (*Apology* 30a–b)

Plato also tells us about the nature of beauty. Beauty has nothing essentially to do with the body or with the world of material things. *Real* beauty cannot "take the form of a face, or of hands, or of anything that is of the flesh" (*Symposium* 221a). Yes, there are beautiful things, but they only are entitled to be described that way because they "partake in" the form of Beauty, which itself is not found in the material world. Real beauty has characteristics which merely beautiful *things* cannot have; real beauty

> is an everlasting loveliness which neither comes nor goes, which neither flowers nor fades, for such beauty is the same on every hand, the same then as now, here as there, this way as that way, the same to every worshipper as it is to every other. (*Symposium* 221a)

Because it is only the soul that can know the Forms, those eternal and unchanging denizens of Reality, only the soul can know real Beauty; our changing, decaying bodies only can put us in touch with changing, decaying pieces of the material world.

Plato also examines love. His famous discussion of love in the *Symposium* ends up being a celebration of the soul over the body. Attraction to and appreciation for beauty of another's body is but a vulgar fixation unless one can use such appreciation as a stepping stone to understanding Beauty itself. One can begin to learn about Beauty, while one is still embodied, when one notices that this body is beautiful, that that body is beautiful, and so on, and then one begins to realize that Beauty itself is something beyond any particular body or thing. The kind of love between people that is to be valued is not the attraction of one body for another, but the attraction of one soul for another. There is procreation of the spirit as well as of the flesh (*Symposium* 209a). All that bodies in unison can create are more bodies – the children women bear – which are mortal, subject to change and decay. But souls in unison can create "something lovelier and less mortal than human seed," for spiritual lovers "conceive and bear the things of the spirit," that is, "wisdom and all her sister virtues" (*Symposium* 209c). Hence, spiritual love between men is preferable to physical love between men and women. At the same time, physical love between men is ruled out, on the grounds that "enjoyment of flesh by flesh" is "wanton shame," while desire of soul for soul is at the heart of a relationship that "reverences, aye and worships, chastity and manhood, greatness and wisdom" (*Laws* 837c–d). The potential for harm in sexual relations is very great – harm not so much to one's body or physique, but to one's soul. Young men especially shouldn't get caught up with older men in affairs that threaten their "spiritual development," for such development is "assuredly and ever will be of supreme value in the sight of gods and men alike" (*Phaedrus* 241c).

So, then, one has no hope of understanding the nature of knowledge, reality, goodness, love, or beauty unless one recognizes the distinction between soul and body; and one has no hope of attaining any of these unless one works hard on freeing the soul from the lazy, vulgar, beguiling body. A philosopher is someone who is committed to doing just that, and that is why philosophers go willingly unto death; it is, after all, only the death of their bodies, and finally, once their souls are released from their bodies, these philosophical desiderata are within reach.

The offices and attributes of the body vis-à-vis the soul are on the whole interchangeable, in Plato's work, with the offices and attributes of one part of the soul vis-à-vis another part. The tug-of-war between the soul and body has the same dynamics, and the same stakes, as the tug-of-war between "higher" and "lower" parts of the soul. For example, sometimes Plato speaks as if the soul should resist the desires not of the body, but of part of its very self (*Gorgias* 505b). Sometimes he describes internal conflict as the struggle between soul and body, and sometimes as the battle among the rational, the spirited, and the appetitive parts of the soul. The spirited part of the soul is supposed to help out the rational part in its constant attempt to "preside over the appetitive part which is the mass of the soul in each of us and the most insatiate by nature of wealth"; unless it is watched, the appetitive part can get "filled and infected with the so-called pleasures associated with the body" (*Republic* 442a–b).

The division among parts of the soul is intimately tied to one other central and famous aspect of Plato's philosophy that hasn't been mentioned so far:

Plato's political views. His discussion of the parts of the soul and their proper relation to one another is integral to his view about the best way to set up a state. The rational part of the soul ought to rule the soul and ought to be attended by the spirited part in keeping watch over the unruly appetitive part; just so, there ought to be rulers of the state (the small minority in whom reason is dominant), who, with the aid of high-spirited guardians of order, watch over the multitudes (whose appetites need to be kept under control).

What we learn from Plato, then, about knowledge, reality, goodness, beauty, love, and statehood, is phrased in terms of a distinction between soul and body, or alternatively and roughly equivalently, in terms of a distinction between the rational and irrational. And the body, or the irrational part of the soul, is seen as an enormous and annoying obstacle to the possession of these desiderata. If the body gets the upper hand (!) over the soul, or if the irrational part of the soul overpowers the rational part, one can't have knowledge, one can't see beauty, one will be far from the highest form of love, and the state will be in utter chaos. So the soul/body distinction, or the distinction between the rational and irrational parts of the soul, is a highly charged distinction. An inquiry into the distinction is no mild metaphysical musing. It is quite clear that the distinction is heavily value-laden. Even if Plato hadn't told us outright that the soul is more valuable than the body, and the rational part of the soul is more important than the irrational part, that message grinds out in page after page of his dialogues. The soul/body distinction, then, is integral to the rest of Plato's views, and the higher worth of the soul is integral to that distinction.

Plato's view of the soul and body, and his attitude toward women

Plato, and anyone else who conceives of the soul as something unobservable, cannot of course speak as if we could point to the soul, or hold it up for direct observation. At one point, Plato says no mere mortal can really understand the nature of the soul, but one perhaps could tell what it resembles (*Phaedrus* 246a). So it is not surprising to find Plato using many metaphors and analogies to describe what the soul is *like*, in order to describe relations between the soul and the body or relations between parts of the soul. For example, thinking, a function of the soul, is described by analogy to talking (*Theaetetus* 190a; *Sophist* 263e). The parts of the soul are likened to a team of harnessed, winged horses and their charioteer (*Phaedrus* 246a). The body's relation to the soul is such that we are to think of the body vis-à-vis the soul as a tomb (*Gorgias* 493a), a grave or prison (*Cratylus* 400c), or as barnacles or rocks holding down the soul (*Republic* 611e–612a). Plato compares the lowest or body-like part of the soul to a brood of beasts (*Republic* 590c).

But Plato's task is not only to tell us what the soul is like, not only to provide us with ways of getting a fix on the differences between souls and bodies, or differences between parts of the soul. As we've seen, he also wants to convince us that the soul is much more important than the body, and that it is to our peril that we let ourselves be beckoned by the rumblings of the body at the expense of harkening to the call of the soul. And he means to convince us of this by holding up for our inspection the silly and sordid lives of those who pay too much attention to their bodies and do not care enough for their souls; he wants to remind us of how unruly, how without direction, are the lives of those in whom the lower part of the soul holds sway over the higher part. Because he can't *point* to an adulterated soul, he points instead to those embodied beings whose lives are in such bad shape that we can be sure that their souls are adulterated. And whose lives exemplify the proper soul/body relationship gone haywire? The lives of women (or sometimes the lives of children, slaves, and brutes).

For example, how are we to know when the body has the upper hand over the soul, or when the lower part of the soul has managed to smother the higher part? We presumably can't see such conflict, so what do such conflicts translate into, in terms of actual human lives? Well, says Plato, look at the lives of women.[5] It is women who get hysterical at the thought of death (*Phaedo* 60a, 112d; *Apology* 35b); obviously, their emotions have overpowered their reason, and they can't control themselves. The worst possible model for young men could be "a woman, young or old or wrangling with her husband, defying heaven, loudly boasting, fortunate in her own conceit, or involved in misfortune or possessed by grief and lamentation – still less a woman that is sick, in love, or in labor" (*Republic* 395d–e). He continues:

> When in our own lives some affliction comes to us you are aware that we plume ourselves . . . on our ability to remain calm and endure, in the belief that this is the conduct of a man, and [giving in to grief] that of a woman.
>
> (*Republic* 605c–d)

To have more concern for your body than your soul is to act just like a woman; hence, the most proper penalty for a soldier who surrenders to save his body, when he should be willing to die out of the courage of his soul, is for the soldier to be turned into a woman (*Laws* 944e).[6] Plato believed that souls can go through many different embodied life-times. There will be certain indications, in one's life, of the kind of life one is leading now; and unless a man lives righteously now, he will as his next incarnation "pass into a woman" and if he doesn't behave then, he'll become a brute! (*Timaeus* 42b–c, 76e, 91a).

Moreover, Plato on many occasions points to women to illustrate the improper way to pursue the things for which philosophers are constantly to be searching. For example, Plato wants to explain how important and also how difficult the attainment of real knowledge is. He wants us to realize that not just anyone can have knowledge, there is a vital distinction between those who really have knowledge and those who merely think they do. Think, for example, about the question of health. If we don't make a distinction between those who know what health is, and those who merely have unfounded and confused opinions about what health is, then "in the matter of good or bad health . . . any woman or child – or animal, for that matter – knows what is wholesome for it and is capable of curing itself" (*Theaeteus* 171c). The implication is clear: if any old opinion were to count as real knowledge, then we'd have to say that women, children, and maybe even animals have knowledge. But surely *they* don't have knowledge! And why not? For one thing, because they don't recognize the difference between the material, changing world of appearance, and the invisible, eternal world of Reality. In matters of beauty, for example, they are so taken by the physical aspects of things that they assume that they can see and touch what is beautiful; they don't realize that what one knows when one has knowledge of real Beauty cannot be something that is seen or touched. Plato offers us, then, as an example of the failure to distinguish between Beauty itself, on the one hand, and beautiful things, on the other, "boys and women when they see bright-colored things" (*Republic* 557c). They don't realize that it is not through one's senses that one knows about beauty or anything else, for real beauty is eternal and invisible and unchangeable and can only be known through the soul.

So the message is that in matters of knowledge, reality, and beauty, don't follow the example of women. They are mistaken about those things. In matters of love, women's lives serve as negative examples also. Those men who are drawn by "vulgar" love, that is, love of body for body, "turn to women as the object of their love, and raise a family" (*Symposium* 208e); those men drawn by a more "heavenly" kind of love, that is, love of soul for soul, turn to other men. But there are strong sanctions against physical love between men: such physical unions, especially between older and younger men, are "unmanly." The older man isn't strong enough to resist his lust (as in woman, the irrational part of the soul has overtaken the rational part), and the younger man, "the impersonator of the female," is reproached for this "likeness to the model" (*Laws* 836e). The problem with physical love between men, then, is that men are acting like women.

To summarize the argument so far: the soul/body distinction is integral to the rest of Plato's views; integral to the soul/body distinction is the higher worth and importance of the soul in comparison to the body; finally, Plato tries to persuade his readers that it is to one's peril that one does not pay proper attention to one's soul – for if one doesn't, one will end up acting and living as if one were a woman. We know, Plato says, about lives dictated by the demands and needs of inducements of the body instead of the soul. Such lives surely are not good models for those who want to understand and undertake a life devoted to the nurturance of the best part of us: our souls.

To anyone at all familiar with Plato's official and oft-reported views about women, the above recitation of misogynistic remarks may be quite surprising. Accounts of Plato's views about women usually are based on what he says in book 5 of the *Republic*. In the dialogue, Plato startled his contemporaries when, as part of his proposal for the constitution of an ideal state, he suggested that

> There is no pursuit of the administrators of a state that belongs to woman because she is a woman or to a man because he is a man. But the natural capacities are distributed alike among both creatures, and women naturally share in all pursuits and men in all.
>
> (*Republic* 455d–e)

The only difference between men and women, Plato says at this point, is that women have weaker bodies than men, but this is no sign that something is amiss with their souls.

Plato also says, in a dialogue called *Meno*, that it doesn't make sense to talk about "women's virtues" or "men's virtues," because virtue as virtue is the same, whether it happens to appear in the life of a woman, a man, or a child. This view is part of Plato's doctrine of the Forms, referred to earlier. Virtue, like any other Form, is eternal and unchanging; so it can't be one thing here, another thing there; it is always one and the same thing. Virtue as virtue does not "differ, in its character as virtue, whether it be in a child or an old man, a woman or a man" (*Meno* 73a).

Well now, what are we to make of this apparent double message in Plato about women? What are we to do with the fact that on the one hand, when Plato explicitly confronts the question of women's nature, in the *Republic*, he seems to affirm the equality of men and women;[7] while on the other hand, the dialogues are riddled with misogynistic remarks? I think that understanding the centrality and importance of the soul/body distinction in Plato's work helps us to understand this contradiction in his views about women. As we've seen, Plato insists, over and over again in a variety of ways, that our souls are the most important part of us. Not only is it through our souls that we shall have access to knowledge, reality, goodness, beauty; but also, in effect we *are* our souls; when our bodies die and decay, we, that is our souls, shall live on. Our bodies are not essential to our identity; in their most benign aspect, our bodies are not essential to our identity; in their most benign aspect, our bodies are incidental appendages; in their most malignant aspect, they are obstacles to the smooth functioning of our souls. If we *are* souls, and out bodies are not essential to who we are, then it doesn't make any difference, ultimately, whether we have a woman's body or a man's body. When one thinks about this emphasis in Plato's thought, his views about the equality of women and men seem integral to the rest of his views. If the only difference between women and men is that they have different bodies, and if bodies are merely incidental attachments to what constitutes one's real identity, then there is no important difference between men and women.[8]

But as we have also seen, Plato seems to want to make very firm his insistence on the destructiveness of the body to the soul. In doing so, he holds up for our ridicule and scorn those lives devoted to bodily pursuits. Over and over again, women's lives are depicted as being such lives. His misogyny, then, is part of his somatophobia: the body is seen as the source of all the undesirable traits a human being could have, and women's lives are spent manifesting those traits.

So the contradictory sides of Plato's views about women are tied to the distinction he makes between soul and body and the lessons he hopes to teach his readers about their relative value. When preaching about the overwhelming importance of the soul, he can't but regard the kind of body one has as of no final significance, so there is no way for him to assess differentially the lives of women and men; but when making gloomy pronouncements about the worth of the body, he points an accusing finger at a class of people with a certain kind of body – women – because he regards them, as a class, as embodying (!) the very traits he wishes no one to have. In this way, women constitute a deviant class in Plato's philosophy, in the sense that he points to their lives as the kinds of lives that are not acceptable philosophically: they are just the kinds of lives no one, especially philosophers, ought to live. It is true that Plato chastises certain kinds of men: sophists, tyrants, and cowards, for example. But he frequently puts them in their place by comparing them to women! We've already seen some examples of that, such as male homosexuals being ridiculed for their likeness to women. Another example comes from the same dialogue in which Plato's argument about equality occurs. At one point in the *Republic* (579c), Plato tries to convince us that tyranny does not pay, by saying that a tyrant is someone who "must live for the most part cowering in the recesses of his house like a woman, envying among the other citizens anyone who goes abroad and sees any good thing."

Plato had what I have described elsewhere[9] as a case of psychophilic somatophobia. As a psychophile who sometimes spoke as if the souls of women were not in any important way different from the souls of men, he had some remarkably non-sexist things to say about women. As a somatophobe who often referred to women as exemplifying states of being and forms of living most removed from the philosophical ideal, he left the dialogues awash with misogynistic remarks. Of course, one can be a dualist without being a misogynist, and one can be a misogynist without being a dualist. However, Plato was both a dualist and a misogynist, and his negative views about women were connected to his negative views about the body, insofar as he depicted women's lives as quintessentially body-directed.

In summary, Plato does not merely embrace a distinction between soul and body; for all the good and hopeful and desirable possibilities for human life (now and in an afterlife) are aligned with the soul, while the rather seedy and undesirable liabilities of human life are aligned with the body (alternatively, the alignment is with the higher or lower parts of the soul). There is a highly polished moral gloss to the soul/body distinction in Plato. One of his favorite devices for bringing this moral gloss to a high luster is holding up, for our contempt and ridicule, the lives of women. This is one of the ways he tries to make clear that it makes no small difference whether you lead a soul-directed or a bodily directed life.

Feminism and "somatophobia"

There are a number of reasons why feminists should be aware of the legacy of the soul/body distinction. It is not just that the distinction has been wound up with the depreciations and degradation of women, although, as has just been shown, examining a philosopher's view of the distinction may give us a direct route to his views about women.

First of all, as the soul or mind or reason is extolled, and the body or passion is denounced by comparison, it is not just women who are both relegated to the bodily or passionate sphere of existence and then chastised for belonging to that sphere. Slaves, free laborers, children, and animals are put in "their place" on almost the same grounds as women are. The images of women, slaves, laborers, children, and animals are almost interchange-able. For example, we find Plato holding that the best born and best educated should have control over "children, women and slaves . . . and the base rabble of those who are free in name," because it is in these groups that we find "the mob of motley appetites and pleasures and pains" (*Republic* 431b–c). As we saw above, Plato lumps together women, children, and animals as ignoramuses. (For Aristotle, there is little difference between a slave and an animal, because both "with their bodies attend to the needs of life" (*Politics* 1254b20–24).) A common way of denigrating a member of one of these groups is to compare that member to a member of one of the other groups – women are thought to have slavish or childish appetites, slaves are said to be brutish. Recall too, that Plato's way of ridiculing male homosexuals was to say that they imitated women. It is no wonder that the images and insults are almost interchangeable, for there is a central descriptive thread holding together the images of these groups. The members of these groups lack, for all intents and purposes, mind or the power of reason; even the humans among them are not considered fully human.

It is important for feminists to see to what extent the images and argument used to denigrate women are similar to those used to denigrate one group of men vis-à-vis another, children vis-à-vis adults, animals vis-à-vis humans, and even – though I have not discussed it here – the natural world vis-à-vis a man's will (yes, man's will). For to see this is part of understanding how the oppression of women occurs in the context of, and is related to, other forms of oppression or exploitation.

There is a second reason why feminists should be aware of the legacy of the soul/body distinction. Some feminists have quite happily adopted both the soul/body distinction and relative value attached to soul and to body. But in doing so, they may be adopting a position inimical to what on a more conscious level they are arguing for.

For all her magisterial insight into the way in which the image of woman as body has been foisted upon and used against us, Simone de Beauvoir can't resist the temptation to say that woman's emancipation will come when woman, like man, is freed from this association with – according to the male wisdom of the centuries – the less important aspect of human existence. According to *The Second Sex*, women's demand is "not that they be exalted in their femininity; they wish that in themselves, as in humanity in general, transcendence may prevail over immanence" (de Beauvoir, 1952: 123). But in de Beauvoir's own terms, for "transcendence" to prevail over "immanence" is for spirit or mind to prevail over matter or body, for reason to prevail over passion and desire. This means not only that the old images of women as mired in the world of "immanence" – the world of nature and physical existence – will go away. It will also happen that women won't lead lives given over mainly to their "natural" functions: "the pain of childbirth is on the way out"; "artificial insemination is on the way in" (de Beauvoir, 1952: 111). Although de Beauvoir doesn't explicitly say it, her directions for women are to find means of leaving the world of immanence and joining the men in the realm of transcendence. Men have said, de Beauvoir reminds us, that to be human is to have mind prevail over body; and no matter what disagreements she has elsewhere with men's perceptions and priorities, de Beauvoir here seems to agree with them. Explicitly de Beauvoir tells us not to be the people men have dreamt us up to be; but implicitly, she tells us to be the people men have dreamt themselves up to be.

I'm not insisting that de Beauvoir should have told us to stay where we are. The burden of her book is to describe the mixture of fear, awe, and disgust in men's attitudes toward the physical world, the body, the woman. Men have purchased one-way tickets to Transcendence in their attempt to deny, or conquer and control, the raging Immanence they see in themselves and project onto women. De Beauvoir says that this attitude toward corporeality has informed men's oppression of women, and yet her directions for women seem to be informed by just the same attitude. But can we as a species sustain negative attitudes and negative ideologies about the bodily aspects of our existence and yet keep those attitudes and ideologies from working in behalf of one group of people as it attempts to oppress other groups? Let me cite some examples to show how unlikely it is that such entrenched values can linger without doing some harm.

The first example comes from Plato. The contradiction we saw in Plato's views about women comes precisely from the source we have just been talking about. For it is just insofar as Plato continues to regard our bodily existence as cause for disappointment, embarrassment, and evil, that he finds the lives of women (and others) the occasion for scorn and ridicule – and this despite his insistence elsewhere in his writings on the equality of women and men.

A second example comes from Betty Friedan. She may seem too easy a target, but I think that something closely connected to what I'm going to point out about her thought can also be found in feminists considered much more radical than she is. Very early in *The Feminine Mystique*, Friedan (1963) remarks on the absence, in women's lives, of "the world of thought and ideas, the life of the mind and spirit" (Friedan, 1963: 36). She wants women to be "culturally" as well as "biologically" creative – she wants us to think about spending our lives "mastering the secrets of the atoms, or the stars, composing symphonies, pioneering a new concept in government or society" (Friedan, 1963: 247). And she associates "mental activity" with the "professions of highest value to society" (Friedan, 1963: 277). Friedan thus seems to believe that men have done the more important things, the mental things; women have been relegated in the past to the less important human tasks involving bodily functions, and their liberation will come when they are allowed and encouraged to do the more important things in life.

Friedan's analysis relies on our old friend, the mind/body distinction, and Friedan, no less than Plato or de Beauvoir, quite happily assumes that mental activities are more valuable than bodily ones. Her solution to what she referred to as the "problem that has no name" is for women to leave (though not entirely) women's sphere and "ascend" into man's. Certainly there is much pleasure and value in the "mental activities" she extols. But we can see the residue of her own negative attitude about tasks associated with the body: the bodily aspects of our existence must be attended to, but the "liberated" woman, who is on the ascendant, can't be bothered with them. There is yet another group of people to whom these tasks will devolve: servants. Woman's liberation – and of course it is no secret that by "woman," Friedan could only have meant middle-class white women – seems to require woman's disso- ciation and separation from those who will perform the bodily tasks which the liberated woman has left behind in pursuit of "higher," mental activity. So we find Friedan quoting, without comment, Elizabeth Cady Stanton:

> I now understood the practical difficulties most women had to contend
> with in the isolated household and the impossibility of women's best
> development if in contact the chief part of her life with servants and
> children . . .
>
> (Friedan, 1963: 93)

Friedan at times seems to chide those women who could afford to have servants but don't: the women pretend there's a "servant problem" when there isn't, or insist on doing their own menial work. The implication is that women could find servants to do the "menial work," if they wanted to, and that it would be desirable for them to do so (Friedan, 1963: 184–185). But what difference is there between the place assigned to women by men and the place assigned to some women (or men) by Friedan herself?

I mentioned that feminists considered more radical than Friedan share something very close to her attitudes about the body: Shulamith Firestone is a case in point. In *The Dialectic of Sex*, Firestone traces the oppression of women to what she calls a "fundamental inequality" produced by nature: "half the human race must bear and rear the children of all of them" (Firestone, 1970: 205). Apart from the fact that we need some explanation of how Nature dictated that women should *rear* children, we also need to understand what it is about bearing children that Firestone finds oppressive. According to Firestone, the fact of their childbearing capacity has been used to justify the oppression of women. But it is not just this that concerns and bothers her. She also thinks that in and of itself childbearing is dreadful; the way in which she describes pregnancy and childbirth tells us that she would find them oppressive even in the absence of oppressive institutions set up around them. She calls pregnancy "barbaric"; and says that "childbirth *hurts*" (Firestone, 1970: 198). Curiously, Firestone elsewhere is angered at the male image of what women ought to look like – "Women everywhere rush to squeeze into the glass slipper, forcing and mutilating their bodies with diets and beauty programs" (Firestone, 1970: 152); and in the fact she reminds her readers that, contrary to male myths, *human* beauty allows for "growth and flux and decay" (Firestone, 1970: 155). Yet she doesn't hesitate to describe pregnancy as a "deformation" of the body (Firestone, 1970: 198). The disgust and fear she expressed reminds one of de Beauvoir's many descriptions of male attitudes toward specifically female and specifically physical functions. As Adrienne Rich has pointed out, "Firestone sees childbearing . . . as purely and simply the victimizing experience it has often been under patriarchy" (Rich, 1976: 174).

Undoubtedly, woman's body has been part of the source of our oppression in several senses. First, pregnancy and childbirth have in fact made women vulnerable, for a long time in the history of the species, and even for a short time in the history of the most economically privileged of women. Second, woman has been portrayed as essentially a bodily being, and this image has been used to deny her full status as a human being wherever and whenever mental activity as over against bodily activity has been thought to be the most human activity of all. But is the way to avoid oppression to radically change the experience of childbirth through the technology, as Firestone suggested, and insist that woman *not* be seen as connected to her body at all, that is, to insist that woman's "essential self," just as man's, lies in her mind, and not in her body? If so, then we are admitting tacitly that the men – from Plato on down – have been right all along, in insisting on a distinction between mind or soul and body, and insisting that mind is to be valued more than body. They've only been wrong in ungenerously denying woman a place up there with them, among the other minds. Women's liberation, on this view, is just a much belated version of the men's liberation that took place centuries ago, when men figured out ways both to dissociate themselves from, and/or conquer, the natural world and that part of them – their bodies – which reminds them of their place in that natural world. And one would think, reading feminists as different as de Beauvoir, Friedan, and Firestone, that indeed what woman's liberation ultimately means is liberation from our bodies – both in fact, and in definition.

By the way, this same view of liberation appears also in any version of androgyny that rests on the assumption that the kind of body we have puts no limits on the personalities we might develop; this is really just like Plato's assumption that any kind of soul or mind can exist in any kind of body – our minds just accidentally and contingently exist in our bodies. The problem androgynists address is that differences between women and men have been used to try to justify two different and unequal sets of rights and privileges. But the solution to that problem does not have to lie in denying all differences between women and men – any more than the solution to unequal treatment based on skin color requires that people have the same skin color! The solution, or part of the solution, lies in realizing that whatever the differences there are between women and men (and we still have a whole lot to learn about what those differences, big or little, are), they should not be used to try to justify the unfair distribution of society's goods.

There is of course much more to be said about de Beauvoir, Friedan, and Firestone than my brief remarks here. And of course there is much more to feminist theory than what they have said, although their theories have been influential for different segments of the women's movement, and their works constitute important landmarks in the development of feminist theory. Even in the recent work of Mary Daly, who knows the ways of the Church "Fathers" too well to describe women's liberation simply in terms of a spirituality divorced from embodiment, it is difficult to see in any detail what women free from shackles of patriarchy will be like: "Spinsters" appear to have none of the characteristics of personal identity which are related to embodiment: color, culture, specific histories. In her insistence on all women's overcoming the barriers that have been used to divide us, Daly ends up with a general notion of woman that seems to be abstracted from any of the particular facts about us which make us different from one another. As Judith Plaskow has remarked, Daly offers "a vision of wild and ecstatic, but essentially contentless and disembodied, freedom."[10]

What I have tried to do here is bring attention to the fact that various versions of women's liberation may themselves rest on the very same assumptions that have informed the depreciation and degradation of women, and other groups, in the past. Those assumptions are that we must distinguish between soul and body, and that the physical part of our existence is to be devalued in comparison to the mental. Of course, these two assumptions alone don't mean that women or other groups have to be degraded; it's these two assumptions, along with the further assumption that woman is body, or is bound to body, or is meant to take care of the bodily aspects of life, that have so deeply contributed to the degradation and oppression of women. And so perhaps feminists would like to keep the first two assumptions (about the difference between mind and body, and the relative worth of each of them) and somehow or other get rid of the last – in fact, that is what most of the feminists previously discussed have tried to do. Nothing that has been said so far has amounted to an argument against those first two assumptions: it hasn't been shown that there is no foundation for the assumptions that the mind and body are distinct and that the body is to be valued less than the mind.

There is a feminist thinker, however, who has taken it upon herself to chip away directly at the second assumption and to a certain extent at the first. Both in poetry, and explicitly in her recent book, *Of Woman Born*, Adrienne Rich has begun to show us why use of the mind/body distinction does not give us appropriate descriptions of human experience; and she has begun to remind us of the distance we keep from ourselves when we try to keep a distance from our bodies. She does this in the process of trying to redefine the dimensions of the experience of childbirth, as she tries to show us why childbirth and motherhood need not mean what they have meant under patriarchy.

We are reminded by Rich that it is possible to be alienated from our bodies not only by pretending or wishing they weren't there, but also by being "incarcerated" in them (Rich 1976: 13). The institution of motherhood has done the latter in its insistence on seeing woman only or mainly as a reproductive machine. Defined as flesh by flesh-loathers, woman enters the most "fleshly" of her experiences with that same attitude of flesh-loathing – surely "physical self-hatred and suspicion of one's own body is scarcely a favorable emotion with which to enter an intense physical experience" (Rich 1976 : 163).

But Rich insists that we don't have to experience childbirth in that way – we don't have to experience it as "torture rack" (Rich 1976: 157); but neither do we have to mystify it as a "peak experience." The experience of childbirth can be viewed as a way of recognizing the integrity of our experience, because pain itself is not usefully catalogued as something just our minds or just our bodies experience.[11] Giving birth is painful, indeed; but painkillers are not necessarily the appropriate way to deal with pain, for we are no less estranged from our bodies, no less put at men's disposal, when "rescued" from our pain by drugs. The point of "natural childbirth" should be thought of not as enduring pain, but as having an active physical experience – a distinction we recognize as crucial for understanding, for example, the pleasure in athletics.

Rich recognizes that feminists have not wanted to accept patriarchal versions of female biology, of what having a female body means (Rich 1976:

39). It has seemed to feminists, she implies, that we must either accept that view of being female, which is, essentially, to be a body, or deny that view and insist that we are "disembodied spirits" (Rich 1976: 40). It perhaps is natural to see our alternatives that way:

> We have been perceived for too many centuries as pure Nature, exploited and raped like the earth and the solar system; small wonder if we not try to become Culture: pure spirit, mind.
>
> (Rich 1976: 285)

But we don't *have* to do that, Rich reminds us; we can appeal to the physical without denying what is called "mind." We can come to regard our physicality as "resource, rather than destiny":

> In order to live a fully human life we require not only *control* of our bodies (though control is a prerequisite); we must touch the unity and resonance of our physicality, our bond with the natural order, the corporeal ground of our intelligence.
>
> (Rich 1976: 39)

Rich doesn't deny that we will have to start thinking about our lives in new ways; she even implies that we'll have to start thinking about thinking in new ways. Maybe it will give such a project a small boost to point out that philosophers for their part still squabble about mind/body dualism; the legacy of dualism is strong, but not unchallenged by any means. And in any event, as I have noted earlier, one can hardly put the blame for sexism (or any other form of oppression) on dualism itself. Indeed, the mind/body distinction can be put to progressive political ends, for example, to assert equality between human beings in the face of physical differences between them. There is nothing intrinsically sexist or otherwise oppressive about dualism, that is, about the belief that there are minds and there are bodies and that they are distinct kinds of things.[12] But historically, the story dualists tell often ends up being a highly politicized one: although the story may be different at different historical moments, often it is said not only that there are minds (or souls) and bodies, but also that one is meant to rule and control the other. And the stage is thereby set for the soul/body distinction, now highly politicized and hierarchically ordered, to be used in a variety of ways in connection with repressive theories of the self, as well as oppressive theories of social and political relations.[13] Among the tasks facing feminists is to think about the criteria for an adequate theory of self. Part of the value of Rich's work is that it points to the necessity of such an undertaking, and it is no criticism of her to say that she does no more than remind us of some of the questions that need to be raised.

A final note about the significance of somatophobia in feminist theory

In the history of political philosophy, the grounds given for the inferiority of women to men often are quite similar to those given for the inferiority of slaves to masters, children to fathers, animals to humans. In Plato, for example, all such subordinate groups are guilty by association with one another and each group is guilty by association with the bodily. In their eagerness to end the stereotypical association of woman and body, feminists such as de Beauvoir, Friedan, Firestone, and Daly have overlooked the significance of the connections – in theory and in practice – between the derogation and oppression of other groups on the basis of, for example, skin color and class membership. It is as if in their eagerness to assign women a new place in the scheme of things, these feminist theorists have by implication wanted to dissociate women from other subordinate groups. One problem with this, of course, is that those other subordinate groups include women.

What is especially significant about Rich's recent work is that in contrast to these other theorists she both challenges the received tradition about the insignificance and indignity of bodily life and bodily tasks and explicitly focuses on racism as well as sexism as essential factors in women's oppression. I believe that it is not merely a coincidence that someone who attends to the first also attends to the second. Rich pauses not just to recognize the significance attached to the female body, but also to reevaluate that significance. "Flesh-loathing" is loathing of flesh by some particular group under some particular circumstances – the loathing of women's flesh by men, but also the loathing of black flesh by whites. (Here I begin to extrapolate from Rich, but I believe with some warrant.) After all, bodies are always particular bodies – they are male or female bodies (our deep confusion when we can't categorize a body either way supports and does not belie the general point); but they are black or brown or biscuit or yellow or red bodies as well. We cannot seriously attend to the social significance attached to embodiment without recognizing this. I believe that it is Rich's recognition of this that distinguishes her work in crucial ways from that of most other major white feminists. Although the topic of feminism, sexism, and racism deserves a much fuller treatment,[14] it is important to point out in the context of the present paper that not only does Rich challenge an assumption about the nature of the bodily that has been used to oppress women, but, unlike other feminists who do not challenge this assumption, she takes on the question of the ways in which sexism and racism interlock. Somatophobia historically has been symptomatic not only of sexism, but also of racism, so it is perhaps not surprising that someone who has examined that connection between flesh-loathing and sexism would undertake an examination of racism.

Feminists may find it fruitful to examine the extent to which attitudes toward and ideologies about the body have played a role not only in sexist institutions and analyses, but also in the analyses feminists themselves are developing in response to such institutions and theories. A theory of embodiment, which must include a theory of the social significance of embodiment, is part of the needed feminist theory of self referred to earlier. Such a theory might reveal some deep connections among sexism, racism, and classism. It might also help expose some of the relations between homophobia and racism, insofar as both historically have such strong connections to fear of sexuality.[15] We also need to ask what theories of embodiment are presupposed by feminist analyses of women's health. All these examinations are part of our refusal to pay homage to a long tradition of somatophobia – a tradition it has been hard for us to shake.

Notes

I want to thank the Women's Resource Center at Smith College for inviting me to give an early version of parts of this essay in April 1979. I am grateful to the editors of *Feminist Studies* for some very helpful suggestions about an earlier draft.

1 There is no reason to think philosophers used "man" or its equivalent in other languages generically. For example, in discussing the conditions of happiness for "man," Aristotle raises the question of whether a "man's" being self-sufficient is compatible with his having a wife (*Nicomachean Ethics 1097b11*).
    All references to Plato are from *Collected Dialogues of Plato,* ed. Edith Hamilton and Huntington Cairns (New York: Pantheon, 1963), and are supplied in parentheses in text.
2 For example, Alice Rossi noted in her introductory essay to *Essays on Sex Equality* by John Stuart Mill and Harriet Taylor Mill (Chicago: University of Chicago Press, 1970, p. 5 and especially note 3) that major collections of John Stuart Mill's works typically do not include *The Subjection of Women*.
3 Our tasks are not, of course, unconnected, but they are distinct. It is always conceivable that a philosopher's remarks not be motivated by nor have consequences for the historical and political events in which his life is framed. It is the task of historians to trace the extent to which in any given case such motivations existed and such consequences followed. My task here, however, is to look at the logical connections between parts of a philosopher's works, whatever the actual connection was between those works and the particular historical moment in which they were created. At the same time, one reason I find the philosophical exercise interesting and worthwhile is just because the mind/body distinction – whatever its particular place in the history of Western philosophy – appears to be so deeply connected with political and social institutions used to define and shape women's lives.
4 See, for example, Christine Garside Allen, "Plato on Women," *Feminist Studies* 2, no. 2–3 (1975): 131–38; Julia Annas, "Plato's *Republic* and Feminism," *Philosophy* 51, (1976): 307–21; Anna Dickason, "Anatomy and Destiny: The Role of Biology in Plato's View of Women," in *Women and Philosophy*, ed. Carol C. Gould and Marx Wartofsky (New York: Putnam's 1976), pp. 45–53; Susan Moller Okin, *Women in Western Political Thought* (Princeton: Princeton University Press, 1979), pt. 1; Martha Lee Osborne, "Plato's Unchanging View of Women: A Denial that Anatomy Spells Destiny," *Philosophical Forum* 6, no. 2–3 (1975): 447–52; Sarah Pomeroy, "Feminism in Book V of Plato's *Republic*,"

Apeiron 8 (1974): 32–35; and my "Metaphysics and Misogyny: Souls, Bodies and Women in Plato's Dialogues," unpublished manuscript.

5 Although Plato objects to certain types of men – sophists, tyrants, and so forth – his disdain for women is always expressed as disdain for women in general and not for any subgroup of women. Moreover, one of the ways he shows his disdain for certain types of men is to compare them to women.

6 In passages like this we see Plato assuming that a certain kind of body implies the presence of a certain kind of soul. This is at odds with his explicit view elsewhere that what is really important about someone is that the person has a soul, no matter what kind of body she has.

7 In contrast, see the articles by Julia Annas and others cited in note 4.

8 This line of thinking may remind us of some contemporary discussions of androgyny; it also has fascinating connections to the complicated phenomenon or transsexualism. In *Conundrum* (New York: Signet, 1974), Jan Morris insists that "she" had always had a woman's soul housed in a man's body. That she could think about herself in this way suggests that she thought her bodily identity not to be indicative of what her soul was like. On the other hand, that she felt compelled to change her body suggests – among many other things – that she felt her body had to properly reveal the kind, the gender of soul she had.

9 Spelman, "Metaphysics and Misogyny."

10 Judith Plaskow, from a lecture entitled "Woman as Body: The History of an Idea," Oberlin College, Oberlin, Ohio, April 1979. I learned about this lecture long after I first entitled this essay.

11 By the way, Rich (*Of Woman Born*, New York: Norton, 1976), here echoes Descartes, the "father of modern philosophy," who otherwise so insisted on the distinction between mind and body. Despite the fact that he provides elaborate attempts to justify the necessity of distinguishing between mind and body, Descartes finds it difficult to *apply* the distinction when talking about pain: the fact of experiencing pain and other common sensations makes Descartes realize that

> I am not only lodged in my body as a pilot in a vessel, but that I am very closely united to it, and so to speak so intermingled with it that I seem to compose with it one whole. For if that were not the case, when my body is hurt, I, who am merely a thinking thing, should not feel pain, for I should perceive this wound by the understanding only, just as the sailor perceives by sight when something is damaged in his vessel.
>
> (*Meditations on First Philosophy*, VI)

12 There are other formulations of dualism; the position usually associated with dualism is that according to which there are two separate and distinct kinds of entities, minds and bodies, which together constitute the entity we call a person; but the position according to which there is one entity, a person, with two different "aspects," psychological and physical, has also been called dualistic.

13 See my "Aristotle and the Politicization of the Soul," in *Discovering Reality: Feminist Perspectives on Epistemology, Metaphysics, Methodology, and the Philosophy of Science*, ed. Sandra Harding and Merrill Hintikka (Dordrecht: Reidel, 1981).

14 See my "Feminism, Sexism, and Racism," forthcoming in *Quest*.

15 This point was suggested to me by Jacquelyn Zita.

Chapter 3

On the definition of 'woman' in the sport context*

Angela J. Schneider

Any discussion of the status of women in the sport context would benefit greatly from examining the underlying premises regarding the definition of 'woman' within (and outside) that context. Even on the surface level it becomes readily apparent to even the less-informed reader that the story to be told of women's participation in sport in general is the story of two ideals in apparent conflict. For example, from inception, the ancient and modern Olympic Games, and the ideal of the Olympic athletes, applied specifically and exclusively to men. From Pausanias' references to dropping women from the side of a cliff if they even observed the ancient Olympic Games, to de Coubertin's ideal that the goals that were to be achieved by the athletes through participation in the Olympic Games were not appropriate for women (de Coubertin 1912), one can easily see that the place of women in sport has been, for the most part, foreign at best. It is this basic idea, the idea that sport, (or sometimes even physical activity) particularly high-level competitive sport, is somehow incompatible with what women are, or what they should be, that must dominate any discussion of the unique issues for women in sport. Philosophies of ideal sport, and ideal women, lie behind discussions of permitting women to compete, of choosing the types of sport in which women can compete, in developing judging standards for adjudicated (as opposed to refereed) sports – contrast gymnastics and basketball – in attitudes to aggression, and competition, and indeed to the very existence of women's sport as a separate entity at all.

Before examining some of these issues in detail, it is worth making a point and a distinction at the outset. The point is that many of the issues, even moral issues, that arise in sport, arise equally for men and women. At the personal level, the decision whether or not to cheat, or what attitude you will take to your opponents or the unearned win, are moral problems any athlete must face. At the institutional level, decisions about rules prohibiting drug-

---

* Originally published as 'On the definition of "woman" in the sport context' in *Values in Sport*, Tännsjö, T., Tamburrini, C. eds. © Routledge 2000.

use, or equipment limitations designed to improve participant safety, should apply equally to women as to men. As such, concerns common to the realm of sport, important as they are, are more appropriately discussed elsewhere.[1] This chapter is devoted to the moral issues that arise because it is women, by virtue of the definition of who they are, who are the athletes. Thus the discussion that follows below will be focused on gender and sport, and the inter-relationships between them.

The philosophy of 'woman' versus the ideal athlete

Ideal woman

The battles that represent the basis for contentious issues for women in sport will be fought over conceptions of women – their bodies and their minds. The traditional ideals of woman during the ancient Olympic Games and the revival of the modern Olympic Games (up to and including some current ideals) are intimately tied to a particular view of woman's body. Some of these characteristics are soft, graceful, weak, and beautiful. The desirable qualities for a woman in the time of the ancient Olympics can generally be summarized as beauty, chastity, modesty, obedience, inconspicuous behaviour, and being a good wife, and a good mother (Lefkowitz & Fant 1985). Of course, these characteristics are tied to the roles of wife, mother, and daughter. They are not similar to those of the traditional ideal of man as hard, powerful, strong and rational, which are tied to the roles of leader, warrior and father. But, more importantly, if we examine the underlying characteristics of the traditional ideal athlete, we can plainly see that the ideal man and the ideal athlete are very similar, particularly in the role of warrior.[2] Conversely, we can plainly see that during the times of the ancient Olympic Games (and during the rebirth in the modern Olympic Games), the ideal woman and the traditional ideal athletes are almost opposites, so much so that women were hardly ever mentioned in conjunction with sport.

In contrast to these infrequent and casual references to women's sport, accounts of men's sport and athletics abound in ancient Greek literature. Homer vividly describes events from chariot racing to boxing. Pausanias furnishes a detailed account of the Olympic Games, and Herodotus, Thucydides, and other Greek authors refer to the Olympic Games and athletic festivals such as the Pythian, Isthmian, and Nemean Games (Spears 1988: 367).

There were also some exceptional counterexamples from ancient Greece – in the writings of Plato, for example – even though it is not well-known that girls competed in athletic festivals in Greece. Plato, at the peak of his writing, argued that women should be accorded the right to soar to the highest ranks he could conceive of in human excellence – the philosopher ruler; and be equally educated in the gymnasium by exercising naked with the men (Harris Bluestone 1987). Other exceptional counterexamples, from ancient Greece that stress physicality and a warrior nature for woman are the archetypes of Artemis, Atalanta and the Amazons, who all rejected the traditional role for women (Creedon 1994).[3]

Of course, book V of Plato's *Republic* is not nearly so well cited by feminist critics as Aristotle's 'On the Generation of Animals' and 'Politics,' and quite rightly so, because of the extremely negative philosophy of woman put forward by Aristotle. However, the fundamental issues in this entire discussion is who gets to choose which images of woman are permitted, desired or pursued in life and in sport. The primary question behind the role for women in sport is inextricably linked to the question of power and autonomy. At the institutional level, if it is the case that men decide, for example, the sports that women are permitted to attempt; the standards of physical perfection that are to be met in adjudicated sports; or the levels of funding accorded to women's as opposed to men's sport; then women have a legitimate grievance of not being treated with due respect. Just as it is the responsibility of each male to decide for himself, his conception of the type of body, and indeed, the type of life he wishes to pursue, moral or otherwise, it is the responsibility and right of each woman to deal with the challenges female athletes must deal with.

Paternalism and autonomy

The *Oxford Dictionary of Philosophy* defines paternalism as 'government as by a benign parent.' Paternalism is not necessarily sexist, although it often has been in sport and sport medicine (it could be called maternalism in a case where it was another woman making the decision on behalf of the individual, or perhaps parentalism), and it is often well-meaning. It occurs when one person makes a decision on behalf of (or speaks for) another, in what he or she takes to be the latter person's best interest. In the case of children, this of course is a necessary part of the parenting process until the child becomes an adult. Paternalism is also morally acceptable in cases where the person concerned is unable, for good reason, to speak or make decisions for himself or herself. It becomes morally troubling when it occurs on behalf of competent adults.

The concept of autonomy in ethical decision-making is very important. Autonomy is defined as the 'capacity for self-government'; furthermore, 'agents are autonomous if their actions are truly their own.' The crucial point here is that an essential part of being human is having the right and the capacity to make the choices and decisions that most affect oneself. Each competent human adult has the right to choose to pursue the projects and endeavours that he or she most cares about. That right is naturally limited by the rights of others to pursue their own desires and interests, but what the concept of autonomy takes for granted is, that no one is entitled to speak on another's behalf, without that person's permission.

Sport paternalism and women's participation

Is there any reason why women should not participate in sports that men have traditionally played? It is instructive to look at what could possibly count as a morally acceptable answer. If there were a sport practised by men that was physiologically impossible for women, it would count as a reason for women not participating. But there is no such sport. To qualify, the sport would probably have to centrally involve male genitalia – funnily enough, we have no institutionally sanctioned sports of this type.

A second possibility would be if there were a sport, played by men, that no women in the world actually wanted to play. It is logically possible that such a sport might be invented, that not one woman anywhere would want to play, but then the reason the women would not be playing would be that they have *chosen* not to play, not that someone else has decided that they should not. Morally unacceptable answers for prohibiting women from playing sport would include: 'It would be bad for women to participate' or 'There is not enough money to allow women to participate.' Each of these two responses requires independent examination.

'It would be bad for women to participate' is the standard line that has been used throughout the history of sport. The exact nature of the harm that would befall women changes. It could be that it 'defeminises' (which might mean that it would make some women less attractive in the eyes of some men – either physically or mentally), or that it would be harmful for women, that they (or sometimes their not-yet-conceived children) would suffer some physiological damage. (For a good discussion of these points see Cahn 1994.) There are two points to be made here. The first is practical. Assertions that strenuous physical exertion harms women but not men, are simply not true. But it is the second point which is more important – women have the right, just as men do, to decide what risks of harm they will run. Subject to the normal limitations on every person's freedom, it is immorally paternalistic to decide, on behalf of another competent adult, what personal risks he or she can choose to accept.

The argument that 'there is not enough money to allow women to participate' can be a more difficult case to answer. It cannot be morally required to do the impossible, however, 'there is not enough money' often masks an inequitable distribution of the resources that are available. If there is money available for anyone to participate in sport, then that money must be available on an equitable basis for both women and men. Men's sport is not intrinsically more important or more worthwhile than women's sport, and therefore, has no automatic right to majority funding.

Specific challenges to women athletes

In the discussion that follows, some of the challenges women athletes face will be examined from a philosophical point of view. Some challenges are a result of the institutional climate for women in sport (e.g. biased, resistant and 'chilly'), and will thus require policy and practice changes in sport. Others – physical, mental and indeed, spiritual – occur at a personal level.

From a physical perspective these challenges may include, but are not limited to, body composition and development issues related to the health and well-being of the athlete. Three issues in particular – disordered eating, amenorrhea and osteoporosis – are called the 'female athlete-triad.' Some of these problems are a direct result of the demands of a particular woman's participation in her sport. *Citius, altius, fortius* – pushing the human limits, male or female, has its effects. For example, many elite-level sports present high risks of injuries and, generally speaking, elite-level training produces fit, but not necessarily healthy, athletes. The results of those pressures can be, and are, in many cases, different for men and women, but the choice whether on not to train and compete is parallel. However, there is a special class of cases where the sport (such as gymnastics) is essentially judged (Suits 1988) – here the physical requirements and resulting risks are directly caused by decisions about what counts as excellent sport. The judging criteria for these sports should be tailored so as to minimise the health risks they impose on the athletes.

This is particularly a problem for women's events as women athletes have a much higher prevalence of disordered eating than men. Women athletes have, at various times, faced different ideals (Creedon 1994; Hargreaves 1995), but the greatest tension is the initial tension – between the traditional ideal athlete and the traditional ideal woman. This modern tension is readily identified in the brief history of women's competitive body building and the conflicting judging practices. Further, if it is true that most women in the general population have eating problems as well (Szekely 1988; Bordo 1990; Sherwin 1992: 189), based on the problem of unattainable ideals (in North America, for example, the two ideals have been Barbie doll and the super-waif model), then this problem is cultural and medical control may not be the best, and certainly not the only, way of addressing the issue.

Amenorrhoea and pregnancy are unique to women athletes and raise issues that are tied to the implications that all women have faced when reproductive aspects of their lives have been designated as illness; and the tension between the two conflicting traditional ideals of woman and athlete. An essential part of the traditional ideal woman is fertility because it is necessary for child-bearing. Fertility and child-bearing are not only not essential to the ideal athlete, they are antithetical to the role of athlete as warrior; for example, the Amazons. In many ways the Amazons were viewed as monstrosities because they rejected the essential biological role of woman as primary.

It is also the case, historically, that some medical authorities have created a series of double binds, situations where options are reduced for oppressed groups to a very few, all of them exposing these groups to penalty, censure or deprivation (Frye 1983: 2; Sherwin 1992: 179), through the decision to view menstruation, pregnancy, menopause, body size and some feminine behaviour forms as diseases (Lander 1988; Broverman et al. 1981). For the female athlete the situation becomes even more complicated because she can be classified as even more abnormal when reproductive changes become evaluated in the context of the traditional male sports arena. For example, if the normal healthy woman is standardly, from a medical perspective, an unhealthy adult, because the ideal healthy adult is based on being male (Broverman et. al. 1981), then it follows that the female athlete starts out an unhealthy adult because she is a woman. But, further, if the female athlete shows signs of becoming masculine, such masculinisation is thought of as further abnormality because it is not normal for a woman to have masculine characteristics. Following this kind of medical classification, when a woman bleeds, she is ill ('Woman...is generally ailing at least one week out of four...woman is not only an invalid, but a wounded one'; Lander 1988: 48), and if she does not bleed (due to amenorrhoea, menopause and pregnancy), she is ill, because it is not normal for her to be unable to conceive, thus make successful use of her biological organs (Sherwin 1992; Martin 1987; Lander 1988; Zita 1988). Pregnancy, then, theoretically constituting a state of health for the traditional ideal woman, should not be treated as disease requiring a significant amount of specialised treatment. However, women and women athletes in particular, are not encouraged to think of themselves, or their lifestyles throughout pregnancy, as healthy. Serious charges of irresponsibility can occur when the relationship between women athletes and their foetuses are characterised as adversarial. (Some countries – Canada, USA, and Australia – have begun to imprison women for endangering their foetuses; see Sherwin 1992: 107.) Most pregnant women athletes, who are falsely charged with harming their foetuses face, at the very least, moral pressure that is based on the view that being pregnant and participating in sport is a socially unacceptable behaviour. However, in some cases, genuine harm to the foetus may occur with participation in sport (oxygen deprivation, for example). But, rather than licensing interference with a female athlete's reproductive freedom, that denies her interest in the health of her foetus and her role as an active independent moral agent, our focus should be on education.

The classification of these reproductive aspects of women's lives as illnesses, can and have, led to wide-scale paternalistic medical management of women under the claims of beneficence (Sherwin 1992: 180). In sport, these so-called illnesses have been part of the basis for excluding women. This does not mean that serious complications requiring medical interventions cannot occur with any aspect of a female athlete's reproductive life or life cycle changes and ageing. (For example, that older women athletes have experienced pain during their menopause has always been a fact. Sport physicians and coaches, predominately male, simply had to learn to take their female Master's-level athletes seriously before they could recognise that this pain was all over women's bodies, not just in their heads.) There will be particular cases where the label of 'illness' or 'disease' is appropriate, provided that ascription does then lead to harming women athletes from a sport policy perspective (for example, banning them from participation in sport rather than educating them about coping with their illness and participating in sport).

The female athlete must also face challenges regarding the mental requirements of sport competition, aggression and violence. Male athletes also face these challenges, but it is considered 'normal' for men and 'abnormal' for women to engage in violence. Traditionally, it has also been predominately men who have committed sexual abuses against women (and minors) in sport. (Some researchers suggest that this predominance may be linked to the socially and legally accepted high levels of violence in some sport; Kirby & Brackenridge 1997.) The control over, and moral responsibility for, violence, abuse, harassment and discrimination, in sport and surrounding sport, lies predominately within the hands of those in the sport community and it is a concern for both men and women. Some women, weary of not having their voices heard on these issues (and for a host of other reasons), advocate completely separate sport for women as opposed to any integration at all.

One argument against integration is that women have to accept the current selection of sports, primarily designed for and practised by men, with an established culture with rewarding and recognising values (such as sport as a battleground on which one conquers one's foes) that most women do not hold; whereas separation might allow women the freedom to create sport based on the values they choose (Lenskyj 1984). Capacities that are viewed as unique to women – sharing, giving, nurturing, sympathising, empathising and, above all, connecting as opposed to dividing – are stressed in this argument. Nevertheless, some would urge women to pay the high price of integration, so that they can have the same opportunities, occupations, rights, and privileges that men have had in sport. This drive for women's sameness with men has sometimes denied women's qualities and how these qualities might contribute in a very positive manner to sport. The argument is that, if women emphasise their differences from men, viewing these as biologically produced and/or culturally shaped differences, they will trap themselves into ghettos, while men will carry on as before.

If we think that women athletes either act as men, if they accept the male ideal, or must be separate and generate their own ideal, the sport experience is highly gender-specific. But, the two views of sport – sport as competition (agon), a test against others to overcome; or as connected co-questers searching and striving for excellence – may well be logically independent of the gender of the athlete.

However, the greatest tension arises for women if we have an 'agonistic' view of sport and women are found to be inherently ('essentially') caring and connected to others (Noddings 1984). In such a model of sport, women may be required to disconnect from their embodied experience. This could be the case for some form of alienation. Most athletes (male and female) find themselves torn between conflicting views of sport because pushing oneself to one's limits challenges even the strongest sense of self, and because in their moments of agony and joy they tend to experience themselves as both radically alone (because no one else can really understand what they feel) and fundamentally united to their team-mates, their competitors, particularly when this experience happens during a major competition.

The logic of gender verification

Entirely separate sport, and even just separate women's events, inevitably leads to the question of the logic of gender verification. If we are to have separate sport, or sporting events for women only, logically it must be possible to exclude any men who may wish, for whatever reason, to compete. This means that there must be a rule of eligibility that excludes men. (Conversely, if we have such a rule for excluding men, should we, for consistency, have such a rule excluding women from men's events even if the women believed they would inevitably lose, but wanted to take part anyway?) This in turn requires that we have a test of gender and/or sex, that can be applied fairly to any potential participant. There are at least three methods of applying any such test: the first would be to test all contestants; the second, random contestants; the third, targeted individuals.

Before looking any more at testing further, we must first deal with the response that we do not need to test because a man would never wish to compete in a women's event. 'Never' is a very strong word. It is not beyond the realm of imagination that a money-hungry promoter might decide that it was a great publicity stunt to enter men in a women's event. A male may even, with good intentions, choose to enter a women's event (such as synchronised swimming) as a form of protest against gender discrimination. Without a test to decide just who is eligible, we could be forced to accept, in women's events, participants who were quite obviously and unashamedly male, but who merely professed to be female.

There is a great deal of debate about how sex roles and gender are established (Travis, Hubbard and Lowe, Schreiber, Blau and Ferber, and Lindsey). Mercier, in her gender verification report (1993), takes the position that sex is one's biological characteristics, and gender is one's socially learned characteristics. The standard practice in the Olympic Games is to have medical experts verify gender. But, by delegating gender verification to medical experts, the sport community (and society in general) has given great power to medical experts on an issue that is in great dispute by researchers. Gender may not be merely a medical question, though it involves medical questions. Dialogues on gender, and gender in sport, have serious social, political and legal dimensions, making the medical story only part of the story.

In 1976 a new player, Renée Clarke, appeared on the US women's tennis circuit, who 'soundly thrashed' the defending champion in the women's division. She was subsequently shown to be Renée Richards, who had recently undergone a sex-change operation and who had previously been a male elite level tennis player (Birrell & Cole 1994: 207–237). The US Women's Tennis Federation wanted to exclude, as unfair competition, a player who was genetically male, but was reconstructed physiologically and now (presumably), psychologically female. The United States Tennis Association and the United States Open Committee therefore introduced the requirement that players take the Barr test (Birrell & Cole 1994: 207). Richards refused, and went to court to demand the right to participate in women's events. In court she was deemed to be female on the basis of the medical evidence produced by the surgeons and medical professionals who had overseen his transformation from male to female. In the media this story played as an example of a courageous individual fighting for personal rights against an intransigent and uncaring 'system' (Birrell & Cole 1994). There are other ways of viewing the story, however.

What makes a woman a woman? Is it chromosomes, genitalia, a way of life or set of roles, or a medical record? It is not clear why medical evidence of surgery and psychology should outweigh chromosomal evidence. In fact it is not clear why any one answer should be taken as categorically overriding any other.

How to approach issues for women in sport

In the field of bioethics, Rosemarie Tong (1995) has suggested that there are three standard elements of methodology that can be used to deal with concerns for women. I believe this methodology may also be very useful for issues regarding women in sport. The first element suggested involves asking what was originally referred to as 'the woman question' and is now called by some researchers 'the gender biased question' (Tuttle 1986: 349). This question challenges the supposed objectivity of scientific research findings regarding the nature of woman and the objectivity of the professions (such as sport medicine) based on that research (Dreifus 1977; Corea 1985; Okruhlik 1995; Schiebinger 1989, 1993). Underpinning this question is the suggestion that many of the 'facts' about female 'nature' actually result from values founded on biased social constructions.[4] The precepts and practices of sport can be, and are, misshaped by gender bias.[5] This gender bias works almost unconsciously and occurs when decision-makers, physicians and coaches in sport treat all athletes, all human bodies, as if they were all male athletes and male bodies. They would then view athletes, or their bodies, as dysfunctional if they failed to function like male bodies, or expressed little or no curiosity or interest in the problems unique to women. There are issues in sport that are, for the most part, unique to women (for example, the female athlete triad – eating disorders, amenorrhoea and osteoporosis, gender verification, reproductive control and pregnancy, sexual harassment, etc.). There are issues unique to men. There are issues unique to certain sports. There are common issues for participants across regions, sports and particular quadrennial cycles. Physicians, coaches and sport organisers need to be aware enough of sex/gender similarities and differences to deal with these issues.

The second suggested part of this methodology is that of consciousness-raising, which requires that women be seriously invited to contribute their personal experiences into sport, so that it has wider meaning for all women. It is postulated that women who share sexual stereotyping or harassment stories in sport, for example, often come to realise that their feeling of having been treated as a girl, rather than a woman, or treated as a man, are not unique to them but common to most women. Such women, if given the opportunity, routinely gain the courage and the confidence to challenge those who presume to know what is best for them, as they become increasingly convinced that it is not they, but (in this case) the sport 'system', that is crazy. The purpose of this consciousness-raising is to achieve fundamental changes by connecting the personal experiences of women to developments in sport. Consciousness-raising suggests that women, sharing among themselves, will become empowered and able to take on some of the responsibility of changing the sport world.

The last part of Tong's methodology is based on at least three philosophical moral theorists: Aristotle's *Nicomachean Ethics* (1976: book 8), Rawls' *A Theory of Justice* (1971) and Mill's *Utilitarianism* and *On Liberty* (1972). She suggests it is an attempt to gain a Rawlsian reflective equilibrium between principles, rules, ideals, values and virtues on the one hand, and actual cases in which moral decisions must be made on the other.[6] It is also proposed that Aristotelian practical reasoning assumes that moral choices are made, for the most part, between several moral agents, rather than isolated within one individual. Finally, Mill's views on the importance of listening, as well as speaking, in the course of a moral dialogue is stressed. Tong's claim that the practice of ethics requires communication, corroboration, and collaboration, and we are not alone when we grapple with applying ethics, is true and can be utilised in the realm of sport.

Such a methodology may assist us in discovering mutually agreeable ways to weaken patterns of male domination and female subordination in the realm of sport. As suggested, this type of discussion requires adopting a particular set of questions. The answers to these questions must be dealt with and understood within the context of women's experiences in sport. If we truly seek understanding of these issues, we must understand the perspective, and thus the social, psychological and political predispositions, that we, ourselves, bring to the discussion. For example, differences in race, gender, education, social/political position, nationality, religion and sexuality are going to bring different perspectives and contexts to the questions of gender, ethics and sport. This fact does not mean that we cannot reach some agreement on important issues, but it does mean that we must be willing to listen, and give due respect, to differing perspectives in our search for justice. This search for justice also requires an understanding of where the power to make changes lies, and the willingness, of those who hold it, to share that power. So far the predominant male power-brokers in sport have not demonstrated this willingness.

If we apply this methodology to the questions surrounding gender verification in sport – by taking the three steps of asking 'the woman of gender-biased question'; raising consciousness by connecting the personal experiences of women to developments on gender verification in sport and sport medicine; and using practical reasoning that attempts to gain a reflective equilibrium and accepts our limited ability to explain and justify our decisions, while simultaneously insisting that we try harder to find the appropriate ways – women themselves will (and should) be the guardians and decision-makers concerning women's sport.

Some women argue that any gender or sex test is demeaning (especially visual confirmation of the 'correct' genitalia) and discriminates against women athletes if it not also applied to men. Clearly the use of any test, given the complexity of human sex and gender, may lead to anomalies and surprises. Yet many women wish to have sporting competitions that exclude men. The best result we can achieve will be one that arises through discussion, debate and consensus and it will be the fairest we can reach. A coherent understanding of the causes of women's subordination to men in sport, coupled with a refined programme of action designed to eliminate the systems and attitudes that oppress or neglect women in sport, must guide this complex approach. A detailed analysis of the distribution of power in each case can identify a particular factor as the primary cause of women's subordinate status in sport, which, for the most part, has traditionally been based on biology. Researchers can, and should, attempt to ascertain the actual status of women in sport and determine how far that condition deviates from what justice prescribes.

The current sport conditions may be made more objective by providing more facts, as opposed to myths or stereotypes, about women athletes, thus alleviating or even eliminating the past and ongoing injustices. The knowledge required to create good, just and rational sport practice can be acquired; it is a matter of discovering and acknowledging all of the true facts.

Everyone's knowledge about sport, sport science, and the health and wellbeing of all athletes, including women athletes, is limited. If we wish to understand a broader experience in sport than just the dominant male one; we must talk to, and take seriously, as many athletes as possible. Women athletes are now beginning to be credited with being able to see things about the reality of sport that men do not typically see (Messner and Sabo 1990). The dominant position in any set of social relations – the general position of men vis-à-vis women in sport – tends to produce distorted visions of the real regularities and underlying causal tendencies in social relations. Men experience their power over women in sport as normal – even beneficial – and this is not women's experience. Women see symptoms of male domination and female subordination in sport as abnormal and harmful.

Political, social and psychological position are not irrelevant. These criteria contribute significantly to the way in which we see the fundamental facts about the athlete's body and mind. Women in sport may possibly find truth and justice, but right now they are nebulous and, unfortunately for women athletes, it may still be some time before they emerge. Right now, however, not all reasonable people necessarily see the same thing when the facts about women and sport stare them in the face.

Notes

1   See Schneider (1992, 1993), and Schneider & Butcher (1994, 1997).
2   For a current personal account of the relationship between masculinity and sport in North America, see Messner and Sabo (1994).
3   However, Coubertin apparently never saw women as having central roles in Olympism. He preferred them as spectators and medal-bearers for presentation to the victors.
4   See Ehrenreich and English (1989) and Fausto-Sterling (1985) for this critique of medicine.
5   See Tong (1995) and Sherwin (1992) for this discussion in the profession of medicine.
6   Tong has suggested this for the area of bioethics (1995: 27).

References

Aristotle (1941) *Ethica Nicomachea* (Nicomachean Ethics). In R. McKeon (ed.) *The Basic Works of Aristotle*. New York: Random House. pp. 935–1127.

Bartlett, K. (1993) 'Feminist Legal Methods.' In D. K. Weisberg (ed.) *Feminist Legal Theory: Foundations*. Philadelphia: Temple University Press. pp. 558–566.

Bender, D. & Leone, B. (eds.) (1995) *Male/Female Roles: Opposing Viewpoints*. Opposing Viewpoints Series, San Diego, CA: Greenhaven Press.

Bluestone, N. (1987) *Women and the Ideal Society: Plato's Republic and Modern Myths of Gender*. Amherst, Massachusetts: The University of Massachusetts Press.

Bordo, S. (1990) 'Reading the Slender Body.' In M. Jacobus, E. Fox Keller & S. Shuttleworth (eds.) *Body/Politics: Women and the Discourses of Science*. New York: Routledge.

Broverman, I., Broverman, D., Clarkson, F., Rosenkrantz, P., & Vogel, S. (1981) 'Sex Role Stereotypes and Clinical Judgments of Mental Health'. In E. Howell & M. Bayes (eds.) *Women and Mental Health*. New York: Basic Books.

Butcher, R. B. & Schneider, A. J. (1993) *The Ethical Rationale for Drug-Free Sport*. Canadian Centre for Drug-Free Sport, Ottawa, Ontario, Canada.

Cahn, S. (1994) *Coming on Strong: Gender and Sexuality in Twentieth-Century Women's Sport*. New York: The Free Press.

Cohen, G. (1993) *Women in Sport: Issues and Controversies*. Newbury Park, CA: Sage Publications.

Corea, G. (1985) The *Hidden Malpractice: How American Medicine Mistreats Women*. Revised Edition. New York: Harper Colophon Books.

Coubertin, P. de (1912) 'Women in the Olympic Games.' *Olympic Review*.

Creedon, P. (ed.) (1994) *Women, Media and Sport*. California: Sage Publications.

Darlison, L. (1996) 'The Starting Line.' *Women Sport International*.

De Frantz, A. (1993) 'The Olympic Games: Our Birthright to Sports'. In G. Cohen (ed.) *Women in Sport: Issues and Controversies*. California: Sage Publications.

Dreifus, C. (ed) (1977) *Seizing Our Bodies: The Politics of Women's Health*. New York: Vintage Books, Random House.

Ehrenreich, B. & English, D. (1979) *For Her Own Good: 150 Years of the Experts' Advice to Women*. Garden City, New York: Anchor Books.

Fausto-Sterling, A. (1985) *Myths of Gender: Biological Theories About Women and Men*. New York: Basic Books.

Frye, M. (1983) *The Politics of Reality: Essays in Feminist Theory*. Freedom, California: Crossing Press.

Hargreaves, J. (1995) 'A Historical Look at the Changing Symbolic Meanings of the Female Body in Western Sport.' In F. van der Merwe (ed.) *Sport as Symbol, Symbols in Sport*. ISHPES Studies, Volume 4, pp. 249–259. Germany: Academia Verlag.

Kirby, S. & Brackenridge, C. (1997) *Coming to Terms: Sexual Abuse in Sport*. Unpublished.

Kittay, E. & Meyers, D. (eds.) (1987) *Women and Moral Theory*. New Jersey: Rowman & Littlefield.

Lander, L. (1988) *Images of Bleeding: Menstruation as Ideology*. New York: Orlando Press.

Leigh, M. (1974) *The Evolution of Women's Participation in the Summer Olympic Games, 1900–1948*. Unpublished doctoral dissertation, The Ohio State University, Columbus, Ohio, USA.

Lefkowitz, M. & Fant, M. (1982) *Women's Life in Greece and Rome: A Source Book in Translation*. Baltimore, Maryland: The Johns Hopkins University Press.

Lenskyj, H. (1984) *Sport Integration or Separation*. Ottawa: Fitness and Amateur Sport.

Lenskyj, H. (1986) *Out of Bounds: Women, Sport and Sexuality*. Toronto: The Women's Press.

Loland, S. (1994) 'Pierre de Coubertin's Ideology of Olympism from the Perspective of the History of Ideas.' In R. K. Barney & K. V. Meier (eds.) *Critical Reflections on Olympic Ideology: Second International Symposium for Olympic Research*. pp. 26–45. Centre for Olympic Studies, The University of Western Ontario, London, Ontario, Canada.

Lowe. B. (1977) *The Beauty of Sport: A Cross-disciplinary Inquiry*. Englewood Cliffs, New Jersey: Prentice-Hall. pp. 41–43.

MacKinnon, C. (1987) 'Women, Self-Possession and Sport'. In *Feminism Unmodified: Discourses on Life and Law*. Cambridge: Harvard University Press. pp. 117–126.

Mahowald, M. (1978) *Philosophy of Woman: An Anthology of Classic and Current Concepts*. Indianapolis, Indiana: Hackett Publishing.

Messner, M. & Sabo, D. (eds.) (1990) *Sport, Men and the Gender Order: Critical Feminist Perspectives*. Champaign, IL: Human Kinetics.

Messner, M. & Sabo, D. (1994) *Sex, Violence and Power in Sports: Rethinking Masculinity*. Freedom, California: Crossing Press.

Mill, J. (1972) *Utilitarianism, On Liberty, and Considerations on Representative Government*. H. Acton (ed.). New York: E. P. Dutton & Co.

Noddings, N. (1984) *Caring: A Feminine Approach to Ethics and Moral Education*. Berkeley: University of California Press.

Okruhlik, K. (1995) 'Gender and the Biological Sciences.' *Canadian Journal Philosophy. Volume* 20, 21–42.

Plato (1961) 'Republic'. In *Plato: The Collected Dialogues*. E. Hamilton & H. Cairns (eds.). New Jersey: Princeton University Press. pp. 575–844.

Postow, B. (ed.) (1983) *Women, Philosophy, and Sport: A Collection of New Essays*. New Jersey: The Scarecrow Press.

Rawls, J. (1971) *A Theory of Justice*. Cambridge: Harvard University Press.

Rioux. G. (1986) *Propos Liminaires: Pierre de Coubertin educateur (1863–1937)*. In G. Rioux (ed.) *Pierre de Coubertin, Textes Choisis, Tome I, Revelations*. Zurich: Weidmann. pp. 19–21.

Schiebinger, L. (1993) *Nature's Body: Gender in the Making of Modern Science*. Boston: Beacon Press.

Schiebinger, L. (1989) *The Mind Has No Sex? Women in the Origins of Modern Science*. Cambridge, Massachusetts: Harvard University Press.

Schneider, A. J. (1992) 'Harm, Athletes' Rights and Doping Control.' In R. K. Barney & K. V. Meier (eds.) *First International Symposium for Olympic Research*, pp. 164–172. University of Western Ontario, Centre for Olympic Studies, London, Ontario, Canada.

—— (1993) 'Doping in Sport and the Perversion Argument.' In G. Gaebauer (ed.) *The Relevance of the Philosophy of Sport*. pp. 117–128. Berlin, Germany: Academia Verlag.

—— (1995) 'Gender, Sexuality & Sport in America.' In *The Journal of the Philosophy of Sport*, Vol. XXII, pp. 136–143.

Schneider, A. J. & Butcher, R. B. (1993) 'For the Love of the Game: A Philosophical Defence of Amateurism.' In *Quest*, Vol. 45 (4), 460–469.

Schneider, A. J. & Butcher, R. B. (1994) 'Why Olympic Athletes Should Avoid the Use and Seek the Elimination of Performance-Enhancing Substances and Practices in the Olympic Games.' *Journal of the Philosophy of Sport*, Vols. XX & XXI, 64–81.

Segrave, J. (1988) 'Toward a Definition of Olympism.' In *The Olympic Games in Transition*. Champaign, IL: Human Kinetics Books, pp. 149–162.

Segreave, J. & Chu. D. (eds.) (1988) *The Olympic Games in Transition*. Champaign, IL: Human Kinetics.

Sherwin, S. (1992) *No Longer Patient: Feminist Ethics and Health Care*. Philadelphia: Temple University Press.

Spears, B. (1988) 'Tryphosa, Melpomene, Nadia, and Joan: The IOC and Women's Sport.' In J. Segrave and D. Chu (eds.) *The Olympic Games in Transition*. Champaign, IL: Human Kinetics Books. pp. 365–374.

Suits, B. (1988) 'Tricky Triad: Games, Play and Sport'. *Journal of Philosophy of Sport*. Volume xiii, 1–9.

Szekely, E. (1988) *Never Too Thin*. Toronto: The Women's Press.

Tong, R. (1995) 'What's Distinctive About Feminist Bioethics?' In F. Baylis, J. Downie, B. Freedman, B. Hoffmaster, & S. Sherwin (eds.) *Health Care Ethics in Canada*, Toronto: Harcourt Brace Canada.

Tuttle, L. (1986) *Encyclopaedia of Feminism*. Essex: Longman.

Zita, J. (1988) 'The Premenstrual Syndrome: Dis-easing the Female Cycle.' *Hypatia* 3 (1), 77–99.

Part 2

Objectification

Chapter 4

Sexualization and sexuality in sport*

Paul Davis

Much has been written in recent years about the sexualization of the athlete.[1] I do not wish to rehash it, nor do I wish to quibble with any of it. However, one upshot of the realizations involved in this work is a pervasive distrust of anything that seems to connect sport with the sexual.

I will try to argue that this feeling is exaggerated. This will require the challenging task of attempting to distinguish between sexualization and sexuality. By combining this distinction with ordinary reflections on the essential nature of sport, I will argue that the sport arena is peculiarly unfitted to be unisexual.

I wish first to distinguish two species of athlete sexualization. The first is grounded in sport performance, and the second is not. This distinction matters for two reasons. First, the performance-specific kind serves to confirm that sport as a practice offers unusually generous possibilities of sexualization and will, in turn, vivify the unavoidable phenomenon of sexuality in sport. Second, the other kind more clearly demonstrates the continuity between athlete sexualization and sexualization in general. This should, in turn, improve the prospects of providing a general account of sexualization and of saying why, unlike sexuality, it is objectionable.

The performance-specific species of sexualization is the sexualized imagery of athletic performance commonly found in newspaper and television coverage of sport. Three qualities are (variously) in evidence here:

- The deliberate focus on particular, sexually significant body parts for the purpose of sexual titillation.
- The attunement to bodily postures that, through freezing or emphasis, are intended to be sexually titillating.
- In the case of photographs in either of the preceding categories, an accompanying, frequently punned caption confirms the moment as one of sexualized comic relief.[2]

---

* Originally published in *Ethics in Sport*. Edited by William J. Morgan, Klaus V. Meier, and Angela J. Schneider. Champaign IL: Human Kinetics, 2001, pp. 285–292.

The sport performance is necessary to this sexualization in that it is the movements made and poses struck whilst in the arena that are sexualized.

Sexualization of the athlete not grounded in the sport performance takes diffuse forms. The most familiar, historically, is probably the public observation of the attractiveness of female athletes offered by male journalists and television hosts and commentators. A less banal example is provided by a recent British television talk show hosted by a well-known male soccer player.[3] As the show kicks in, the host is filmed showering and dressing. A camera focused at crotch level highlights sexually significant parts in, arguably, a sexually significant state. It is tempting to conclude that this example is that of a sexualized celebrity who happens to be an athlete, a conclusion made more alluring by the fact that the show is not essentially about sport (the host chats with singers, for instance, without involving sport in the conversation). However, the conclusion is perhaps too abrasive in this case, since some classes of athletes have socially evolved into the intrinsically sexy, grounding context-indifferent sexualization of their members. Some attention has been given in recent years, for instance, to the sexualization of the black male athlete,[4] and it is probably no accident that the host of this show is a black male athlete.

I will not concern myself here with the shady commerce between athlete sexualization and variables such as sex, race, class, and sexual orientation, important though these topics are. This is instead an a priori inquiry into the distinction between sexuality and sexualization and the application of this distinction to the social practice of sport.

Consider another phenomenon, a not uncommon one, that might look at first like another clear case of sexualization: that of swimmers at a club who feel a sexual interest in a locker room photograph of a prolific swimmer in the act of swimming. This case is ambiguous. It would be highly premature to regard it as simply another instance of sexualization. In this context, the photograph is infused with an important generality of meaning. The picture is inscribed with the message that *our sport*—swimming, in this case—is sexy, that swimming is a sexy thing to do. In addition, there is a critical particularity about the photograph and the sexual stimulus elicited. Swimming is something those who enjoy the picture can identify with deeply, something that excites them at a fundamental level and probably has done so since a point in their lives at which talk of *sexual* responses is not an issue. Not just any picture will do, nor is the sexual response of club members an undifferentiated excitation. The sexual response is highly precise and is uniquely caused by the sight of a quality swimmer in the act of swimming.[5]

In addition, qualities of this case sharpen, perhaps in a critical way, the contrast with the preceding cases. Two interrelated features exist here. The first concerns the content of the picture. There is no attempt by the photographer to focus on sexually significant body parts such as the breasts, buttocks, or crotch. The photo does not attempt to reveal a sexually marketable body posture. There is no tawdry caption; all that might appear beneath the photo is the name of the swimmer and the event the photograph is taken from. These qualities distinguish this case sharply from the others, each of which is characterized by at least one of the aforementioned features.

The second feature is that the photograph does not result from an extraneous agenda, nor, relatedly, does it require any contrivance or discordance of content and context. This is in contrast to the performance-specific class of sexualization, in which the shot or photograph is clearly motivated by considerations extraneous to the sport context. The context in the example of the swimming photo is one in which the appropriate considerations are sporting ones, but this is farcically at odds with a shot or photograph that is explicitly shaped to sexually titillate. The appropriate context—if any—for such a shot or photograph is a magazine or video geared towards teenagers. In the case of the television show, similarly, the opening shots are more suited to the beginning of a soft porn video than to the beginning of a talk show. (The aforementioned sexual accolades offered by male journalists and television hosts and commentators are appropriate in—at best—a beauty contest.) Again, none of this grotesquery is present in the case under consideration—a shot of a swimmer swimming, driven by a photographer's ambition, perhaps, of capturing the distinctive character of this particular swimmer or something of the kinaesthetic character of high-powered competitive swimming in general. The photograph appears in a swimmers' locker room, and some of the swimmers find it sexually stimulating.

I propose that we consider this instance not sexualization of the athlete but rather unobjectionable sexuality in sport. It also offers an intimation of how sport is particularly unfitted to be unsexual. Clarification of these suggestions requires a brief theoretical detour on the nature of both sport and sexual response.

In his book *Sexual Desire*, Roger Scruton articulates a persuasive case on the essential character of human sexual response (Scruton, 1986). Integral to the phenomenon of sexual desire, he argues, are metaphysical shadows of which we cannot disburden ourselves. Because the "I" seems transparent to itself, the idea irresistibly arises that what I am essentially is "this self-knowing I . . . who lies concealed within, behind or beyond the organism, but who cannot be identical with the organism, for the very reason that the bodily states and the substance of this organism remain obscure to me, while my mental life is thoroughly and completely known" (Scruton, 1986: 56). We therefore take ourselves to be "pure, unified individuals, havens of possibility, located outside the limits of natural causality, capable of acting freely and integrally, so as to be responsible for the present action at every future time" (Scruton, 1986: 58).[6] This is what it is to be a person. I constantly identify myself without reference to my body and react to you as though you were not identical with your body but operating through it. We are capable of experiencing a quite radical estrangement from our bodies, for example, when examining the state of them, or when considering whether we should lose weight or what we should wear tonight. We can experience even profound alienation from our bodies; when ill or incapacitated, I might think of my body as a prison in which the self is trapped. From the first-person point of view, a person seems essentially a perspective, a willing, experiencing, thinking subject, contingently connected to a body. This theory of the human agent is given considerable and distinguished exposition in the shape of the Cartesian ego, the Leibnizian apperception, the Kantian "transcendental unity of consciousness" and "transcendental self," the Hegelian *Fürsichsein*, and the Sartrean "*pour-soi*." Only when we detach ourselves from the first-person perspective might it seem to rest on an illusion. But we cannot abandon the first-person perspective. We might conclude that we cannot live with it. But neither can we live without it.

If we cannot evade this self-mystification, then neither can we escape its metaphysical counterpoint of embodiment.[7] How can putatively transcendental subjects be individuated except through their bodies? How can I implement my (free) will except through my body (even if this amounts to nothing more than using my voice)? Isn't it true that someone who hits my body has hit *me*? Helmuth Plessner has argued that I stand to my body in a relation that is at once instrumental and constitutive: I *have* my body, but I also *am* my body.[8] Consequently, the relation of self to body has essentially an enigmatic, frequently troubling quality.

In sexual desire, we aspire to suspend this fraught relation of self and body. It is not a body that is desired. The desired is, *qua desired*, a perspectival, freely willing, and responsible being. The desiring wishes his or her own perspective to figure in the perspective of the desired, and wishes himself or herself to be freely desired.[9] At the same time, the aim of desire is the complete embodiment of each point of view. In sexual desire the embodiment of persons is itself the object of our interest. What is desired is the *person as body-subject*. We seek to reveal the life of another in the life of the body, through a largely involuntary gamut of responses such as smiles, stares, blushes, and changes in the sexual organs. We seek to unite the desired with his or her body, and at the ideal limit of sexual response we are profoundly united with our bodies. A critical fact about human sexual response is that the very incitements to desire are often the smiles, the walk, the movements, the expressions, the voice—in short, the *bodily agency*—of the desired, especially when, significantly, it seems not to be self-conscious. In sexual desire we celebrate, perhaps as in no other realm, the fact that our subjecthood is, for all the vaunted glories of free will, responsibility, and the like, a marvellously corporeal phenomenon.[10] This is what gives human sexuality its character as existential triumph. What might be a prison becomes for a time a hospitable home.

Consider sport. Here too the embodiment of the person is the object of our interest. Here too we are, as performer or spectator, interested in neither bodies nor immaterial soul, but the person as body-subject. In its well-documented noninstrumentality, sport is, indeed, a celebration of the body-subject.[11] The athlete is conceived, qua athlete, as a perspectival, freely willing, and responsible being (for that reason, spectators tend to be disappointed by a competitor, and especially a victor, who looks robotic).[12] Again, the athlete seeks the unity of self and body. At the ideal limit of sport, also, a person is profoundly united with his or her body; free will, responsibility, and the rest roundly converge with materiality. Paraphrasing Yeats, we do not know the dancer from the dance.[13] As spectators, we tend to find sport particularly pleasing when, significantly, it manifests a bodily agency that seems not to be self-conscious. (In performance of both sport and sex, indeed, we tend to mess up if we become conscious of our bodies).[14] The common celebration of the embodied subject makes the idea that sexuality should or could be expunged from sport a singularly fishy one. It is, indeed, the shared centrality of the body that makes sport as a practice particularly vulnerable to performance-specific sexualization. In this respect, sport is distinctive, and the possibilities for sexualization that it offers provide a discontinuity with most of the rest of life. The practice of chess, for instance, is not similarly vulnerable to sexualization. The fact that sport is intrinsically so sexualization-friendly should cast doubt on the ambition of banishing or marginalizing the sexuality that is within it.

The preceding reflections are intended to lend some persuasive force to my suggestion that the phenomenon exemplified in the picture in the locker room is sexuality and not sexualization. In this case, the object of sexual intrigue is the uncompromised, unmediated person as body-subject, manifested in sport. Whatever sexual ramifications the picture has emerge out of the shot of the subject swimming. There is no clash between content and context. There is no decontextualization of this body-subject, because it is the rich and precise character of the movements of a top-level swimmer that the photographer is hoping to capture. It is significant here, as I have already indicated, that those whose enjoyment of the picture has the precise sexual edge I have emphasized have an intimate engagement with the activity of swimming.

Contrast this with the other cases described in this chapter. Imagine a familiar example of an opportunistically captioned tabloid shot of a female tennis player whose lunge with her racquet reveals a little cleavage. This is sexualization, and is objectionable, for two interrelated reasons: it involves an artificial focus on particular, sexually significant body parts, a focus that temporarily detaches the body from the rich and precise bodily agency on display on the tennis court and reconfigures it into something trivially titillating or comic (or both). An observer could experience the intended titillation or amusement without any appreciation of the game of tennis. Conversely, the essentially precise sexual response of the swimmers could not be paralleled with innocuous tennis film or photography if the respondent does not have a serious appreciation of tennis.

The talk show example also clearly involves a dramatic rupture of content and context. (And the same is true, again, of the inappropriate comments of male journalists and television commentators and hosts.) The inappropriate footage aggressively detaches the body of the show's host from the context in which his agency is present. In this feature athlete sexualization is continuous with sexualization in general. The critical characteristic is the decontextualization of the body-subject. This provides sexualization, in contradistinction to sexuality. And this is objectionable.

If my argument is sound, then it follows that sexual responses to sport and athletes do not inevitably betoken ideological invasion. Many such responses no doubt do, and those who are sexually titillated by examples such as those presented in this chapter ought not to be, and should retrain their responses.

However, as I have tried to illustrate, a sexual component in the enjoyment of sport needn't always be a guilty secret.

Notes

1 See, for instance, Paul Willis, 1994, "Women in Sport in Ideology," in *Women, Sport, and Culture*, ed. S. Birrell and C. Cole (Champaign, Ill.: Human Kinetics), 31–45, esp. 35, 41–42; M. MacNeill, "Active Women, Media Representations, and Ideology" (ibid., 273–87), and A. Blasamo, "Feminist Bodybuilding" (ibid., 341–52), esp. 343–45.
2 I borrow this felicitous expression from the essay of M.C. Duncan, M.A. Messner, L. Williams, and K. Jensen, "Gender Stereotyping in Televised Sports," in S. Birrell and C. Cole, 251. The authors apply the description to the use of female spectators in television coverage of sport.
3 "Friday Night's All Wright" (London Weekend Television, 1998).
4 See, for instance, E. Cashmore, 1982, *Black Sportsmen* (London: Routledge) and Pieterse, J.N., 1992, *White on Black: Images of Africa and Blacks in Western Popular Culture* (New Haven: Yale University Press).
5 For powerful criticism of theories of the emotions that reduce emotion to apprehension plus an undifferentiated general excitement, see R.W. Hepburn, "Emotions and Emotional Qualities," 1965, in *Collected Papers on Aesthetics*, ed. C. Barrett, (Oxford: Blackwell), esp. 195. Hepburn's comments are in discussion of emotions evoked by artworks. For a recognition of specificity of affect in discussion of art and sport, see Terence J. Roberts, "Sport, Art, and Particularity: The Best Equivocation," 1995, in *Philosophic Inquiry in Sport*, ed. W.J. Morgan and Klaus V. Meier (Champaign, Ill: Human Kinetics), esp. 417–18.
6 Roger Scruton, 1986, *Sexual Desire* (London: Weidenfeld and Nicolson). See also Thomas Nagel, 1986, *The View From Nowhere* (New York City: Oxford University Press), 110–26, and also Thomas Nagel, 1979, "Subjective and Objective," in *Mortal Questions* (Cambridge: Cambridge University Press).
7 Kantian philosopher Strawson has stated that persons are essentially the sort of things to which M(material)-predicates and P(psychological)-predicates apply. See P.F. Strawson, 1959, *Individual* (London: Methuen), 87–116.
8 Helmuth Plessner, 1970, *Laughing and Crying: A Study of the Limits of Human Behaviour*, transl. James Spencer Churchill and Marjorie Grene, Evanston: Northwestern University Press.
9 On the reflective perspectival interplay of sexual response, see Nagel, "Sexual Perversion," in *Mortal Question*.

10 This summation of the nature of persons is that of Michel de Montaigne (*Essays III, viii*). Charles Taylor (1990) quotes it in *The Sources of the Self* (Cambridge: Harvard University Press), 181.
11 See, for instance, Iris Marion Young, "The Exclusion of Women From Sport: Conceptual and Existential Dimensions," reprinted in Morgan and Meier, esp. 263. Also Joseph H. Kupfer, "Sport: The Body Electric," reprinted in Morgan and Meier, esp. 392–93 and 403–4.
12 For endorsement of the notion that sport is properly a competition between persons, see Robert L. Simon, "Good Competition and Drug-Enhanced Performance," in Morgan and Meier, 109–14. For an interesting recent discussion suggesting that our paradigms of freedom and responsibility (and related reactive attitudes such as praise) may be exaggerated in sport as elsewhere, see David Carr, 1999, "Where's the Merit If the Best Man Wins?" *Journal of the Philosophy of Sport* 26 (1999): 1–9.
13 "O body swayed to music, O brightening glance, / How can we know the dancer from the dance?" W.B. Yeats, "Among School Children," in *Collected Poems* (1982) (London: Macmillan), 242–45.
14 I am indebted to Gunnar Brevik for making this point in his presentation to the 1999 International Association for the Philosophy of Sport conference in Bedford, England ("The Self in Bodily Movement").

Chapter 5

Mere and partial means

The full range of the objectification of women*

Carolyn McLeod

Kant discussed the moral wrong of treating people as *mere* means or as a means *only*.[1] To treat people as means is to treat them as objects for our use. It is to objectify them. To treat people as a mere means is to treat them wholly as objects, rather than partially so. It is to have an objectifying manner that is absolute or unmitigated. Whether Kant meant to suggest that we commit a moral wrong only when we treat people as means absolutely, rather than partially, is debatable.[2] My concern is how feminist theorists writing on the objectification of women have followed Kant in emphasizing the extreme case of the mere means. These feminists have implied that the moral wrong of objectification occurs only with absolute objectification, as though between it and respecting someone's autonomy there were no degrees of objectification that are morally suspect.

The relevant feminists' work centres on such topics as women's reproductive freedom, their sexual freedom, and gender equity in employment. In discussing women's objectification in reproductive health, feminists often depict women either as 'breeders' or as choosing beings; they are either the 'mere maternal environment' or conscious moral agents. In illustrating women's sexual objectification, feminists tend to use such stark examples as the Playboy Bunny or the rape victim. A central case in Sandra Lee Bartky's work on objectification is that of a woman interviewed for a philosophy job who had the chair stare at her breasts throughout the entire interview. Bartky writes, "In this situation, the woman is a bosom, not a job candidate" (Bartky 1990: 27). She is *mere* bosom.

But what about the woman who is both bosom and job candidate? Are there not gradations of the objectification of women? And what do we miss by assuming there are not? Perhaps there is no such thing as objectifying people to degrees; objectification involves seeing another *as an object*, not as

---

* Originally published as 'Mere and partial means: the full range of the objectification of women' in *Moral Philosophy*, *Canadian Journal of Philosophy*, 2002, suppl. vol. 28. Edited by Samantha Brennan. © University of Calgary Press 2002.

part-object, part-person. Perhaps what I am calling degrees of objectification are simply instances of treating persons without the full respect they deserve. Such treatment is disrespectful, but not objectifying.

I shall answer objections of that sort while defending the claims that objectification admits of degrees and that a significant portion of the objectification of women in contemporary Western society—the objectification that contributes to their oppression—is what I call 'partial objectification.' To acknowledge the full range of objectification in women's lives, feminists need a theory of how objectification can be degreed. They need to be able to say that women can be both bosom and legitimate job candidate, both breeder and health care patient, both sex object and intimate partner.

I. Preliminary comments on objectification

Objectification as a concept is exceedingly complex. Drawing on previous feminist work as well as a narrative of my own experience, I begin by sketching dimensions of objectification insofar as they are relevant to my thesis. Later, I use an analysis of objectification by Martha Nussbaum as the building blocks of my theory that objectification comes in degrees (Nussbaum 1995: 249–91).

Let me begin with the narrative. When I was a teenager, I was in a tennis tournament in a small town where the McLeods of my family first settled in Ontario, Canada. I was in the finals of 'ladies singles.' The next day, a picture of me appeared in the sports section of the local newspaper. I was lunging for a ball, and like a good 'lady' of tennis, I was wearing a little skirt. Clearly the photographer had taken the shot while lying on his back, for the most prominent features of it was my crotch. (It became known as 'the crotch shot.') My Aunt Fern fumed (my mother laughed), and Fern almost boiled over when she found out that some men at the nearby hydro plant (what we call 'Hydro') put the picture on the wall in the men's changing room.[3] The whole thing was discomforting for me, especially becoming a target for the sexist jokes and fantasies of men at Hydro. (I'd worked at Hydro, so I knew about the jokes.) Never before had I imagined myself so thoroughly as something that could just get men off. I was angry with the photographer, although I later found out that it was a photographer's trick to point a camera upward if you want only one figure in a shot and no background objects to distract attention from it. It is possible that the photographer did not intend to produce a crotch shot.

I want to highlight features of the story that will help to illuminate the concept of objectification. First, notice that the men at Hydro who put up my picture essentially reduce me to one of my sexual parts. It may be that *my* crotch was particularly appealing to them because it was a part of what was then a pretty athletic body; nonetheless, they wanted a crotch. They treated me as if a part of me could represent me, which is one element of objectification (Bartky 1990: 26, 27). It alone does not define objectification (which is something that Bartky assumes), for it is not unique to it, and, in fact, appears in one form of 'subjectification.' Consider how we sometimes identify people by special or quirky aspects of them (e.g., their laugh, their expressions, their way of walking, even their bodily parts), which is something we do most often in close personal relationships. We do not necessarily objectify them, particularly, if, for us, the part is a consummate expression of them as subjects.[4] We allow the part to represent the whole, but in a way that is *subjectifying*, not objectifying. To give an example with which everyone could identify would be difficult. One that works for me is how my friend Sue's beautiful sigh represents her in all of her particularity. It fully captures her disillusionment with mainstream society and the distinct way she expresses that. It also reveals, among other things, the side of her that is playful, because an air of laughter comes out in the sigh.

Second, for the men at Hydro, the part that represented me was not one that defined me as a subject in relation to them. (I did not even know these men; my crotch could not have been the consummate expression of my subjectivity for them.) Hence, they made me out to be an object. Another feature of objectification, the most important no doubt, is that parts of the subject are represented in such a way that she becomes an object or like an object. Objectification in general involves treating that which is not an object (i.e., a subject) as though it were an object (Nussbaum 1995: 257).

Third, the experience changed the way I thought about myself at the time: now I could be 'something that just gets men off.' In other words, I internalized the gaze of the Other by becoming object-like (an effect that was not permanent, I do not think). An important question about the nature of objectification is whether the one objectified *always* has to take on qualities of objects for objectification to occur. In other words, is objectification necessarily a relation between someone (or something) with an objectifying perspective and someone who is actually objectified by it? Catherine MacKinnon and Andrea Dworkin seem to say 'yes.' For them, objectification is the dynamic of women's subordination, so that to be a woman is to be objectified and hence subordinated. For objectification to have the effect of subordination, it must be embodied in the subject such that the subject becomes object-like, one would think. MacKinnon says that women's objectification "becomes *embodied* because it is enforced" (Dworkin 1987: 142). Dworkin writes, "the brilliance of objectification as a strategy of dominance is that it gets the woman to take the initiative in her own degradation" (Dworkin 1987a: 142).

Note that a woman could embody her objectification or take the initiative in her own degradation without *internalizing* the objectifying gaze. I internalized the attitude of the men at Hydro to some degree, but I did not have to do so to be objectified (i.e., to be made into an object). Say that I had worked at Hydro still at the time that my picture went up and I frequently encountered men joking about it. I did not defend myself in part because these men had significant power over me, because they were men, most of them were older than me, and they had seniority at Hydro. I even made the effort to make them think that their comments did not faze me—that I even thought they were funny—because to seem all irritated by them would have brought on a new insult: being labelled as a bitch. Hence I took some initiative in my own degradation, but I never believed that I deserved to be treated that way.

So the one objectified can, at least superficially, embody an objectifying gaze without internalizing it. The question still remains of whether the attitude *must* be embodied for the objectification to occur. Sally Haslanger writes that, for MacKinnon, "the relation of objectification that constitutes gender requires both attitudes and act. Gender is a distinction of power that is *read* into and imposed *upon* women" (Haslangler 2002: 225). I think that objectification can be pure attitude, in which case it is not imposed on anyone, at least not anyone who is real. For example, one could imagine the photographer on the sidelines catching glimpses of my crotch forming an objectifying attitude towards me by allowing that part of me to represent me in a way that it surely does not. He does not have to act at all to be objectifying me. Objectification can still be a relation of one person objectifying another when it is pure attitude; the other simply becomes an object only in the objectifier's mind.

We are beginning to see how complex objectification is. To add even more complexity, consider that it need not have an effect on the one objectified not only because it can be pure attitude, but also because some *acts* even of objectification will not produce an effect.[5] Such acts can be successful or unsuccessful.[6] What makes them successful depends on our ends in objectifying others, and our ultimate end may not be to have them become like objects. Usually our purpose *is* to do that: to have the ones objectified be passive, predictable, that which can be manipulated like objects, so that they satisfy a particular desire we have, which they would not do otherwise. We objectify others when we feel the need to control them, instead of allowing them to grow and change with their changing environments. Thus, men who want women to take on traditional female roles may do so in part by objectifying women. However, consider that a man might treat a woman as though she were an object only to increase his sense of power over women. Perhaps the only goal the men at Hydro had in putting up my picture was to enhance their feelings of what Dworkin calls "raw phallic power" (Dworkin 1981: 128). In the case, whether I, or any woman was objectified in reality by having the crotch shot on the wall was irrelevant to whether the act of putting it there was successful.

While more needs to be said about whether objectification can be simply an attitude and what would make it successful or unsuccessful as an act, I think it is clear that objectification does not have to be '*read* and imposed *upon*' (Haslanger 2002: 225). Still, objectification is probably a relation in which that person is made into an object at least in the objectifier's mind. Even when men objectify women only to bolster their own sense of phallic power, they must imagine the women to be object-like through their gaze. I raise the issue, of whether objectification must be the sort of relation I have described, because it is relevant to an objection to my thesis that objectification admits of degrees.

Fourth, my story is almost mundane because of sexism. That I, a woman, have had such an experience is not altogether surprising, which suggests that oppressive social structures play a role in determining how or whether one is objectified. They make it common for female athletes to be valued more for their looks than their athletic ability, for example, and consequently objectified for their looks. They probably even explain in part why the photographer in my story took the picture that he did. He might not have *intended* to produce a crotch shot yet could have strived for one unconsciously because he knew that it would sell papers.

A final point about my story is that my objectification, by different people at different times, admitted of degrees. When my picture first hit the newspaper, it served at least two purposes: 1) to show off a sexual part of me, and 2) to introduce readers to one of the finalists in women's singles (me). The crotch shot was not entirely gratuitous (unlike shots of Anna Kournikova, who rarely makes it to the finals of singles anyway). However, the act of posting my picture at Hydro was gratuitous in that the only purpose the picture served at that point was to give men something to ogle at while they changed into their coveralls for work. So my objectification was both partial and absolute, assuming that the idea of partial objectification makes sense, which we shall consider shortly. But first observe how feminists have portrayed women's objectification so narrowly that cases resembling mine (when I was both finalist and sex object) are excluded. Their work leaves little room for conceptualizing such acts as putting the crotch shot in the newspaper as objectification.

II. The narrow range of objectification in feminist work

I shall focus on work relating to women's sexual lives as well as their reproductive lives, particularly those of women who are patients in fertility clinics. This work comes from such radical feminists as Dworkin, MacKinnon, Janice Raymon, and Gena Corea. Their description of women's objectification are radical in at least two respects: 1) they assume that all objectification of women is morally wrong or sexist; and 2) they focus on absolute objectification to the exclusion of partial objectification. More moderate feminists, such as Martha Nussbaum and Sandra Lee Bartky, have responded to 1) but not 2): they have rejected the claim that all objectification of women (or men) is bad—objectification can be benign in their view—but they continue only to use examples where women are objectified absolutely. Thus, I contribute with this paper to a moderate feminist theory of objectification by arguing that degreed forms of objectification exist and that it is relevant to modern sexism and other forms of oppression in the West. Women are sometimes objectified only to degrees, but that can still be oppressive.[7]

Before turning to the singular attention by feminists on absolute objectification, let me explain how objectification can be either benign or malign. Nussbaum's whole purpose in "Objectification" is to show why this distinction is plausible. She writes, "[i]n the matter of objectification, context is everything" (Nussbaum 1995: 271), that is, it determines whether objectification is wrong or permissible. What matters most about context for her is whether there is "mutual respect and rough social equality" (Nussbaum 1995: 275). The former, mutual respect exists in her view, it appears, if the one objectified consents to be objectified and the objectifier is aware of that and respects the limits of it. Bartky gives an example of where a woman might consent or desire to be objectified: she writes, "surely there are times, in sexual embrace perhaps, when a woman might want to be regarded as nothing but a sexually intoxicating body and when attention paid to some other aspect of her person—say, to her mathematical ability—would be absurdly out of place" (Bartky 1990: 26). How would one know, however, whether the woman *really* wants that, especially if the person she is embracing has greater social power than she does? Nussbaum adds the criterion of rough social equality to eliminate the perhaps intractable problem of having to adjudicate whether consent is true or desire is authentic when the one being objectified is socially subordinate to the objectifier.

An important phenomenon that Nussbaum leaves out in determining how objectification can be benign is that of adaptive preferences.[8] Even with a person who is roughly her equal in society, a woman's desire to be 'nothing but a sexually intoxicating body' can be suspect. In analysing such a desire ethically, one has to consider its content. For example, does the woman want to be intoxicating in the way that some nameless, pouty model is (deemed) intoxicating? If so, we could legitimately wonder whether her preference is an adaptation to a sexist social environment. While adaptations are not in themselves suspect, certain environments are. And when the environment to which one adapts oneself is hostile to one's flourishing, we need to be able to criticize the relevant preferences (i.e., presumably using some account of our flourishing).

The tricky thing upon acknowledging that people can modify their preferences to adapt to oppressive circumstances is deciding what to do upon discovering that someone's preferences *are* adaptive in that way. Should one force the person to adopt new preferences? Would such an act not itself be oppressive? Alternatively, one might try to persuade the person to change

her preferences, assuming that it beards on the question of whether objectification is benign or malign not only what preferences a person should have,
but also what preferences she does have (or ends up with after attempts at
persuasion). Perhaps, objectification is benign only if the person prefers it
and her preferences are not adaptive in an oppressive way. This point will
be relevant in our discussion below of how objectification admits of degrees.

By including the case in which women are objectified benignly, Nussbaum
and Bartky broaden the range of women's objectification beyond what we
get from MacKinnon and others. But is the range that even they acknowledge
broad enough? I say 'no,' for neither treats the objectification of women as
a degreed notion. Let us now see how starkly they and other feminists characterize women's objectification, distinguishing work on sexual objectification from work on reproductive objectification.

Women's sexual objectification

McKinnon, Dworkin, Bartky, and Nussbaum primarily discuss sexual
objectification. I shall begin with MacKinnon and Dworkin, who have similar
views on the matter. Both argue that the social relations defining gender are
sexual objectifying for women, and they depict such objectification as though
it were absolute. To be a woman is to be pure sex object (simple as that;
although many have argued that it is not so simple). MacKinnon writes,
"objectification itself, with self-determinations ecstatically *relinquished*, is
the apparent content of women's sexual desire and desirability" (MacKinnon
1989, quoted in Nussbaum 1995: 269). Real women are "walking embodiments of men's projected needs" (MacKinnon 1995: 119). They are "*exile[d]*
. . . from every realm of expression outside the strictly male-defined sexual
or male-defined maternal" (Dworkin 1981: 22), becoming that "thing that
enables [men] to experience raw phallic power" (Dworkin 1981: 128).

Here is further evidence that, for Dworkin and MacKinnon, men's sexual
objectification of women is absolute. "[M]ost men cannot really tell the
difference between [the average, educated woman] and Linda [Lovelace],"
'star' of the pornographic film, *Deep Throat* (MacKinnon, 1997: 12). That
is true in part because women are "seen *in* and *as* our violation" (MacKinnon
1997: 12). "[Woman] is defined by how she is made, that hole, which is
synonymous with entry" (Dworkin 1987: 123). "He's a citizen; she's a cunt"
(Dworkin 1987: 34).

Unlike Dworkin and MacKinnon, Bartky does not reduce women's
oppression to their sexual objectification, although she sees the latter as an
important element of the former. She illustrates with the story of the job
candidate in philosophy (see my introduction), and with the following:

> It is a fine spring day, and with an utter lack of self-consciousness, I am
> bouncing down the street. Suddenly, I hear men's voices. Catcalls and

whistles fill the air. These noises are clearly sexual in intent and they are meant for me. . . . I freeze. As Sartre would say, I have been petrified by the gaze of the Other. . . . Blissfully unaware, breasts bouncing, . . . I could have passed by without having been turned to stone. But I must be *made* to know that I am a 'nice piece of ass.'

(Bartky 1990: 27)

Here, she is objectified absolutely. She is turned to stone. Rather than being numbed by the gaze of the Other, she is frozen by it.

Nussbaum gives numerous literary and media examples to illustrate objectification, mostly of a sexual nature (and of men as well as women). Her own analyses of the examples suggest that they are of absolute objectification.[9] Many involve completely reducing others to bodily parts, particularly genitals. A example involving men is Alan Hollinghursts's *The Swimming-Pool Library*, in which the protagonist contemplates the penises of anonymous men in the shower room at a club as if their penises defined them (Nussbaum 1999: 255). The example Nussbaum gives of women's objectification that is particularly interesting to me involves the pictures in *Playboy* of actor "Nicollette Sheridan playing at the Chris Evert Pro-Celebrity Tennis Classic, her skirt hiked up to reveal her black underpants. Caption: 'Why We Love Tennis' " (Nussbaum 1999: 253). Nussbaum evaluates the example this way: the 'caption reduces the young actor [sic], a skilled tennis player, to a body ripe for male use: it says, in effect, she thinks she is displaying herself as a skilled athletic performer, but all the while she is actually displaying herself to *our* gaze as a sexual object' (Nussbaum 1999: 254–255). She is a mere sex object, not both skilled athletic performer *and* sex object.[10]

Bartky and Nussbaum both suggest that it can be liberating for women to be sexually objectified, depending on the context. Here, they side with feminists to whom radicals refer not so fondly as "sexual liberals." Left out of this debate is the partial objectification of women; we get only absolute objectification, good or bad.

Women's reproductive objectification

Women's objectification is relevant to feminist reproductive ethics, not only to feminist ethics on women's sexuality. "Just as women have to fight against the degrading identification of themselves with parts of their body in the area of sexuality (for example, as 'cunt' or 'piece of ass', etc.) so, too, must women fight against the psychologically oppressive objectifications of themselves in the area of reproduction" (Morgan 1989: 73). And they must do so in particular surrounding the use of artificial reproductive technologies (ARTs), as many feminists have argued.

Radical feminists Raymond and Corea claim that ARTs and practices (e.g., *in vitro* fertilization, surrogacy) inherently objectify women. They can only be acceptable to a society in which women are already objectified as 'breeders,' and they promote such a society. Hence, the titles of two of Raymond and Corea's works: *Women as Wombs* (Raymond 1993) and *The Mother Machine* (Corea 1985), respectively. Raymond writes that the technologies and relevant procedures are a "form of medical violence against women"; they are "brutality with a therapeutic face" (Raymond 1993: vii, xix). Corea says that they buttress "male power over women" by objectifying women as breeders. Women who consent to them are "agents of male power" (Corea 1985: 4).

Some feminists have countered such pessimism by pointing out that some women find ARTs beneficial and are in positions to resist being mere mother machines.[11] Such theorists acknowledge that women's oppression and liberation in the realm of reproduction occur along a continuum (and therefore can be degreed). They do so when they criticize radical feminists for invoking dualistic constructions in which the technologies themselves are either repressive or liberatory, women's desire to reproduce is either socially constructed or natural, and the like (siding in each case with the left side of the binary). However, the moderates highlight the positive end of the continuum (having reproductive freedom) more than the negative (being a breeder). They emphasize that some women have freedom of choice or that some can resist. They do not discuss the potential harm of objectifying women partially.

Moderates therefore tend to replace the emphasis by radicals on women's objectification with an emphasis on their agency or autonomy in feminist debates about ARTs. They do not refer to good objectification over bad, as feminists do in the sexuality debates. However, radicals and moderates in both domains (sexuality and reproduction), who focus on how women are objectified, tend only to use cases where women are treated as mere means. Perhaps their intent is merely to provide clear cases for analysis. But if that is true, clarity comes at the expense of obscuring the reality of women's objectification. Let us now turn to what reality is.

III. The broader range in reality

The quotations above from feminist work exhibit absoluteness in terms of either the gaze of the objectifier or the potential effect on the one objectified. In both cases, partialness is possible as well as absoluteness. In this section, I illustrate how partial objectification is directed towards and affects women in ways that are oppressive. How much such objectification occurs is an empirical question that may be ripe for analysis but is not answerable here. I make only tentative generalizations on that subject.

Think of the objectifying gaze first and consider MacKinnon's statement about objectification being the content of women's desirability. In other words, women are desirable to men only as objects not subjects.

Sex object and intimate partner

Surely women are sometimes both sex object and intimate partner. They are desirable not only for their bodies or for how well they conform to oppressive stereotypes about women's sexuality, but also for themselves as subjects. They are not mere Linda Lovelace equivalents. To assume otherwise, as Dworkin and MacKinnon do, is overly pessimistic. Still, to presume that women are normally desired *only* for their personalities and not at all in terms of how well they live up to oppressive standards for women would be overly optimistic. Most of us (men and women) have internalized such standards to some degree. We have to make a concerted effort *not* to allow them to mediate our interactions with intimate others, if that is our ideal. So although absolute malign objectification may not characterize all intimate partnerships, partial malign objectification is probably a feature of many of them.

Bosom and legitimate job candidate

Partial sexual objectification occurs not only in sexual relations, but also in workplace relations. Consider again Bartky's example of the breast-obsessed chair. One could easily imagine (and one may have experienced) a chair not staring fixedly at a candidate's breast in an academic interview, but showing an inappropriate interest in them. Nonetheless, the chair thinks of the candidate seriously as a potential future colleague; to him, she is both potential colleague and object for sexual gratification. His objectification of her is partial, and given the context (an academic interview, the inequality of power in the relationship), it is almost certainly malign objectification.

The above example is probably more representative of women's objectification in the workplace, particularly for female professionals, than the example where the candidate is mere bosom. Affirmative action programs in most professions are not so strong that women are hired *only* because they are women, or bosoms (contrary to what some people claim). Women's professional skills are also relevant. However, so is their conformity to social standards of femininity, which explains why many people deem it appropriate to criticize female professionals harshly if their demeanour or appearance is masculine, even though their work may be exemplary.

Breeder and health care patient

Similar complexity exists in how female patients are valued in infertility treatment contexts; it is doubtful that they are mere breeders. Raymond and Corea say that ARTs objectify women absolutely, which implies that all women who find them helpful, even if only to a degree, are mere dupes.[12] Such an assumption is uncharitable as well as extreme. Raymond and Corea's view also suggests that physicians who work in reproductive endocrinology have little to no concern for women's welfare; they could not if they are willing to impose such violent technologies and procedures upon women. But surely that is unfair. My experience of working with some of these physicians has taught me that some care a lot about their patients. Nonetheless, my interactions with and research on women who have undergone infertility treatment reveal that *partial* malign forms of objectification by physicians do occur in some clinics. To illustrate, consider this remark by a patient: "They praised my 'good response' (shown in blood work and ultrasound results) to the medication used to induce ovulation, while playing comparatively little attention to my concern that I had lost fifteen pounds because of the stress of one treatment cycle."[13] This patient made it clear to me and to her physicians that she was not willing to get pregnant at any cost. She did not objectify herself as a mere reproductive vessel. However, her care providers objectified her in that way *to some degree* when they valued her success in treatment (defined in terms of getting a baby in the end) more than her psychological well-being, which they did not ignore entirely, but to which they paid insufficient attention. She was not a *mere* member to them—a potential breeder that might improve their success rates, but she was not fully respected as a person either; that is, as someone with her own goals and preferences.

We have considered how the objectifying gaze on women can be and is perhaps often partial. Now think about the one objectified and whether she embodies that gaze only to degrees, if at all.

Grasping self as object and moral agent

Is it true that today most women in the West are 'walking embodiments of men's projected needs?' Do they see themselves or behave as though they were pure objects of male desire? I doubt it. While many women experience objectification by men and embody it, many are also partially autonomous at least, which we would not be if we were mere things designed to fulfill male needs. Surely, we are made to feel like complete objects some of the time, such as when strange men leer at us in a piercing way or when we experience unwanted advances by men who really do see us as pieces of meat. But many of us respect ourselves enough and are respected by others enough that we do not always embody such malign perspectives. Still, we might see ourselves as partial objects much of the time. The steady, but not singular, concern that many women have with their weight, or with their appearance in general, suggests that many women internalize partial objectification.

In this section, I have shown that partial, malign objectification of women occurs both from the perspective of the objectifier and from that of the one objectified. But one might ask whether the phenomenon I have illustrated throughout is truly objectification. Is a woman *objectified* who feels the pressure of society's beauty standards for women but who does not define her worth solely or even primarily in terms of those standards? The term 'objectification' may be too extreme in this contest. Why is that *not* the case?

IV. How objectification admits of degrees

Nussbaum's theory of objectification is particularly useful for showing that partial objectification exists. In a number of ways, the theory allows for and even presupposes degrees of objectification. I shall explain why that is true and describe other virtues of the theory to justify my use of it here.

It is Nussbaum who writes that objectification is about "treating *as an object* what is really not an object, what is," as she adds, "a human being" (Nussbaum 1999: 257). The notion of humanity she adopts (and which others before her adopt, e.g. MacKinnon) is Kantian: a human being is a rational, self-determining being who should be respected as such.[14] Nussbaum goes on to say that human beings can be treated as objects in multiple ways; and hence, that objectification comes in a variety of forms (Nussbaum 1999: 257).

1   *Instrumentality*: The objectifier treats the object as a tool of his or her purposes.
2   *Denial of Autonomy*: The objectifier treats the object as lacking in autonomy and self-determination.
3   *Inertness*: The objectifier treats the object as lacking in agency, and perhaps also in activity.
4   *Fungibility*: The objectifier treats the object as interchangeable (a) with other objects of the same type, and/or (b) with objects of other types.
5   *Violability*: The objectifier treats the object as lacking in boundary-integrity, as something that is permissible to break up, smash, break into.
6   *Ownership*: The objectifier treats the object as something that is owned by another, can be bought or sold, etc.
7   *Denial of Subjectivity*: The objectifier treats the object as something whose experience and feelings (if any) need not be taken into account.[15]

Implicit here is a certain conception of objects, as well as of persons or subjects. Usually (but not always), objects are passive, inert matter that can, with impunity, be manipulated, owned, used, and substituted for one another. Ideally, the same is not true of persons. I want to assume that these conceptions are roughly correct.

Nussbaum explains how each form of objectification is distinct from the others. For example, we can deny someone's autonomy without treating that person as an instrument for our use. We can claim to own someone without denying his subjectivity (which involves failing to ask such questions as 'what is this person likely to feel if I do X?') (Nussbaum 1999: 265). Further, we can deny subjectivity without presuming fungibility; that is, deny that a person is a subject without assuming that he is interchangeable with other subjects, which he may not be if his body, and his body alone, satisfies a particular desire we have, say for *his* chest, with its own special shape and feel.

According to Nussbaum, we sometimes treat any one of the different forms of objectification as sufficient for objectification to occur (258), which she does not find troubling, although I think that she should, particularly with regard to the denial of autonomy. Clearly we can deny the autonomy of animals or of children without objectifying them, which of course does not mean that we cannot objectify them. Nussbaum makes room for their objectification by suggesting that each form of objectification could be sufficient. Deny the subjectivity of a gorilla and we objectify the gorilla.

To apply this theory to a specific case, consider again my narrative with which we began this paper. Any or all the forms of objectification Nussbaum identifies could have been present in the attitudes of the men who put up my picture at Hydro. They could have imagined me lacking autonomy and subjectivity, being inert and even owned by them. They probably saw me at least as an instrument of sexual pleasure and as fungible with other women whose bodies resembled mine. (I must have been fungible to them because they did not even know me. Their attention could not have been drawn to anything other than general qualities that I could easily share with other women.) The effect of their act on me was to have me see myself as a sexual tool. (Again, I was something that could get men off.) The only form of objectification that I embodied was instrumentality.

One might consider it unusual for the one objectified to feel like an instrument specifically. Normally, the impact of objectification is more general than that: the person just feels more 'bodily' or feels a heightened sense of embodiment. If that were true, distinguishing among various forms of objectification as Nussbaum does would be inappropriate from the perspective of the one objectified. However, the view here about objectification is false for two reasons. One is that people can be objectified for their minds (as child protégés are), which surely would not enhance a sense of embodiment. The other is that people can certainly feel objectified in ways that correspond to the different forms on Nussbaum's list. For example, my partner cheats on me and I feel fungible. He questions whether my decisions really match my values, making me believe that I am less autonomous than I actually am. In each case, I may feel more embodied than usual (e.g., feel like a body rather than an autonomous being), but that is not all that I feel, and different actions of my partner produce different sorts of feelings.

Beyond being accurate in terms of how we can be objectified and objectify others, Nussbaum alludes to a further advantage of separating out the different forms of objectification: it allows us to see how objectification can be benign.[16] Failing to separate them makes that more difficult (which is a criticism Nussbaum makes of MacKinnon and Dworkin: 270). If one thought that treating someone as an object meant treating them in all or most of the ways Nussbaum describes—as inert, lacking in subjectivity, as an instrument, *et cetera*—it would be hard ever to condone objectification. If the objectification of a patient by a heart surgeon meant that the patient was not only violable and fungible with other bodies with hearts, but also a mere instrument, one that could be owned by the surgeon, the practice of surgery would raise much greater moral concern than it does already.

A further advantage of Nussbaum's account, to which she does not allude, is that it helps us to see how objectification can be degreed. It does that in a number of ways. One is that each of the forms it identifies admits of degrees. For example, we deny someone's subjectivity to different degrees when we approach such questions as 'What is the person likely to feel?' with different levels of seriousness. Consider a physician who, accompanied by a group of medical students, enters an exam room of a patient whom she had never met before. She says to the patient, "You don't mind if these people join us, do you?" Clearly, she does not take seriously the question of what the patient would feel or want. But neither does she ignore that question altogether. If she did, she would not even ask whether the patient minded the intrusion.

Other forms of objectification can also come in degrees. We can think of others as fungible, violable, or lacking in autonomy to different degrees. Just as we can be partial owners, we can treat people as partially owned. Further, we can recognize someone to be mostly inert, but not entirely so, such as a child who is petrified by lightning; but who could still run if he really had to. Finally, someone can be an instrument for us, but not wholly an instrument. For example, if I am chatty and nice to the checkout boy as I use him as a means to get out of the grocery store in the proper fashion, I probably do not treat him as a mere means.

A second reason why Nussbaum's theory allows us to conceive of degrees of objectification is that by "uncoupling" (to use her term) the different forms from one another—by noticing that they do not necessarily accompany one another—it is just easier to think of degrees of objectification. The point is similar to the one Nussbaum makes about benign objectification: if the different modes were inseparable, it would be hard to imagine how objectification could be benign. Similarly, if every time we objectified someone, we had to assume that the person had all the qualities we normally associate with objects (e.g., fungibility, lacking autonomy and subjectivity, inertness, and the like), then the person could not be much more than an object in our minds, one would think. Dworkin and MacKinnon create the impression of men's objectification of women by suggestion that, for men, women are not only instruments of sexual pleasure, they also lack autonomy, subjectivity, and are both violable and fungible (as the quotations in Section II illustrate). In other words, Dworkin and MacKinnon portray absoluteness in men's treatment of women as objects not only by making such bold claims as 'man is citizen; woman is cunt,' but also by suggesting that the different forms of objectification always come together, including when men objectify women.

Perhaps disentangling the different forms makes room for degrees of objectification in another way. One might assume that some forms can only be absolute in conjunction with others: perhaps, pure instrumentality can only exist along with the denial of subjectivity, for example. But if each mode were sufficient for objectification to occur, as Nussbaum allows, then partial objectification must be possible. Consider first whether pure instrumentality requires the denial of subjectivity. Unless I assume that the checkout boy has no feelings or desires of his own, I do not treat him as a mere instrument. But surely that must depend on my purpose in instrumentalizing him. If I want to get through the checkout without having to acknowledge anyone (I would prefer an automatic checkout, but it is rare where I live), then for the boy to be a pure instrument for me, I would have to deny his subjectivity. But what if what I wanted was to have my groceries packed well, with the stuff that could get squashed on top? If that were my main goal, it would be wise to acknowledge the boy, which would probably make him a better instrument for my purposes. (He would not just pack the bags any old way, thinking what a *jerk* I am.)

Similarly, one might think that denying autonomy is essential for other forms to be absolute, such as fungibility; but that would be a mistake. Someone who is autonomous has a mind of her own, which implies that she could not be entirely fungible (or entirely an instrument, a piece of property, et cetera). However, consider that a sadist for whom one tortured person is as good as any other may not ignore or deny the autonomy of his victims. (And note that denying autonomy is not the same as lacking respect for it; once one denies someone's autonomy, one cannot have respect for it.) In fact, the victim's autonomy or capacity for autonomy may be important to him because it means that they can be tortured more than they could otherwise be. Still, they are completely interchangeable to him insofar as they are roughly equal in their ability to be tortured.[17]

I think it is possible for each form of objectification to be absolute on its own, which means that assuming each to be sufficient on their own for objectification to occur does not open up conceptual space for partial objectification. However, Nussbaum's theory might create that space in yet another way. Recall that the main point of her paper is to establish that objectification can be benign. I suggested that whether it is in fact benign depends on whether the one objectified prefers it and whether her preferences are adaptive to an oppressive social environment. If her *actual* preferences are relevant (as opposed to the preferences she should have), then the person objectifying her should be aware of them and how they might change over time to avoid objectifying her in a malign way. Such awareness precludes absolute objectification in the forms of denying subjectivity or autonomy. And if that is true, benign objectification of those forms will always be partial. People who objectify one another benignly in a sexual encounter, for example, do not deny one another's subjectivity absolutely. Doing so would be a recipe for sexual assault.

Thus, if objectification can be benign and if it comes in distinct forms that admit of degrees, partial objectification is possible. Women therefore can be partially objectified, presumably in both malign and benign ways, and in ways that promote sexism and other forms of oppression. Objections remain, however, to the very idea of partial objectification. Let me turn to them now.

V. Objectification

I shall deal with two potentially serious objections. One concerns whether my view assumes a radical dichotomy of subject/object, which would be problematic; and the other denies that 'partial objectification' is objectification at all as opposed to disrespect.

The first objection emphasizes that subjects are normally embodied and so are not entirely distinct from objects. To assume otherwise would be to accept a radical duality of subject and object, which many feminists and others rightly reject.[18] Treating objects as partial objects *is* appropriate; no difference exists between how we should treat subjects *qua* subject and the partial objectification of the subject. By ignoring this fact, I have implicitly assumed a radical subject/object split.

Note that this objection establishes not that partial objectification does not occur, but that it is appropriate. What the objection fails to explain is that is it not always appropriate, even if we understand persons or subjects to be embodied. To paraphrase Bartky, surely there are times when attention paid to anything *other* than a woman's mathematical ability is absurdly out of place (e.g., in a math class or in an interview for a math job). The same goes for a woman's ability to play tennis (i.e. sometimes, it should be the sole focus of attention). Even though subjects and persons are inherently embodied, their embodiment is not always relevant to how we should treat them.

The second objection goes like this: what I call degrees of objectification are simply instances of treating persons without the full respect they deserve. Such treatment is disrespectful, but not objectifying. Now why would one want to make this distinction? Well, it is obvious that treating someone as a mere means is a form of disrespect that is objectifying. But if treating someone as a partial means is also objectifying, then will not all disrespect be objectification, in which case the two are indistinguishable and that seems counter-intuitive? It does seem that way to me, although it would not to everyone, including Kant for whom disrespect simply involved treating people as means.

My response to this objection is not to admit that all disrespect is objectification, but to distinguish between the two in the following ways: 1) objectification can be benign unlike disrespect; and 2) the former is a relation in a way that the latter is not. Disrespect can exist without the one disrespected being reduced or degraded or without imagining that to be the case. I can act disrespectfully or have a disrespectful attitude toward someone but not diminish that person's self-respect or even think anything of it. By contrast objectification makes the one objectified into an object, partially or absolutely, in reality or only in the imagination of the objectifier. I admit that malign objectification is a form of disrespect, but not even that those two are identical.

VI. Conclusion

Degrees of objectification therefore cannot be reduced to disrespect, they exist, and surely they can be morally wrong just like absolute forms of objectification. Such insights are important for feminists because, in the West at least, much of women's objectification is probably now degreed, but could nonetheless be oppressive. The reason why it would be degreed lies in women's empowerment relative to a time when they were mere chattel, which allows many women to have some say over how they are treated, in both sexual and reproductive contexts. Still, they may not have enough say that no one objectifies them in ways that are morally harmful.

Such speculations require empirical support that I have not given in this paper. What I have done is the conceptual work that should underlie any descriptive account of oppressive forms of the objectification of women. These accounts should investigate how women are treated, not only as mere means, but also as partial means.[19]

Notes

1 The language of 'mere' and 'only' appears in *The Foundations of the Metaphysic of Morals*, trans. T.K. Abott (Buffalo, N.Y.: Prometheus Books, 1988), especially 56–58.
2 It is the subject of a paper by Todd Calder, entitled 'Kant and Degrees of Wrongness,' presented at the Eastern Division conference of the American Philosophical Association in 2002.
3 They were not original in doing so. Someone testified at hearings in Minneapolis about harm posed by pornography about 'working men plaster[ing] women's crotches on the walls of workplaces.' See *In Harm's Way: The Pornography Civil Rights Hearings*, by Andrea Dworkin and Catherine MacKinnon (Cambridge, MA: Harvard University Press, 1997), 6.
4 The term 'consummate expression' is Jeremy Bendik-Keymer's (personal communication). I owe this point to him.
5 I thank Christine Overall and Sue Sherwin for bringing this point to my attention.
6 John Hardwig first gave me the idea that acts of objectification can be successful or unsuccessful.
7 Objectification is sexist, or oppressive in general, if it targets one's membership in an oppressed group (e.g., women) and if it is systemic. See Sandra Lee Bartky, 'On Psychological Oppression.'
8 On adaptive preferences, see Jon Elster, *Sour Grapes: Studies in the Subversion of rationality* (Cambridge, UK: Cambridge University Press, 1983), Amartya Sen, *Inequality Reexamined* (Oxford: Clarendon Press, 1992), and Martha Nussbaum, *Sex and Social Justice* (New York: Oxford University Press, 1999). Nussbaum leaves out this phenomenon despite discussing it in *Sex and Social Justice*, where 'Objectification' also appears.

9 She summarizes what is going on in them and suggests that each is about seeing the other as nothing but an object. See 'Objectification,' 254, 255.

10 Most of the examples here from feminist work involve the objectification of beautiful female bodies. However, people sometimes objectify women for their ugliness rather than their beauty (as Rebecca Kukla stressed to me at the conference where we presented our work for this volume). This point comes out clearly in Iris Marion Young's, 'The Scaling of Bodies,' *Justice and the Politics of Difference* (Princeton, NJ: Princeton University Press, 1990). She describes how oppression can be 'aversive,' where dominant groups feel repulsed by those whom they dominate. Some women's bodies are defined as objects to be averted.

 Young is somewhat of an exception among feminists who have written on objectification in that she implicitly acknowledges the degreed nature of women's objectification. She refers to the 'aesthetic scaling of bodies' in Western culture. Beautiful, youthful bodies form the apex of the scale and 'degenerate' bodies, the nadir (128). Oppressed people have degenerate bodies, which are objectified in her view (as are beautiful bodies, but Young does not acknowledge that). The idea that bodies are 'scaled' suggests that degrees of degeneracy exist. And if all degenerate bodies are objectified, then degrees of objectification must also exist.

11 See Anne Donchin, 'Feminist Critiques of New Fertility Technologies: Implication of Social Policy,' *Journal of Medicine and Philosophy* 21 (1996): 475–98; and Jan Sawicki, 'Disciplining Mothers: Feminism and the New Reproductive Technologies,' in *Disciplining Foucault: Feminism, Power and the Body* (New York: Routledge, 1991).

12 Donchin makes that point in 'Feminist Critiques.'

13 The statement comes from an unpublished narrative that this patient wrote about her treatment and which she kindly shared with me.

14 The definition excludes the objectification of animals, which is problematic, for animals are not objects, although they can be treated as such. However, in filling out her account, Nussbaum makes room for their objectification, as we shall see.

15 I endorse the idea that objectification comes in these different forms, but one might think that is inconsistent with my title, which emphasizes only one form; namely instrumentality. Treating people as mere means involves treating them as instruments for our use. But is that necessarily true of Kantian means? One could read Kant as saying that treating people as means involves placing them in the class of objects, that, *among other things*, can be mere instruments (see Dennis Klimchuk's 'Three Accounts of Respect for Persons,' *Kantian Review* (forthcoming). Instrumentality does not have to be their defining property. Support for such a view comes from examples of disrespect in Kant that do not involve someone getting something out of being disrespectful. (So the person disrespected does not have to be a means to the other person's ends.)

16 Given how this advantage supports her thesis (that objectification can be benign), it is surprising that Nussbaum does not make the point more forcefully than she does.

17 I owe this example to Betsy Postow.

18 MacKinnon herself does that in *Toward a Feminists Theory of the Sate*, 120, 121, and so does Evelyn Fox Keller in *Reflections on Gender and Science* (New Haven, CT: Yale University Press, 1985).

19 Earlier versions of this paper were presented to audiences at the University of Tennessee, Knoxville, at the 2002 conference of the North American Society for Social Philosophy, and at the conference organized for this volume. I wish to thank them all for their helpful comments. Special thanks to Jeremy John Hardwig, Dennis Klimchuk, Jim Okapal, Christine Overall, and Susan Sherwin.

References

Bartky, Sandra (1990) 'On Psychological Oppression' in *Femininity and Domination: Studies in the Phenomenology of Oppression*, New York: Routledge.

Corea, Gena (1985) *The Mother Machine: Reproductive Technologies from Artificial Insemination to Artificial Wombs*, New York: Harper & Row.

Dworkin, Andrea (1981) *Pornography: Men Possessing Women* New York: Perigee Books.

—— (1987) *Intercourse*, New York: The Free Press.

Haslanger, Sally (2002) 'On Being Objective and Being Objectified,' in Louise Anthony and Charlotte Witt (eds), 2nd edition, *A Mind of One's Own: Feminist Essay on Reason and Objectivity*, Boulder, CO: Westview Press.

McKinnon, Catherine (1987) *Feminism Unmodified: Discourse on Life and Law*, Cambridge, MA: Harvard University Press.

—— (1989) *Toward a Feminist Theory of the State*, Cambridge, MA: Harvard University Press.

Morgan, Kathryn Pauly (1989) 'Of Woman Born? How Old-Fashioned! – New Reproductive Technologies and Women's Oppressions' in Christine Overall (ed) *The Future of Human Reproduction*, Toronto: The Women's Press.

Nussbaum, Martha (1995) 'Objectification', *Philosophy and Public Affairs*, 24: 249–91.

Raymond, Janice (1993) *Women as Wombs: Reproductive Technologies and the Battle over Women's Freedom*, San Francisco: HarperSanFran.

Chapter 6

Unraveling the ideological concept of the female athlete

A connection between sex and sport

Charlene Weaving

Introduction

There are sonorous parallels, at the levels of discourse and ideology, between sex and sport.[1] Sharp awareness of these parallels is key to understanding persisting sex inequalities within sport, for example, the disparities in funding, athletic scholarships, sponsorships, professional leagues, salaries, and media coverage. It is fundamental to understanding and eradicating a broader sexism also.

Our conception of sexual relations between women and men inflects our conception of the respective sporting endeavors of the sexes. Two overlapping but distinct features bulk large. The first is the incompatibility between the female athlete and the (ideologically) ideal woman. Athletes are expected to be strong and powerful. However, the ideal woman is less of an athlete and more of a Barbie (tall, long legs, long blond hair, thin, and not *too* muscular). Angela Schneider has commented:

> It is the basic idea, the idea that sport (sometimes even physical activity), particularly high-level competitive sport, is somehow incompatible with what women are, or what they should be, that must dominate any discussion of the unique issues for women in sport.
>
> (2000: 122)

The second feature is that in the discourse of heterosexual sex, women are typically configured as harmed objects. This is manifested in the language often used to describe the female and her role in heterosexual sex, a language regularly inscribed with metaphors from sport. Conversely, contemporary sport is supercharged with sexual innuendos that in turn reinforce this conception of the female's sexual role.

These two features critically overlap, since creatures with Barbie-like passivity and docility are especially vulnerable to harm, and perhaps easy to view as *eligible to be harmed*. If women, or even just athletically disposed women, were ideologically encouraged to celebrate their athleticism, then it would be much more difficult to view women as harm-apt or even just vulnerable to harm. However, the distinctly unsportish ideological pressure upon women in sport is in hoc to the preceding, passive-and-harmed configuration of women in sexual activity.

In the remainder of this essay, I first address conceptions of the female in heterosexual sex. I then argue that these conceptions reinforce trivializing ways of talking about women. I follow with examples of how the discourses of heterosexuality and sport thematically reflect one another, in turn reinforcing the disparagement of the female athlete. I then consider and reject the typical discourses of both male and female rugby culture. I argue, finally, that female empowerment, including the power to be an authentically female athlete, involves the cessation of the sex-harm discourse.

The sexual object and sexual objectification discourse

In this section, I describe and critique the cultural discourse of women, and try to show its implications for cultural conceptions of the female in heterosexual sex. Robert Baker suggests that the way in which we identify something reflects our conception of it; and that the conception of women embedded in our language is male and chauvinistic:

> Perhaps the most striking aspect of the conceptual discrimination reflected in our language is that man is, as it were, essentially human, while woman is only accidentally so.
>
> (1994: 253)

For Baker, therefore, the root of the problem is social structures of sexual identification. Baker observes the following five ways that women are typically identified in our language:

1   Neutral terms: lady, gal, girl, sister, broad (pregnant cow)
2   Animal: chick, bird, fox, vixen, filly, bitch
3   Plaything: babe, doll, cuddly
4   Gender: typically associated with a type of clothing, worn by those in that specific gender (skirt, purse, makeup)
5   Sexual: snatch, cunt, ass, twat, piece of ass, lay, pussy, sweat hog (254).

While some of Baker's examples may seem dated, it is undeniable that we continue to identify women by derogatory labels. Contemporary examples include *pussy, ho, skank, bitch*, and *slut*. Women refer to themselves, revealingly, in some of these ways. Both sexes have therefore adopted a negative conception of women and the female role in sexual activity.[2]

Baker proposes that a sex object is an object that one desires to have sex with. He considers it "prudish" to think that women should not be sex objects. The problem, he feels, is when the sex object is also *dehumanized*:

The point is not that men ought not to think of women in sexual terms but that they ought to think of them as human beings; and the slogan men should not think of women as sex objects is only appropriate when a man thinking of a woman as a sexual partner automatically conceives of her as something less than human.

(260)

And, for Baker, a sexist society that already imperils the autonomy and subjectivity of women provides soil that is particularly fertile for the reduction of women to dehumanized sex objects. Conversely, a society that isn't sexist "all the way through" would not leave women's sexuality so liable to dehumanization.

Baker argues that the most effective approach for feminists is to get individuals to think differently about women and sex. Neither sex should, again, think of women as exclusively sex objects. Both sexes are human beings. We will still desire, innocuously, to have sex with individuals. Baker suggests, however, that feminists attempt to change the language used in describing sex, and therefore help diminish sexist configurations of women.

Baker's program of discursive therapy is both do-able and desirable. The hegemonic (though not exclusive) conception of sexual intercourse configures women as depersonalized objects instead of humans. This conception pervades North American society, resulting in emphasis upon a raunch style of sexual interaction that involves little variation or imagination. It also involves "cookie cutter" forms of idealism and stereotyping of sexiness and sexuality. For example, young women are deemed "sexually progressive" if they enjoy pornography and watching female striptease performances.

Our language of sex roles is inextricably in cahoots with this regime. As Baker tellingly states, "The limits of our language are the limits of our world" (266). He notes that passive constructions such as "screwed," "fucked," "banged," and "had" connote a sex role that is both female and harmed. Complaints such as "I got fucked" and "I got screwed" signify a parallel between being harmed, deceived, or exploited, and the female sexual role. Among the most powerful of insults are, again, "screw you!" "up yours!" and "go fuck yourself!" And the most pungent insult for a male athlete is the label, "pussy." The next section considers further sport-specific examples of the discourse.

Baker counters that anatomical differences should not determine how we conceptualize the difference between the penis and vagina in sexual intercourse. There is no a priori prohibition on a discourse in which the female subject requires active verb constructions, e.g. "Blossom engulfed Joe," instead of "Joe screwed Blossom." Therefore, the typical use of passive constructions for the female in copulation reflects, not differences determined by human anatomy, but rather differences generated by human culture (263).

Sport-specific examples

This section involves analysis of five examples from sport. Their significance lies in the illustration of the connections between the respective sexist languages of sport and heterosexual sex, and in their capacity to illuminate how women are in turn subordinated in sport, and consequently experience a tension.

Sport hunting

Consider this description of a cartoon that appeared in the magazine *Hustler*:

> Two white men, dressed as hunters, sit in a black Jeep. The two men carry rifles . . . The men and the Jeep face into the camera. Tied onto the hood of the black Jeep is a white woman. She is tied with thick rope. She is spread-eagle. Her pubic hair and crotch are the dead center of the car hood and the photograph. Her head is turned to one side, tied down by rope that is pulled taut across her neck, extended to and wrapped several times around her arms, crisscrossed under her breasts and over her thighs, drawn down and wrapped around the bumper of the Jeep . . . Between her feet on the car bumper, in orange with black print, is a sticker that reads: I brake for Billy Barter. The text under the photograph reads 'Western sportsmen report beaver hunting was particularly good throughout the Rocky Mt. region during the past season. These two hunters easily bagged their limit in the high country. They told Hustler that they stuffed and mounted their trophy as soon as they got her home'.
>
> (Dwyer 1995: 49)

The description promotes the traditional view that men have power over women, depicting the woman as prey that is to be hunted and then harmed. The words used describe women as animals that are hunted, preyed upon, and owned. In this cartoon, the power of sex is identified with the power of conquest, a power prevalent in the language of hunting.

The concepts involved in sport hunting echo the concepts implicated in the subordination of women. In sport hunting language, sexual contact is implicit. There is a strong conceptual connection between hunting terms and expressions used in sexual language. We often refer to courting women as "chasing beaver", "chasing tail" and "hunting for cougars." There is a parallel between conquering animals and conquering women sexually.[3] These conceptions of women are embedded in our sporting language. They make it inevitable that women have little place within the hunting world. Indeed, the preceding cartoon description, especially the description "stuffed and mounted", suggests scarce qualitative distinction in the hunting world between putting a moose head over one's fireplace and placing an open-legged woman over the same.

Mountaineering

The discourse of mountaineering is, like that of hunting, inscribed with a feminized nature. A brief historical overview of the sport helps chart the development of this discourse.

Women have participated in mountaineering in Canada for over 100 years. However, a feminization of the mountain occurred in the twentieth century (Fairley and Marty 1995: 177). The imagery of mountain "conquering" began to involve sexual, even violently sexual, scenarios. Mountaineering became a metaphor for sex; sometimes forced sex, strongly evident in this retrospection upon a 1953 expedition to Everest: "There might have been a more sporting ethic about the conquest of the world's highest mountains: less rape and more seduction" (Fairley and Marty 1995: 178). The sexual discourse surrounding mountaineering seems to have expanded since. The following passage, again, shows mountaineering as a metaphor for sexual acts:

> As for the female character of the mountain, the anthropomorphism has been automatic, its roots found in a tangle of male psychology and mountaineering tradition. The usage varies, the climbers' approach to the image is personal. [Ron] Fear's sweet lady and delicate lover is [Jim] Morrissey's siren, whore and bitch: only the eyes of the beholder are different . . . well let's climb this pig, he was calling on an image not of the barnyard but of a college freshman mixer.
>
> (Blanchard and Arbic 1994: 265)

This post-war mountaineering culture did not seem to have a positive place for women among its peaks, since women were viewed as sexual encounters leading to conquests, rather than peers within the climbing community. However, the 1970s was the high water mark of Second Wave Feminism and the Sexual Liberation Movement, resulting in fewer rules and inhibitions surrounding sex, especially female sexual activity.

An all-women North American expedition to Annapurna occurred in 1978. The members sold some fifteen thousand T-shirts to fund themselves for the expedition. The slogan on the T-shirt was "A woman's place is on top . . . Annapurna." This climb was liberating, not only for women in mountaineering, but also for women sexually, since women were portrayed in active rather than passive positions. The sexual metaphors typically involved in mountaineering support the connections Baker draws between women, sex and inequality. However, the T-shirt would be considered by Baker to be a positive portrayal of sexual activity, as it configures women in a powerful position using an active verb conjunction.

However, the oppositional flavour of the all-women expedition could not prevent the following joke circulating within the Sherpa community throughout it:

> Did you hear the one about the Sherpa who said trekking work is very easy? You only need one word of English "yes". Sherpa climb high? "yes", Carry load? "yes", Cook dinner? "yes", Memsahib [female mountaineer] wants to *fuck*? "yes".
>
> (Blum 1980: 18).

Its point is that these North American women were in Annapurna to achieve success, not on the mountain, but in the bedroom or tent as the case may be. When women's role in a sport is primarily one of sexual service, it is difficult to view men and women equally. The Annapurna women were accomplished mountaineers, yet were reduced, ideologically, to a servicing sexual role. This consolidates the ideological tension typically felt by female athletes.

Squash advertisement

The third and final sport-specific example is a women's squash tournament promotion. The advertisement announces the 2007 Toronto Squash Open Tournament. The main focus of the image is a typical squash court. However, the centre squash line is the heart of the image and a pair of very shapely woman's legs (from a front view) straddles the line. The top of the photograph cuts off the rest of the body and a tiny trim of a short skirt dangles, while three-quarters of a racquet rests against the left thigh. Through the woman's spread legs, a large group of males have their faces pressed up against the court's glass back door. The caption reads, "Women's professional squash. It's irresistible." This running header sustains the illusion that the males' gaze is directed at the player's backside. Additionally, the squash line that the woman straddles doubles as a phallus that leads to the prize—between the woman's legs.

The advertisement is an undisguised attempt to draw a crowd via the heterosexuality of the women athletes. It implies that the women's ability and skill at squash is second fiddle to how their buttocks look in a short skirt. The athlete is showcased as a sexual object. The foregoing sexual ideology— that configures women as passive, dehumanized, and harmed objects— multiplies the potency of the image. The ideological tension between being and athlete and being a woman is in turn powerfully reinforced. The next section considers examples from our sporting language that fuel the ideological tension of the female athlete.

The male pussy

Sports are primarily heteronormative and masculinist. According to Toby Miller (2001), the most pungent insult a coach can visit upon a male player is to associate him, as already indicated, with the "womanly" (19). Basketball coach Bobby Knight's 1985 outburst toward a male player provides a memorable example:

> You never push yourself. You know what you are, Daryl? You are the worst fucking pussy I've ever seen play basketball at this school. The absolute worst pussy ever. You have more goddamn ability than 95 percent of the players we've had here, but you are a pussy from the top of your head down to the bottom of your feet. An absolute fucking pussy.
>
> (Miller 2001: 49)

This common sporting language, like the preceding languages of hunting and mountaineering, degrades women and insults their sexuality, since their genitalia are conceived as weak and useless, suggesting in turn that women are weak and useless in sport. Women in sport also use the term "pussy" to describe someone that does not take risks, or is not as strong as the others. Therefore, women have themselves adopted this disparaging view of female genitalia—the last word in masculinist hegemony.

Sex as victory

This bumpy road takes one in the opposite direction too. Heterosexual sex is similarly described in imagery borrowed from sport. For instance, success in the pursuit of sexual intercourse is regularly described as "scoring." Whilst there is, for sure, a constituency of women who use this word, it is predominantly used by males to applaud their attainment of heterosexual sex. It likens sex with a female to victory in a competition. Young individuals are often taught to associate different levels of sexual activity with baseball bases, where the ultimate goal is to score a "home run." Other examples include "sinking the putt," "getting in the shot," "digging in," and "splitting the uprights."

Male rugby culture as hegemonic masculinity

An entire text could be written on rugby subculture. Although it is now changing, rugby was well known for its acceptance of excessive drinking and "dirty," degrading songs about women. Typical male rugby songs express hostile, brutal, and fearful attitudes towards women and sex (Nelson 1994: 89). An explicit example is "S and M Man," sung to the tune of "Candy Man":

> Who can take a chain saw?
> Cut the bitch in two
> Fuck the bottom half
> And give the upper half to you?

The S & M man, the S & M man,
The S & M man cause he mixes it with love
And makes the hurt feel good!
Who can take a bicycle?
Then take off the seat
Set his girlfriend on it
Ride her down a bumpy street?
Who can take an ice pick?
Ram it though her ear
Ride her like a Harley,
As you fuck her from the rear?

(Nelson 1994: 90)

The song suggests that the rape and the murder of women are socially acceptable acts, supporting Baker's argument that women are ideologically defined by harm-through-sex. It is, moreover, expressive of the dominant paradigm of manliness, which is partly defined by a certain type of heterosexual sex. As journalist Mariah Burton Nelson (1994) has put it:

Real men are aggressive in sex. Real men get cruel in sex. Real men use their penises like weapons in sex. Real men leave bruises. Real men think it's a turn on to threaten to harm. A brutish push can make an erection feel really hard. That kind of sex makes you feel like someone who is powerful and it turns the other person into someone powerless. That kind of sex makes you feel dangerous and in control-like you're fighting a war with an enemy and if you're mean enough you'll win but if you let up you'll lose your manhood. It's a kind of sex men have in order to have a manhood.

(143)

Real men essentially require, naturally, their complement: the *feminine*.[4] Women are, conversely, socially expected to be ladylike, gentle, polite, and decorous (the set entails pressure to be sexually reactive and not proactive).[5] Otherwise, they are liable to be damned as "unwomanly," "masculine," "butch," and/or "lesbian." This presents difficulty for the female athlete, whose essential qualities are, as already noted, in conflict with the preceding requirements of femininity.

However, not all female athletes surrender meekly to this ideological conflict. There are female sport subcultures that robustly try to celebrate alternative ways of being female. One is the subculture of female rugby, and merits some reflection.

Female rugby subculture: oppositional?

The following lyrics are those of a song sung by many women's rugby teams:

> We are the _____ team so worship us
> We are the drunken sluts so sleep with us
> We are going to smoke and fool around,
> Champion bound, _____ rugby team
> We aren't the basketball, soccer lamos
> We aren't the football, hockey homos,
> We are just a bunch of drunken nymphahose,
> So let's go, _____ rugby team
> We have a drinking rule
> And we are proud of it
> So the soccer team can deal with it
> Eat my shit, suck my tit, lick my clit
> _____rugby team.
> You can tell that we are superior,
> Just look around at all the girls here,
> We are going to drink lots of beer,
> With no fear, no pukers here,
> _____ rugby team.
>
> (Washington Rugby Club Song Book, 1997)

The lyrics in this song are typical of most women's rugby songs. They redefine female sexuality as active, selective, and diverse. They also "turn the tables around." Instead of questioning the sexuality of women, they make remarks that stereotype the sexuality of male football and hockey players. Most of the traditional male rugby songs now contain lyrics providing the female rebuttal for various lines in the males' songs. Despite this, it seems that both songs can involve, critically, the degrading sexualization of female sexuality within the sport context.

Female rugby players might yet experience significant tension through their participation in such a traditionally masculine sport.[6] First, their femininity, heterosexuality, and womanliness are, again, often questioned because they act aggressively and powerfully. There might be a limit to the indifference their oppositional bravura can offer. Additionally, they seem to also feel the need to uphold the ethos of the (male) rugby subculture, where one is encouraged to sing about one's sexuality and in turn participate in songs that degrade both men and women. So it might be that female rugby players experience a profound ambivalence at the level of ideals. Their raucous counter-orthodoxy might also be threatened with implosion, since their songs definitively look over their shoulders to how women are ideologically positioned in heterosexual sex. The impression of sexual empowerment might therefore be illusory, or it might result from an empowerment not worth having, since it seems to replicate the sex-harm logic of masculinist culture. As Ann Garry argues, the fact that women are not the ones dominated or harmed does not make the domination of one individual by another morally acceptable (1994: 139). Genuine female empowerment is perhaps not the pseudo empowerment of beating men at their own game, but is, instead, the cessation of the sex-harm discourse. The results would include the undermining of the ideological conflict that inheres in being female and an athlete, and the robust undermining of the broader sexism in which this conflict figures.

Conclusion

Appreciation of the interdependent languages of sex and sport helps us understand the ideological tension in the concept of the female athlete. Sport is itself regularly sexy or sensual. That is healthy.[7] The problem lies in the symbiotic discourses of sport and heterosexual sex, each of which is inscribed with a conception of females as passive, dehumanized, and harmed sex objects. I have tried to illustrate this in the examples of sport hunting, mountaineering, the squash advertisement, the "male pussy", and sex-as-victory. That females in sport buy into this language rings like the *coup de grâce* of the masculinist hegemony. The "oppositional" discourse of female rugby culture rings like a mere oblique manifestation of the same hegemony.

Sport is not unique in its sexual language. Most sociocultural sub-regions, arguably, are similarly pervaded by sexual allusion, analogy, and innuendo (consider advertising). However, the massive humanizing potential of sport makes redress of the preceding discourses of sex and sport an urgent matter. Only by such redress can sport hope to fulfill its humanizing potential. Only then can the sexes be equal in sport and elsewhere, and only then will ideological tension in the concept of the female athlete disappear.

Acknowledgements

Thanks to Paul Davis for his insightful comments and feedback on earlier drafts of this essay.

Notes

1   I do not consider the question of the definition of sport and furthermore do not think my treatment requires it.
2   The United States National Broadcast Standards strictly limits the use of "vagina." "Penis" is not similarly restricted. This reinforces the notion of female sexuality as uniquely furtive and shameful.
3   This motif is confirmed, again, in a story about a rugby team that travels to play in a tournament. The team captain orders the men's team florescent orange shirts

as its "tour" shirts. When prompted by the players about the colour, he responds, "We need to wear hunter orange, since we'll be chasing cougars all weekend."

4   Saltman, in Chapter 7 of this volume's essays, notes similarly that masculinity and femininity rely on each other for intelligibility.

5   Iris Marion Young states, in this volume's first essay, that the human female is, historically, *body-object*, in contradistinction to the male body-subject.

6   Betsy Postow (Morgan and Meier 1995: 324) distinguishes four senses in which a sport might be considered masculine. Rugby would count as masculine in three of those senses, and fail on the fourth only because it is not an Olympic sport.

7   The essays in this volume by Saltman (Chapter 7) and Davis (Chapter 4) offer pertinent reflections. Saltman notes that some bodybuilders have said that, whilst lifting weights, they feel like a giant pumping penis, and that some felt sexually aroused and experienced orgasms. Davis tries to distinguish sexuality in sport from sexualization of the (typically female) competitor.

References

Baker, Robert and Frederick Elliston (eds) (1994). *Philosophy and Sex*. New Revised Edition. New York: Prometheus Books.

Blanchard, Barry and Peter Arbic (1994). 'The Wild Things', in *Canadian Mountaineering Anthology – Stories from 100 years at the edge*, Fairley and Marty (eds). Vancouver: Lone Pine Publisher.

Blum, Arlene (1980). *Annapurna: A Woman's Place*. San Francisco: Sierra Club Books.

Dwyer, Susan (1995). *The Problem with Pornography*. Belmont: Wadsworth Publishing Company.

Fairley, Bruce and Sid Marty (eds) (1995). *Canadian Mountaineering Anthology – Stories from 100 years at the edge*. Vancouver: Lone Pine Publisher.

Garry, Ann (1994). 'Pornography and Respect for Women', reprinted in *Philosophy of Sex*, Baker, Robert and Frederick Elliston (eds). New York: Prometheus Books, pp. 312–326.

Miller, Toby (2001). *Sportsex*. Philadelphia: Temple University Press.

Morgan, W.J. and Meier, K.V. (eds) (1995). *Philosophic Inquiry in Sport*. Champaign, IL: Human Kinetics.

Nelson, Mariah Burton (1994). *The Stronger Women Get, the More Men Love Football: sexism and the American culture of sports*. New York: Avon Books.

Schneider, Angela (2000). 'On the Definition of "Woman" in the Sport Context', in *Values in Sport*, Torbjorn Tannsjo and Claudio Tamburrini (eds). New York: E & FN Spon, pp. 123–138.

Part 3

Sex boundaries

Construction, naturalisation, and opposition

Chapter 7

Men with breasts*

Ken Saltman

Most women have breasts. Most men don't. Women who have had mastectomies don't have "real" breasts, but many have prosthetic breasts.[1] Men are not usually born with breasts but, like women, men can wear breasts, get breast implants, or take hormones to develop a bust. In American culture, breasts signify nourishing, nurturing motherhood, the object of love, and also libidinal desire. Breasts sell. They sell beer and cars and cigarettes and other products that advertisers want to tell us feel good to use. Breasts feel good to use.[2] When we emphatically tell the truth, we speak from our heart and beat our breasts. We carry our pride there. Those we love fall asleep on our breasts, and we fall asleep on theirs.

Male bodybuilders create massive breast-like mounds of muscle. With the development of muscle and reduction of body fat, great sheaths of pectoral muscle, another kind of breast, replace the breasts of female bodybuilders. The breasts of bodybuilders shine and ripple, pulse with veins, dance, grimace, and shiver. Male bodybuilders who stack[3] steroids eventually develop gynecomastia – the development of breasts atop the pectoral muscle. They get breasts on top of the breasts they have built and refer to this nuisance as "bitch tits." They stack and get stacked.

Norms of sexuality cannot be considered apart from gender norms. Just as the gender categories masculinity and femininity rely on each other for intelligibility, sexual categories of heterosexuality and homosexuality make sense only in opposition. Diana Fuss explains the co-implicatedness of the categories:

> The homo in relation to the hetero, much like the feminine in relation to the masculine, operates as an indispensable interior exclusion – an outside which in inside interiority making the articulation of the latter

* Originally published as 'Men with breasts' in *Journal of the Philosophy of Sport*, 1998, XXV, pp. 48–60. © 1998 by the International Association for the Philosophy of Sport. Reprinted, with permission.

possible, a transgression of the border which is necessary to constitute the border as such.

(Fuss 1991: 3)

In other words, because categories, which make meaning through exclusion, rely upon their excluded outside for intelligibility, this denied outside resides *within* the category. Categorization and naming, so necessary for interacting with others, induces us to forget that identity gets constituted through negation, through what necessarily gets excluded. In bodybuilding these interior exclusions are momentarily remembered; they manifest themselves, allowing brief glimpses at the excluded outside which resides inside.

Men with breasts

A great corpus of literature now exists in philosophy, feminism, cultural studies, and queer theory on the subject of the cultural construction of the body.[4] However, aside from Alphonso Lingis' 1986 essay, "Orchids and Muscles," and his 1994 *Foreign Bodies*, the sport of bodybuilding has only begun to receive academic attention as an important site for the political struggle over gender and sexual meaning. More recently Pamela L. Moore's (1997) edited book, *Building Bodies*, specifically addresses bodybuilding culture, the body, and representational politics. Most of the new studies of bodybuilding argue that it either challenges or reinforces gender and sexual norms. Lingis' essay differs, viewing the built body as the locus of trans-formation – the body giving birth to itself, the ornamental musculature turning away from the consumptive eye of industrial culture which made it and returning to nature, becoming like the orchid. Like Lingis' essay, this paper stresses the transformative dimensions of bodybuilding. While he elaborates on the reversal of the gaze and on the bodybuilder as prototype for a non-predatory humanity, I expand specifically on the gender and sexual reversals that occur as masculinity and femininity pushed to their limit overflow their fleshy containers.

Bodybuilding constantly ruptures itself, revealing its not so straight inside. Men become women, women become men. While it in many ways reinforces popular notions of the "real man" and "real woman," an examination of bodybuilding culture reveals that the "real man" and "real woman" are possible only through the most extreme of artifices; this artifice challenges the naturalness of gender upon which normative heterosexuality rests. Bodybuilding also expands objectification, unsettling dominant power relations, by reversing the gaze. Those who are typically subject to the gaze get to do the looking while those commonly privileged as viewers get surveilled.

One of the few academics to address the political implications of bodybuilding, Susan Bordo, has argued that the "power look" in female bodybuilding subjects women to an oppressive masculine disciplinary regime of the body (1993). In contradistinction, this paper argues that while bodybuilding, in some ways, reinforces gendered body norms and maintains the lines between gender categories, it also subverts itself, creating gender confusion, blurring the lines between gender and sexual categories, and even making a whole new category. Heterosexuality depends upon firmed-up notions of masculinity and femininity both ontologically and in terms of heterosexual practices associated with these categories. What a "real man" is makes sense only in opposition to what a "not-real man" does. Likewise homosexuality relies upon the fixedness of gender categories, because it is defined as transgressing those dominantly defined categories. What a "dyke" does transgresses the borders of what "real women" are supposed to do.[5]

Bodybuilding has the potential to serve as an example of gender multiplicity and the potential to challenge dominant binaries of masculine–feminine and straight–gay. I will in the first section lay out the way bodybuilding works to maintain gender norms and then in the second discuss the way it undermines them.

Bodybuilding reinforces gender norms

The male bodybuilder is Hercules, Tarzan, and Superman – the embodiment of masculine norms of strength, self-sufficiency, power, and heroism. As James McBride expresses in *War Battering and Other Sports* (1995), American masculinity is predicated upon and defined specifically against femininity – women and effeminate men. The distinct way the male body can look when pushed to its limits maintains gender norms by suggesting a "real man" defined against the feminine and the fag.[6] As a glossy public relations campaign for the "real man" male, bodybuilding fuses physical traits and physical practices to gender and sexual categories. It supports versions of gender that define gendered difference by virtue of physicality; it bolsters the tyranny of a limited number of dominant versions of gendered bodies, as well as the current power relations and social roles corresponding to them.

Female bodybuilding maintains gender norms

Female bodybuilding, or one version of it, also works to maintain gendered body norms. It has been split since its inception. Becoming increasingly more prevalent, one of these looks, the authentic *Playboy* bunny look, has been an extension of female body ideals and traditionally submissive feminine roles exemplified by fashion models. TV shows such as "Kiana's Flex Appeal," and former Ms. Olympia Cory Everson's show, "Gotta Sweat," promote a muscular feminine form, large breasts (often silicon), full ass, and almost no body fat.

The February 1997 issue of *Flex* has a swimsuit spread that poses the smoother model-looking bodybuilders against the massive and defined ones. There is even a flip-side centerfold pull-out. On one side, modelesque Monica Brant avails herself, her body smooth and thin, her butt stuck out, legs together, eyes closed. Her pose says, "Take me." Turn the pull-out over and find Natalia Murnikoviene with incredibly large and well-defined muscles, legs spread, arms crossed, staring daringly at the viewer in a black suit with bright red flames, "Come too close and I'll burn you!" She defies both the body ideal and the pose of feminine norms. *Playboy* now offers *Playboy's Hardbodies: Buffed Beauties Soft and Sexy* that goes one step further than the soft and submissive bodybuilders of *Flex* by posing these women naked in typically submissive soft porn poses and with a variety of absurd sports props including stiletto heels. While noticeably more muscular than either emaciated super-models or voluptuous porn stars, these female bodybuilders are not enormous and do not have a "ripped" look, now mandatory for male bodybuilders, which reveals the veins and muscle striations. They are firm and smooth – they are "feminine."

Subversion

Men become women become men

In bodybuilding, men become "real" men – but they also become women. Excess masculinity turns into femininity at the thinly stretched edges of the inflated body. Male bodybuilders develop massive smooth breasts, the center of the physique. They depilate body hair, swathe the corps with tanning cosmetics and oil, and don a delicate g-string. The male bodybuilder's body parodies its own hyperbolic butchness as it transmutates into the feminine. As the male bodybuilder adopts accoutrements of femininity, he engages disciplinary regimes peculiar to femininity: preening and primping, pluming and plucking – disciplines, rituals preparing for pageantry.

Female bodybuilders develop muscles that are hard to distinguish from men's. Their breasts shrink and are replaced by pectoral shields, veins bulge from necks and forearms, smooth skin turns into a pulsing roadmap, the feminine abdominal paunch disappears. Steroids make the jaw muscles protrude, facial hair develops, more body hair sprouts, and the clitoris enlarges, likening itself to a penis.

Male bodybuilders endure tremendous sacrifice, pain, and sometimes ill health to become the object of desire. But who is it that male bodybuilders want to want them? Reading bodybuilding magazines one discovers that bodybuilders try to sculpt their bodies to the perfection that they see in other men. The male readership of magazines such as *Muscle and Fitness, Flex,* or *Ironman* want to look like the men in the photos – Dorian Yates, Shawn Ray, Rich Gaspari, and of course the omnipresent Arnold. The industry is built around this desire. The reader desires to be the object of desire. The reader projects himself into the image and desires himself there. The reader wants to be like the object, wanted by other men. In this way, bodybuilding is inherently homosexual.

The fans know it too. In a letter to a recent issue of *Flex* magazine, a female bodybuilding fan complains of the magazine's failure to condemn breast implants for women the way it has condemned steroid use by men. The letter is noteworthy here because it mentions a usually unspoken fact of male bodybuilding.

> Set aside for the moment the concerns that implants are dangerous and unsportsmanlike, and address another issue. Featuring women with implants gives credibility to a cliché about male bodybuilders that FLEX should want to discourage: namely, that the average bodybuilder doesn't look at female breasts often enough to know the difference between fake and real.
>
> Frieda L. Weber, Fort Edward, NY (*Flex* 1997: 226)

The writer's thinly veiled inference of homosexuality endemic to the sport is more openly confirmed by Sam Fussell's book *Body: Confessions of an Unlikely Bodybuilder* (1991) as well as Harry Crews' novel *Body* (1990). In *Body*, the "roid raging" Russel Morgan, a.k.a. Russel "Muscle," gives supposedly straight men spontaneous erections with only the sight of his tanned and tremendous bulbous slaps of body beef. For example, at the Flamingo Hotel where a bodybuilding competition is to be held, the wormy desk clerk surprised at himself must cover his lap with office papers to hide his erection and yearns for the touch of the big man. Fussell tells his story of being a nerdy bookworm terrified of other people who thoroughly immerses himself in bodybuilding. While he overcomes his fear, he suffers from the unhealthy results of anabolic steroid use and the dehumanizing attitude necessary for success. During Fussell's first experience in the gym, he is jeered by the massive lifters in the free-weight area of the YMCA, punched in the kidney by a massively muscular double amputee, and then adopted by a very thin gay man named Austin who shows him how to use the universal machines.

> Just then, a man dressed in a singlet and what appeared to be a tutu broke from the line for the deltoid press to introduce himself to me.
>
> Quickly, Austin pushed him away, hissing, "Back off, Mary. He's mine!" The man skulked back to his station.
>
> I couldn't let this go on any longer. "Is this a gay gym?" I asked.
>
> "Look, honey," he replied. "*All* gyms are gay."
>
> I examined the men by the machines. There Austin seemed right. "But what about them?" I asked, pointing to the free-weight lifters.

Austin laughed out loud. "*Especially* them," he said. "They just don't know it yet!"

(Fussell 1991: 37)

Common to both of these examples is the accusation of homosexual latency that always shadows the fiction of the "real man." Fussell's book chronicles his movement from the sissy world to the world of real men. Increasingly, he discovers that the bodybuilding culture that accompanies his commitment to transformation is one of complete artifice.

Real men

In order to become "real men," bodybuilders must take artificial hormones, use dyes on their skin, shave off the natural outcropping of hair, load their systems with diet pills and supplements such as creatine monohydrate, and remove their blood and reinject it weeks later. Steroids, which are taken by all pros,[7] cause balding as well as shrinking of the testes and a drastic reduction of the male sex drive. This same issue of *Flex* is filled with advertisements for products guaranteed to improve male sexual performance as well as balding. These "real men" wear diapers in the gym while squatting, because they often lose bowel control while lifting extremely heavy weights.

Before competitions bodybuilders are incredibly weak (Fussell 1991). Having dieted and dehydrated to thin their skins, some can barely walk to the posing dais. In the sport of powerlifting, athletes compete not for body image but for sheer strength measured in the moment of the lift. Powerlifters are invariably much stronger than bodybuilders in any given lift. For example, as Mr. Olympia, Arnold could bench press 460 pounds, while top powerlifters can bench 700 pounds. The kind of prolonged steroid use demanded of bodybuilders causes high blood pressure, "roid rages" (violent mood swings), kidney damage, impotence (in men), and cessation of menstruation (in women). The magazine advertisements recognize this and hawk cures for baldness and impotence. Extreme artifice in bodybuilding bubbles to the surface and exposes the pose as just that – a pose.

And yet the artificiality does not make the endeavor any more absurd. Rather, it is the bodybuilders who don't use steroids who are absurd. The "natural bodybuilders" who reject drugs have their own few magazines and organizations. They lack the *unbelievable* size and definition of the pros. It is specifically the unreality of bodybuilders, both men and women, that makes them so appealing. They are more human than human so as to be unhuman. They are walking anatomy lessons – every muscle, tendon, and artery on display. They are what Jean Baudrillard in *Fatal Strategies* means by obscene: they reveal the workings of power, and that is their appeal.

> All structures turned inside out and exhibited, all operations rendered visible. In America this goes all the way from the bewildering network of telephone and electric wires (the whole system is on the surface) to the concrete multiplication of all the bodily functions in the home, the litany of ingredients on the tiniest can of food, the exhibition of income or IQ, and includes harassment by signals, the obsession with displaying the innards of power, the equivalent of the mad desire to locate the critical function in the lobes of the brain . . .
>
> (Baudrillard 1990: 29)

The revelation of a vast network of veins, the exposure of every muscle striation – the bodybuilder is a moving, breathing anatomy lesson with each part of the physique exploded for easy reading. What can we read in the multiplicity of lines on the body? If we could, like a palm reader, read the multitude of lines on the body of the bodybuilder, we would see written over and over: The Law – the ultimate punishment, the greatest terror, just like Kafka's, "In the Penal Colony" (Kafka 1961). But also the greatest pleasure. To have the law inscribed on the body – what is so real about the bodybuilder is that she or he performs capitalism, the ultimate alienation from one's labor: the body now machine.

Bodybuilding is the only sport in which the product of the athlete's labor has no object outside of himself or herself. Whereas a basketball player trains her body to perform for activities within a game, the bodybuilder's labor remains invested in the body. The body becomes both the catalyst of production and the product of one's labor. Not only is the body the site and end of labor, but each part of the body is continuously reproduced with the specialization of labor, an endless series of repetitions designed specifically to increase mass and better reveal the workings of the product. Bodybuilding incorporates mass production and reproduction onto the body itself.

In enacting the law, the bodybuilder becomes the great scroll on which the law is written. But capitalism is not the only law. There is patriarchy, too.

Real women

As G-spot (a female bodybuilder and friend of Fussell) put it with her winning smile and foghorn voice, "I've fucking reversed the course of nature."

> Menarche had halted with the introduction of steroids to her system. The coarse facial hair and acne started soon after. To counteract the sweat, she used spritz, to counteract the muscles, make-up. In fact, on the sofa, in my arms, G-spot looked like she'd strayed into mommy's make-up cabinet. She wore more rouge, lipstick, and powder than a Regent Street bawd.

Between the two of us, there was close to five hundred pounds on that sofa, and when our grappling session began, you could practically hear the clink and groan of the armor. There was barely room for our lips to meet above our swollen, pumped up chests. When, finally, I reached below her gold dumbbell pendant for her breast, I found it harder than my own.

(Fussell 1991: 158)

The scene Fussell describes highlights the artifice of not only the steroids which make G-spot more "manly" but the artifice of those technologies designed to make her more "womanly." Fussell and G-spot herself fail to see the extent to which the "course of nature" isn't natural at all. The cosmetics that all female bodybuilders wear and the silicone breasts that many implant chafe against the intense masculinization they have undergone. The result is an exceeding obviousness of the unnaturalness of both the feminizing and masculinizing prostheses. Unfortunately, female bodybuilders are seldom understood as breaking down these gender borders and denaturalizing gender norms. Too often they are dismissed as freaks.

Objectification

Male bodybuilders are hyper-masculine. They are more masculine than masculine, and this extremity undermines itself. Masculinity stretched to its limits begins to fray, transmuting itself into the feminine but also the neutered. As men approach this hyper-realness promised by bodybuilding, the genitalia shrink, the effeminate g-string goes on, the hair comes off, and there is not simply a feminizing – another gender is created. It would be impossible to say that these men have become women or look like "real women." This gender is asexual. Female bodybuilders who take steroids and undergo the regimens and push the practice to its limit become masculine and then also enter this neutered zone. Male bodybuilders don't really look like men. Female bodybuilders look like men who don't really look like men.

In bodybuilding, not only the breast but the whole body enters a state of pure objectification. The body becomes a pure sexual and sensual object; the bodybuilder loses genital sexuality. In American culture, breasts signify nourishing, nurturing motherhood; they are also the center of the sexual gaze for heterosexual men. We consider these functions to be at odds – a women breast-feeding in public commits an obscene act, and yet a large-breasted woman at the beach in a small bikini is a sexual object. The nurturing function of the breast, of the person, is usually split off and repressed to turn the breast, and the person, into an object of sexual desire.[8]

Alphonso Lingis, in *Foreign Bodies*, discusses the sexuality of the bodybuilder as not disappearing but rather being reinvested throughout the whole body. He quotes Schwartzenegger in the film *Pumping Iron* who says that getting pumped is like coming all day and in his whole body. In this way, sexuality gets de-genitalized and re-sensualized, re-corporealized. Sexuality expands from between the legs to the entire body. The man becomes that which above all stands for his manhood, his difference – the phallus. After Fussell's last competition, his lifting buddy runs up to him excited:

> "Oh, Sam," he gurgled. "You looked like a fucking human penis! Veins were poppin' every which way!"[9]
>
> (Fussell 1991: 232)

The expansion of sexual objectification in male bodybuilding, in a way, undermines the objectification of women by men. It does so by positioning men – no longer only women – as subject to the scrutiny of others. This unsettles the dominant relation of men as subjects and women as objects. I believe that as spectacular as it is, this is why male bodybuilding is not shown on television as a prime hour sport. It makes men too subject to the gaze of others. Unlike football or baseball, it puts patriarchy in trouble. "We have to accept that bodybuilding is a subculture that will continue to expand but will never be fighting for prime-time space with the World Series . . . The public finds the sight of 260 pound shaved and oiled bodybuilder hitting a side-chest faintly ridiculous"[10] (Flex 1997: 95).

Though de-humanization is potentially dangerous, objectification is not in itself bad. It can have emancipatory effects. Objectification is often portrayed as the twin evil of humanization. To be more human is better; to be less human is worse. In fact, humanization risks reifying categories as much as objectification. Liberation from traditionally considered "natural" roles (a woman's place is in the home) can often yield new normative constructions that equally constrain women (a woman's place is in the factory or office). Romanticizing the so-called human is no safer than romanticizing objectification, artifice, or cyborgs. Increasingly, with the human being defined in mechanistic ways by science, old recourse to "natural" ideals are as much fictions as the artifice they seek to supplant. Humanization and objectification both lend themselves as ideological constructs to be utilized to maintain or contest dominance by one group or another. Here I point to the potentially liberatory appropriation of objectification by women.

The expansion of objectification has other potentially liberatory effects. Female bodybuilding can objectify women in a way different from the objectification of the fashion model. Female bodybuilders enter positions and postures of typically masculine power and authority. This is clear when comparing the bodybuilding shows on ESPN2 with typical muscle magazine spreads. Former Ms. Olympia, Cory Everson, is in a position of authority on her show. She directs male bodybuilders in their workouts. This contrasts with bathing beauties hanging on the arms of male bodybuilders in *Muscle and Fitness*. More importantly, one does not find female bodybuilders hanging on men, admiring a man's physique, promising sex to male hetero viewers the way models do. Female bodybuilders cannot be placed as appendages on men. They demand their own attention, staring hard at the viewer. They proudly pose their *own* physiques. In so doing, they defy the hetero norm of being a female sacrifice for men. Like "bull dykes," female bodybuilders appropriate typically masculine imagery, refusing to become traditional objects of consumption in the masculine economy. But for whom then *are* they objects of consumption? Female bodybuilders are role models for women interested in alternatives to the singular norms of gender offered by fashion models. But female bodybuilders are also the objects of sexual desire. Reconfiguring the feminine as dominant or at least as strong and self-sufficient, they appeal to those of any sex or gender who want to be either dominated, engaged by an equal, or to dominate someone stronger. The expansion of female norms expands the intelligibility of multiple forms of identification and desire.

Expanded gender norms increase gender possibilities and sexual possibilities but also market possibilities. The emancipatory potential of multiply conceived gender and sexual roles functions comfortably within capitalism, a structure which is one of bodybuilding's prime conditions of possibility. This points to: (a) the body and bodily practices as crucial sites of contested and ongoing, constituted meaning-making; (b) the relative autonomy of multiple fronts of social struggle. Gains *can* be made against heterosexism within other oppressive structures such as capitalism; and (c) the need for theoretical work that can merge a cultural politics of recognition with a social politics of economic distributive justice.[11]

Gender confusion or the limits on becoming other

While the pure objectification of the body produces a becoming-other that occurs in both male and female bodybuilding, the two are fundamentally different in relation to challenging or reinforcing common sense about gender. Despite the unraveling of masculinity as it is stretched to its limit, male bodybuilding in current American culture also works in the service of maintaining gender roles by serving as the ideal for a very different masculine culture. Despite what I have detailed as the gay dynamics of bodybuilding, the auto-homo-desire, and the latency found in books and magazines, the male bodybuilder serves as a referent for a more mainstream, macho, patriarchal, heterosexist male culture.

Male bodybuilders, ironically, serve as the very nearly platonic form of manliness that gets expressed through a very different, very "straight" aesthetic in neighborhood gyms and health club franchises. The particulars of the form, the lifters who idolize these god-like men, are often hairy, fat, pale, and slovenly dressed.[12] They come into the gym after a night of drinking beer, eating chicken wings, and watching football on big screen television. Unlike the pro bodybuilders whose bodies are temples, the common lifter's body is more typically battered garrisons, some combination of muscle and fat, armor, thrown up to stand as a defense between the lifter and the world. It is the bulk that most of these lifters are after, unrestricted growth, accumulation, a wealth of flesh. The bodybuilder's body is sacred. Consumption is a religion for pros counting calories, fat, protein, and carbohydrates. The common male lifter's body is profane, his consumption gluttonous, unrestrained, unscrupulous. Both the sexually ambiguous male bodybuilder and the sexually "certain," "straight" male weightlifter are visions of excess, models of successful reinvestment of labor back into the means of production. The bodybuilder, like the action hero, serves as the *ideal* "real man." He is the promise, the advertisement, the seduction. But this common lifter is the real "real man." And an American man doesn't even have to lift weights to be him. He need only consume. If anything, he is the bigger whore.[13] Although, as I have discussed, the "real man" is a fiction, this fiction wields tremendous cultural power. That is why when women become "real men," it is thoroughly subversive. It reveals the fictive nature of the naturalization of gender.

While male bodybuilding has functioned primarily to solidify gender identification by resonating with popular conceptions of masculinity, female bodybuilding has worked primarily to break it down and commit gender confusion. As I have mentioned, at present there are really two competing versions of female bodybuilding. The February 1997 issue of *Flex* shows the smoother, rounder, less-inflated bodies of "fitness champs." This is a new category attempting to appeal to those interested in looking at what they might find in fashion magazines or the *Sports Illustrated* swimsuit issue. However, tremendously muscled and defined bodybuilding champions such as Lenda Murray, Nikki Fuller, and Natalia Murnikoviene thoroughly upset the physicalized norms of femininity – gentility, softness, fragility, and smallness. Not only do they call into question femininity but masculinity as well by showing that supposedly masculine traits can be worn like so much clothing.

Gender traits do not inhere to gender. Rather, any body ideal can be the basis for ideological claims. It is not as if individuals can or should simply exit the gender category in which they find themselves and enter a more liberating one. While gender remains a necessary (if not inevitable) political category, the destabilizing of gender challenges the ideological application of it. Susan Bordo puts it well:

> I view our bodies as a site of struggle, where we must work to keep our daily practices in the service of resistance to gender domination, not in the service of "docility" and gender normalization.
>
> (Bordo 1993: 184)

Bordo goes on to argue that female bodybuilding is simply a taking on of masculine power through strict regimes of disciplining the body. She sees no liberatory potential here:

> To feel autonomous and free while harnessing body and soul to an obsessive body-practice is to serve, not transform, a social order that limits female possibilities. And, of course, for the female to become male is only to locate oneself on a different side of a disfiguring opposition. The new "power look" in female body-building, which encourages women to develop the same hulk-like, triangular shape that has been the norm for male bodybuilders, is no less determined by a hierarchical, dualistic construction of gender than was the conventionally "feminine" norm that tyrannized female body-builders such as Bev Francis for years.
>
> (Bordo 1993: 179)

I think that Bordo's argument, while compelling, is limited in two ways. First, to say that female bodybuilders become male is to abandon muscularity to the category of masculinity. It reinforces the notion that gender is defined by biological difference. The massive muscularity of male bodybuilders is not "natural" for men any more than it is for women. The hulk-like triangular shape is prosthetic. It is clothing for both men and women. Secondly, if our bodies are a site of struggle against gender normalization, then it would seem that the development of alternative and multiple "feminine" beauty forms would contest the one dominant version of female beauty that can be viewed in pornography, the Victoria's Secret catalogue, *Baywatch*, Barbie, and nearly everywhere else in the culture. There is gender subversion always already in bodybuilding, a built-in contradictoriness that needs to be made apparent rather than seeing the phenomenon as wholly on the side of oppression or liberation.

Conclusion

Work needs to be done in classroom education and cultural pedagogy to dismantle restrictive cultural categories to allow for the creation of tentative new categories. This is a very different project from the liberal one of promoting tolerance for difference. This entails the daunting task of calling into question all categories – for example, heterosexuality and homosexuality. Such cultural deconstructive work ought to be attentive to the way structural determinants, such as capitalism and patriarchy, play out through very specific sites and in particular practices and disciplines determining, yet not over-determining, cultural formations. I have sought to show here the way capitalism and patriarchy determine and structure our pleasures in surprising and uncharted ways and also that resistances, such as female bodybuilding, can develop to challenge the limits imposed by these structures.

Ultimately, such deconstructive work should be inextricably bound to a larger political movement concerned not only with a politics of recognition but with greater social and material equity.

I want to insist that cultural artifacts in themselves cannot be relied upon to challenge sexual and gender oppression. That is the role of teachers and other cultural workers: to "out" interior exclusions, to bring them to the surface and penetrate the bounds of normative categorization, to defy categorical borders and, ultimately, to teach the critical engagement of cultural artifacts in order to transform limited meanings into yet unimagined possibilities.

Acknowledgements

My thanks to Alphonso Lingis, Amy E. Smith, and Shawn J. Smith for their helpful comments and colorful conversation on this paper and earlier drafts.

Notes

1 The meaning and definition of the breast, its use, and its relation to other parts of the body has been contested for centuries. In this paper, I question the fixity of gender and sexuality but also the identity of the breast as any one thing. I am concerned with challenging the idea that one kind of breast is any more natural than any other as a corollary to the more central concern of this paper—namely, that one kind of gender and sexual role is any more natural than any other. My concern here is with the use of the breast as it fosters or challenges certain social relations rather than with laying out the contested history of the meaning of the breast itself. For a history of the breast over the last few hundred years, consult Thomas Lacquer's *Making Sex*, Laquer and Catherin Gallagher's edited book, *The Making of the Modern Body*. By defining men's chest as breast, prosthesis as breasts, and women's mammaries as breasts, I suggest that what a breast might be is far more open to interpretation than is usually supposed.

2 Men use their own breasts as well as the breasts of other men, men use women's breasts, women use their own breasts, women use other women's breasts. Breasts are commodified and commodities in part because they are so tied up with pleasure in American culture. This is not an ascetic indictment of pleasure. On the contrary, specifically because breasts feel good to use, resistance to normalization can develop through pleasure, and pleasure can result from resistance. As I explain in the section on objectification, objectification is not all bad but is an inevitable result of utility. However, the objectification of the breast cannot be considered apart from social structures and relations of power that play out in the use of the body. The body is used ideologically in ways which support or challenge social structures, such as capitalism and patriarchy.

3 To stack steroids is to take more than one kind of steroid at a time for maximum muscle growth in a given period of time. All the famous male bodybuilders have done this. There are plastic surgeons who specialize in the removal of "bitch tits." See Fussel or Crews.

4 See, for example, Michel Focault's *History of Sexuality*, Volume 1, Judith Butler's *Gender Trouble*, Susan Bordo's *Unbearable Weight*, Thomas Lacquer's *Making Sex* and Laquer and Gallagher's *The Making of the Modern Body*. There has been

growing interest in masculinity more specifically. See Paul Smith's edited book, *Boys*.

5 In this paper, I use the term "dyke" and "bull dyke" as markers of political categories the way that "queer" is a politicized version of "gay." I recognize the play of appropriation and re-appropriation of meanings in language. I take the liberty of using these terms as an expression of political alliance and at the same time remind readers that I do not subscribe to the kind of authenticity-minded identity politics which holds that one has to be in a category to speak about the category. That would be at odds with my purpose of challenging categorical boundaries.

6 I use the expressions "real men" and "real woman" with an understanding that these terms are also subject to appropriation and used in multiple and contradictory ways. For example, they are used in a resistant way by queers and re-appropriated and used in a homophobic way as well by straights. I am also aware of the danger of reinscribing the boundaries between categories I am attempting to challenge. Language, like gender categories, refuses stasis yet tends toward dominant meanings.

7 The difference between a bodybuilder on steroids and a "natural" one is dramatic. Only with steroids can one develop to the size of an Arnold Schwartzenegger or a Bev Francis. In fact, the size standards have increasingly grown for male bodybuilders since Arnold's heyday. The vascularity (that "ripped to shreds" look) achievable with steroids cannot be attained naturally. Compare the bodybuilders in *Muscle and Fitness* to those in a natural bodybuilding magazine. The difference is drastic and obvious. The telltale signs of steroid use are enlarged jaw and facial muscles, gapped front teeth, a slightly bloated look to the skin of the face, and, of course, muscular development that looks impossible.

8 The breast has many functions. One of these, the nourishing function (not always present), has to be split from the sexual function. The reason why these two functions are so at odds in current American culture, I believe, has to do to a large extent with capitalism and with women being positioned as baby machines or sexual commodities. They cannot be both machine and commodity at the same time in U.S. culture at present. However, in female bodybuilding, they are both. Reproduction is invested in the body of the woman to make more of her rather than to produce a product. The object of reproduction shifts from the baby to the mother. This follows the fundamental law of capital: reinvestment of the product of labor back into the means of production rather than into the product.

9 The redeployment of sexuality from the genitals to the entire body may, in fact, challenge the genital orientation of dominant heterosexual male sexuality. This important question warrants its own paper (if not a book).

10 The quote comes from an article justifying the continued use of steroids by bodybuilders. It argues that the public "finds the sight of a 160-pound bodybuilder hitting the same pose [as the 260-pounder] *totally* ridiculous" – not just "faintly ridiculous." The magazines do not explore why the public sees bodybuilding as a "weird subculture" as opposed to, say, football which is seemingly stranger with its plastic and rubber armor and incredibly complex set of rules. Unlike football and baseball, bodybuilding holds out a promise of glory to anyone willing to work hard (and eventually sacrifice their health). In this way, it is tied to an inherently conservative American dream vision. Schwartzenegger's career is the male bodybuilder's dream. There is far less of a notion of "the natural" athlete in bodybuilding because of the incredible amount of work the sport entails.

11 The theoretical underpinnings of joining deconstructive cultural politics to socialism as two complementary projects of structural change can be found in Nancy Fraser's *Justice Interruptus* (1997), Chapters 1 and 3.
12 This "straight" male aesthetic of unrestrained consumption contrasts drastically with more typically female and "gay" aesthetic of meticulous dress and careful body sculpting.
13 Traditionally, "whore" is a derogatory term for a female who takes in the objects, the penis, and the other indiscriminately. It has not masculine counterpart. Capitalism encourages men to consume indiscriminately, while this is profane for women. Such language operates as the tendrils of patriarchal social control. By this statement, I infer the parallel between consumption and sexual ingestion. Bodybuilders, common lifters, along with nearly every American, are obsessed with consumption, with taking the object, the other into the self. The common slob does so indiscriminately and reveals the workings of power in American culture just as much as the bodybuilder does. See Baudrillard (1990) on the obese in *Fatal Strategies*. The homosexual nature of mainstream male culture is more highly repressed than opposite. That the mainstream male gazes admiringly, lovingly, and *enviously* upon the action hero–bodybuilder (taking him in from the screen) reveals the fact that he wants him and wants to be him, wanted by other men, to be taken in by other men via the screen.

References

Baudrillard, J. (1990). *Fatal Strategies*. New York: Semiotext(e).
Bordo, S. (1993). *Unbearable Weight*. Berkeley, CA: University of California Press.
Butler, J. (1990). *Gender Trouble*. New York: Routledge.
Crews, H. (1990). *Body*. New York: Poseidon Press.
Foucault, M. (1980). *The History of Sexuality, Volume I: An Introduction*. New York: Vintage.
Fraser, N. (1997). *Justice Interruptus*. New York: Routledge.
Fuss, E. (ed.) (1991). *Inside/Out*. New York: Routledge.
Fussell, S. W. (1991). *Muscle: Confessions of an Unlikely Bodybuilder*. New York: Poseidon Press.
Kafka, F. (1961). *The Penal Colony and Other Selected Stories* (W. Muir and E. Muir, Trans.). New York: Schocken.
Laquer, T. (1992). *Making Sex*. Cambridge, MA: Harvard University Press.
Laquer, T., and C. Gallagher (eds.) (1987). *The Making of the Modern Body*. Berkeley, CA: University of California Press.
Lingis, A. (1994). *Foreign Bodies*. New York: Routlege
—— (1995). "Orchids and Muscles." *Journal of the Philosophy of Sport*, 12: 15–26.
McBride, J. (1995). *War, Battering, and Other Sports*. Atlantic Highlands, NJ: Humanities Press.
Moore, P.L (ed.) (1997). *Building Bodies*. New Brunswick, NJ: Rutgers University Press.
Playboy's Hardbodies, January 2007.
Smith, P. (ed.) (1996). *Boys*. Boulder, CO: Westview Press.

Chapter 8

The doping ban
Compulsory heterosexuality and lesbophobia*

Rebecca Ann Lock

> [P]olicing gender is sometimes a way of securing heterosexuality.
> (Butler 1990: xii)

There have been many different kinds of papers written about doping in sport. It is only relatively recently that questions have been asked about what effects doping bans have had (Black 1996; Black and Pape 1997; Burke 1998; Burke and Roberts 1997; Burke and Symons 1999; Davis and Delano 1992). Besides attempting, but clearly failing, to stop drug use in sport, the doping ban has been shown to have better success in promoting a sex or gender order (Burke 1998; Burke and Roberts 1997; Burke and Symons 1999; Davis and Delano, 1992). Like Burke and Roberts (1997), I contend that, by looking at examples of women who are disliked for similar reasons to female dopers, we can appreciate why doping harshly grates on some people's sensibilities. Parallels, then, will be drawn between female dopers, 'unattractive' women, and lesbians, because they are all disliked for how they contravene heterosexual femininity. This analysis builds upon those that suggest that the doping ban functions to promote a sex/gender order, and it asserts that this social order is distinctly heterosexual.

My article focuses on female dopers, for like Burke and Roberts (1997), I think female dopers pose more of a threat to the dominant social order than male dopers do. This is manifested in the lesser response of disgust for male dopers. However, I further illustrate that there is little response of disgust when female dopers do not show so-called masculine side effects.[1] The disgust, then, is not necessarily for doping per se, but for the effects these substances can have on conventional femininity. My point is that people are disgusted by the idea of women dopers, because doping is typically equated with the effects of 'masculinization'.

To make sense of how male dopers and some female dopers are treated less harshly by the media than 'masculinized' female dopers, I explain how

* Originally published as 'The doping ban: compulsory heterosexuality and lesbophobia' in *International Review for the Sociology of Sport*, 2003, vol. 38, no. 4, pp. 397–411.

femininity is not independent of sexuality (Butler 1990). If we are to make sense of how women who do not conform to expectations of femininity are feared and badly treated, we need to consider the significance of sexuality. 'Masculinized' female dopers and non-dopers are insulted and criticized in a way that is similar to those stigmatized as lesbians. The press describes such women in a manner that promotes heterosexual aesthetic values as natural and more attractive. I contrast these insults with descriptions of female dopers who maintain an acceptably feminine appearance. Accordingly, the case can be made that, by taking sexuality into account, we can develop a more complex understanding of the social order that permeates sport. My position, then, is to argue that the doping ban functions to legitimate heterosexuality and demonize lesbianism. My charge against the anti-dopers is that, through their aesthetic values, they are inherently lesbophobic and legislate for aesthetic and athletic performances of compulsory heterosexuality. I argue that female dopers are treated in a similar way to 'masculinized' females who do not cheat, precisely because of myths/stereotypes of sexuality as an identifiable aesthetic.

The heterosexual matrix

There are two major reasons why I am dissatisfied with the exclusion of sexuality from discussions about the effect of doping bans. One is because there is such a striking similarity between how lesbians and female dopers are criticized (which I illustrate in a later section). The other is an epistemological concern that sex and gender are not sexuality-neutral constructs. It is this latter concern that I discuss in this section, which theoretically grounds the relationship between sex, gender and sexuality through Judith Butler's construct of the heterosexual matrix. Butler (1990: 23) suggests:

> 'Intelligible' genders are those which in some sense institute and maintain relations of coherence and continuity among sex, gender, sexual practice, and desire. In other words, the spectres of discontinuity and incoherence, themselves thinkable only in relation to existing norms of continuity, are constantly prohibited and produced by the very laws that seek to establish causal or expressive lines of connection among biological sex, culturally constituted genders, and the 'expression' or 'effect' of both in the manifestation of sexual desire through sexual practice.

There are two key points here that support my objection to how doping and gender have thus far been discussed. First, gender is central to what Butler (1990) calls the 'heterosexual matrix', which is the hegemonic belief in the relationship connecting sex, gender, sexual practice and desire. Each element of the matrix is fundamental to the intelligibility of gender and likewise gender is fundamental to the intelligibility of sex, sexual desire and practice.

For example, masculinity and femininity are understood as genders because there are the biological sexes of males and females to which they can be attached. If there were no differences demarcated between males and females it would be difficult to imagine the performance of gender at all. Furthermore if there were no heterosexuality (a desire that is oppositional), there would be no categorizing of humans into oppositional groups: males and females, or masculine and feminine genders. Put in constructive terms: 'The hetero-sexualisation of desire requires and institutes the production of discrete and asymmetrical opposition between "feminine" and "masculine", where these are understood as expressive attributes of "male" and "female"' (Butler 1990: 23).

The second key point that I have alluded to is that sexuality is also interpreted in appearance. Insulting women who are not feminine and stereotyping non-feminine female athletes as lesbian (which I will detail in the final section of this article) illustrates how sex is situated with gender and gender is situated with sexuality. Such insults express an objection to women who do not have a gender-appropriate appearance. Further, a lack of femi-ninity is presumed as a signifier of lesbianism. Arguably then, the inter-relationship of sex, gender, desire and sexual practice are implicated in the intelligibility of these labels. Within this framework, heterosexuality for females is understood as expressed in a performance of femininity. Thus, the promotion of femininity as *the* legitimate aesthetic, and the criticizing and effacement of non-feminine women, also has the effect of policing non-heterosexual gender expressions of women.

Men who perform masculinity and women who perform femininity are considered to be desirable; the coherency between their sex type and gender makes them fully oppositional to one another and therefore potentially sexually desirable. Not being very feminine and therefore being considered as more masculine, if a person is a biological female, is to fail to be desirable. Thus, if a woman's gender performance is not coherent with her sex, she is judged as ugly. Hence, from here on I will use the term 'heterosexual femininity' because the conventional femininity at any point in time is a gendered performance that is by definition heterosexual.

As Butler (1990) explains, the distinction between sex and gender, by feminists, was intended to undermine biology as destiny formulations, which justified valuing and treating women differently to men. However, this strategy and presumption led to an essentializing of women by second-wave feminists, because gender was set up as socially constructed and it was assumed that biological sex was natural. Interrogations of the social constructedness of sex (Dreger 1998; Epstein 1990; Fausto-Sterling 2000; Laqueur 1990) have shown that sex is as gendered (socially constructed) as gender. In paraphrasing de Beauvoir, Butler (1990: 12) infers, 'there is no recourse to a body that has not always already been interpreted by cultural meanings; hence, sex, by definition, will be shown to have been gender all along'. If there is no causal relationship between sex and gender, then temporal support of difference also crumbles, and using the terms 'sex' and 'gender' as if they denote different things also becomes questionable. In the same vein perhaps we might also recognize gender as sexuality all along. That is, we can see that gender is a social construction that is related to one's sex, but not in any natural way caused by it. So what kind of social construction do we think gender is? Sexuality is arguably implicated in the production and maintenance of gender because socially sanctioned conceptions of gender are read as a signifier of sexuality. Women who conform to femininity are not assumed to be lesbian or bisexual, but heterosexual,[2] and only when one's gender performance is non-feminine do people wonder if the woman is a lesbian. Therefore, we might also think of gender as a socially constructed expression of sexuality.

Having illustrated how the heterosexual matrix links sex, gender and sexuality, the argument can be made that any issue of gender is also an issue of sexuality. A stronger way of putting this is that sexuality is not only relevant but also indispensable to any discussion of gender. At best those who discuss only sex and/or gender presume sexuality, for sexuality is implicit in the meaning of sex and gender. To fail to recognize this is to underestimate the meaning invested in each of these concepts.

Doping and the absence of sexuality

Having argued that sexuality needs to be a part of discussions of sex and gender, because their intelligibility is produced by reference to one another, and because sexuality is read into appearance, I now turn to critiquing articles that have explored sex/gender's relation to doping with reference to the significance of sexuality. I reflect on the limits of articles about doping, which do not adequately acknowledge sexuality, by explicitly illustrating how sexuality is silent in these articles, yet implicated in the arguments.

Burke (1998) discusses sex and gender as he makes the argument that sport scientists, ethicists and legislators help maintain myths about dichotomous sexual categories. Only once, though, does he discuss sexuality as he explains how male power[3] deals with female body-building to reduce the threat it poses to exposing gender dichotomy as a continuum. Burke (1998) describes women as reined in to acceptable femininity by needing to be heterosexually attractive in order to be successful competitors. However, he fails to develop the significance of heterosexuality in defining femininity. Further, he does not discuss how a stereotypical heterosexual femininity is considered the only femininity, therefore the only way to be acceptable/authentic as women. Moreover, when he moves to discuss doping more specifically, he does not refer to sexuality again, but only to dichotomous sex categories as something that female dopers threaten through 'masculinization', which is the effect some dope has on women.

Burke and Symons (1999) continue this discussion following a response to Burke's (1998) article. Again the main focus is on sex and gender. However, they make the interesting point that the term lesbian is used as an insult about female athletes if their muscles are considered too big. Disappointingly, though, they do not interrogate what 'freak, ugly, lesbian and/or a drug taker' (Burke and Symons 1999: 15) have in common. As I explain later in the article, a closer look at these terms reveals a striking connection; the kind of woman who gets called these names does not meet the accepted criteria of heterosexual femininity.

Davis and Delano's (1992) article takes a slightly different approach in that they focus on a number of anti-doping posters that both assume and naturalize sex and gender dichotomies. These campaigns suggest that steroid users' bodies will become more like the 'opposite' gender; the presumed masculine will become feminized and the presumed feminine will become masculinized. Their concern is about how the biological bodies are presented as naturally dichotomous (male and female) and how doping is presented as disrupting these bodies in terms of appearance and function. The 'unnatural' consequences of doping are presented as disgusting, obscene and abnormal. Davis and Delano (1992) interrogate these for how they naturalize an ideology of male/female and nature/artifice dichotomies.

Among the posters Davis and Delano (1992) use to support their position is one that refers to sexual health. The caption reads: 'It's a myth that all the really big jocks take steroids. Extended steroid use can lead to sterility, impotence and atrophied testicles. But that only concerns you if you want a healthy sex life' (cited in Davis and Delano 1992). Healthy sex life is defined in specifically heterosexual terms. First, there is an explicit connection made between healthy sex and reproduction—implying sex to necessarily have reproductive potential. Second, erections are considered essential for sex. Erections are essential to sex when sex is limited to penile penetration of the vagina. The emphasis on erections for healthy sex presumes that the role of the male is exclusively one of penetrating rather than being penetrated, or sex without penetration. My point is that this poster promotes male heterosexuality because the focus on the norm of healthy sex is put in overtly heterosexual terms. Moreover, the notion of 'really big jocks' appeals to a sense of ideal masculinity; the poster prescribes the kind of man one should want to be – a heterosexually active one. Davis and Delano (1992) reduce the effect of the doping ban to sex and gender, and do not consider the relationship they have with sexuality.

Another poster shows a woman with a bulging crotch with the caption: 'Steroids, they'll make a man out of you yet' (cited in Davis and Delano, 1992). Appreciating that the image is a sarcastically exaggerated one, the issue remains that there is an assumption that female genitalia is 'naturally' small. The image and the caption both suggest that an enlarged clitoris is for a female to become like a male.[4] The sarcasm of the poster expresses and promotes disgust for enlarged clitorises. Given that an enlarged clitoris is interpreted as penis-like, the idea of a woman having a small penis disrupts the simplistic idea of males being the ones with penises and penetrative capacities. The female penis is something that physically disrupts the idea that men and women have sex because they 'were built to fit together'; the idea of the complementary opposites is shattered by the notion of the 'female penis'. It is only within a strictly heterosexual discourse of sex that an enlarged clitoris would be likened to a penis, a penis is considered fundamentally valid for penetrating, and a penis is considered oppositional and therefore complementary to a vagina. It is an offence against the heterosexual matrix for a woman's genitalia to defy its complementary relationship to the penis. Davis and Delano (1992) do not consider the heterosexual rhetoric of this poster. To protect one's femaleness from the 'man making' effects of steroids is also to protect and recreate the coherent relationship between the anatomics of the body and heterosexuality.

Burke and Roberts (1997) provide the most comprehensive discussion of a social order that the doping ban helps to maintain. They argue, '[T]he pervasive dislike of athletes using drugs is not explained entirely by the "good" practice of sports and fairness, and that it also has something to do with the fear of transgressing socially constructed, gender boundaries' (100). They suggest that the rationality used to oppose doping and normative descriptions of 'masculinization' as a serious side-effect on women is not rational but a dominant sentimental solidarity.

Burke and Roberts's (1997) discussion includes examples of women who are not accused of doping but are criticized for being too 'masculine', thus grating people's sensibilities. In other words, women dopers are objected to on aesthetic grounds. The first gender transgressor they refer to is Zheng Haixia, an example they use to show the limits of a claim by Fairchild (1989) that a non-doped athletic body, well shaped for a sport, is a body beautiful. They argue that this particular athlete has a body well suited to basketball but is not considered a body beautiful because, she, like some female dopers, does not have a feminine appearance. Burke and Roberts (1997) refer us to a wider social context to understand why some female athletic bodies are responded to in a way that is quite different to male bodies. Exemplary male athletic bodies that are 'abnormal' among the male population are accepted because with men:

> ... we can demarcate sporting bodies from social bodies. We are suggesting that such demarcations are less likely with respect to female athletes because athleticism, especially female athleticism, must be understood in the wider context of socially constructed gender.
>
> (Burke and Roberts 1997: 104)

How is it that only male sporting bodies are easy to demarcate from social bodies? Moreover, what is a male sporting body if not a kind of social body?

If we take it that 'social bodies' is a general term for all other bodies besides sporting bodies, then I agree that attitudes towards female athleticism need to be reflected upon according to the norms concerning female bodies in wider society. Following Butler (1990), though, I would suggest that the wider social norms of femininity are characteristically heterosexual. Furthermore, it is arguable that male athletic bodies equally need to be understood this way – in the wider context of normative notions of sex, gender and sexuality. Is it not traditions of hegemonic heterosexual masculinity that are compatible with, rather than conflicting with, male sporting bodies/expressions? And is it not female sporting bodies/expressions that often conflict with dominant notions of heterosexual feminine bodies/expressions?[5] Even conventionally feminine women disrupt notions of coherent heterosexuality when they transgress into the socially constructed confines of masculine performance. Part of the social context by which male and female athletes are judged is characterized by heterosexuality as one's gender expression. If Zheng, then, is not a body beautiful because her performance as a woman is not acceptably feminine, she does not just disrupt the gender order but renders incoherent the causal connection between female, feminine and heterosexual. Thus, her appearance is not just non-feminine and transgressive of a gender order, but non-heterosexual and transgressive of a specifically heterosexual social order.

The role of sexuality in femininity can be appreciated if we consider what counts as feminine and, therefore, what excludes Zheng from the category of body beautiful. An acceptable female is not simply accepted for being female.[6] An acceptable female is one who appears and/or behaves in certain ways. Consequently we can see that being a woman is a necessary but not sufficient condition for being considered acceptably feminine.[7] So what counts as feminine? Zheng is an interesting example because she is not androgynous. She could not be mistaken for a man; she has the fairly normative features of a woman: long hair, noticeable breasts, a proportionately *normal* jaw, and so forth. The striking thing about her, which is only noticeable when you see her with others, is her height. At 6ft 8ins, she is taller than most men. She is described by Wolff as 'the slowest low post player on earth' (cited in Burke and Roberts 1997). How she moves is also antithetical to heterosexual femininity because she is not graceful and light, but heavy, strong and muscular. These features render her too masculine.[8] Given that these features cause her to be ugly for a woman, we can consider her size, muscularity and her comportment to be outside of the boundaries of an authentic feminine performance. The kind of person who would find Zheng ugly is one who thinks that the attractive physical attributes of a woman are those that can be interpreted as different and physically inferior to men in certain ways. Conversely, such a person would find a woman attractive if she moves gracefully, is more delicate than men, is weaker than men, is smaller than men, and has different body shape to men. The kind of gaze that makes this aesthetic appraisal of women is the hegemonic heterosexual gaze. Thus, a non-body-beautiful for a female is not so much a body that is not beautiful, but a body that does not fully conform to the aesthetic criteria of the heterosexual gaze.

Another interesting case that Burke and Roberts (1997) refer to, that is more obviously about sexuality, is that of Martina Navratilova. Navratilova's muscular athletic body challenged normative ideas of acceptable femininity in sport, and this led to much success in terms of the tennis titles she gained. The body she had developed by Fairchild's (1989) definition is a fine candidate for being reckoned as a body beautiful. However, generally speaking she, 'was not identified with positively', as Burke and Roberts (1997: 104) put it. They suggest that the lack of positive identification with Navratilova was due to her body transgressing the norms of femininity. While I think it plausible that this is a part of her social rejection, it is also plausible that she was not popular because of her lesbianism. Since 1978 Navratilova has been 'out' as a lesbian. In this year publicity about her lesbianism forced her to retire from her position as the head of the Women's Tennis Association (The Lesbian and Gay Staff Association, 2001). Moreover in the early 1980s she was known for climbing into the crowd and kissing her lover after winning matches (Parvin, 2000). Furthermore, she was the innovator of female tennis players having more muscular bodies, yet when this became the norm she still did not win any major sponsorship deals. If her muscularity were the issue, surely she would have been perceived as popular once it became the norm, or the other muscular women would have been unpopular for the same reason. I suggest that what left her unpopular and unmarketable was her sexuality. Arguably then, it is hard to believe that she only transgressed gender boundaries. Moreover, given that femininity is read as an expression of sexuality, and she was not expressing femininity through her appearance, but was openly expressing her lesbianism, it is difficult to imagine that anyone who objected to her femininity-contravening, muscular body would be indifferent to her overt homosexuality.

Some female athletes make the effort to weigh the balance of their appearance towards heterosexual femininity,[9] gratifying the heterosexual gaze. However, Navratilova's open lesbianism illustrates how she was not interested in conforming through a performance of heterosexuality, which happens to be the main criteria of social acceptance for female athletes. Navratilova is disruptive of the heterosexual matrix. As neither feminine nor heterosexual, she clearly undermines the naturalistic and causal understanding of sex, gender and sexuality.

Given that Burke and Roberts (1997) use only the theme of gender in their analysis, they do not consider the threat 'ugly' women, including some female dopers, pose to the social order. Instead, they suggest that women are interpreted by men as threatening because, 'If females can become part of the community of *we* [we men], either through the use of drugs or by surgery, how can *our* superioity be maintained as central to our humanity?' (Burke and Roberts 1997: 106). Although they argue two non-dopers to also be gender transgressors (Zheng and Navratilova), they suggest that the two ways women make this threat to the male category is through doping or surgery. Given that Zheng and Navratilova are also not socially well received because of their non-conformity to femininity, then surely doping and surgery are not the only ways in which women are threatening to the dominant social order?[10] If we take it that being a lesbian, or being too masculine, is also a part of what is threatening to the dominant social order, then perhaps the perceived threat is not women actually becoming men by doping or through surgery. What is disturbed by Zheng Haxia, Martina Navratilova and some female dopers is the coherency and stability of the distinction between men and women. If there is no coherent femininity, and if those called women cease to be clearly different from men, the integrity of the categories 'men' and 'women' are disturbed, and those who are called men or women may no longer feel sure that it is a stable identity. My suggestion, then, is that the threat is more complex than women becoming men, because any woman who does take drugs or has surgery will not be accepted as a 'real' man. Furthermore, the very idea of a 'real' man is invested in a natural origin that is confirmed by heterosexual hegemonic masculinity.

The big, the bad, and the ugly . . . and the heterosexually attractive

Thus far, I have presented the case as to why sexuality is relevant to the discussion of gender and doping. I have highlighted the neglect of sexuality and reworked it into previous analyses. In this section, I address my concern of the similarities in descriptions of female dopers, lesbians and unattractive women by the press. The appearance that is the mythical/stereotypical lesbian aesthetic is precisely what is offensive about some female dopers and unattractive women according to the heterosexual gaze. Finally, I reaffirm the significance of aesthetics in how women athletes are judged and treated by the press, by contrasting these rejected women with female dopers who have maintained their heterosexual femininity and thus their social acceptance.

Dopers

Articles in the popular press about athletes accused of doping, or those who fail doping tests, always take up the size of the athlete in terms of muscularity. Alexander and Curtain (1994) sarcastically commented on the female Chinese swimmers: '[S]ome of them have nice big physiques and lovely big voices just like those very gifted East Germans did'. They also quoted American Kristine Quance who was beaten by Dai Guohong as saying of the victor: 'I have never seen another 17-yr-old look like that . . . I have never seen any woman like that'. Similarly, Spector (2001) described Venolyn Clarke as, 'the five-foot-four sprinter whose arms and shoulders looked like they belonged to a linebacker'. And, the infamous Flo Jo was subject to the following accusations from the Brazilian, Joachim Cruz: 'In 1984 in Los Angeles Florence was an extremely feminine person. Today she looks and runs more like a man than a woman. She must be doing something not normal to break these records' (Chaudhary 1998).[11]

In these instances the accused or tested dopers are insulted because of their muscularity. They are either suggested to be ugly or like men, and in heterosexual discourse, looking like a man means one is ugly for a woman. Being accused of looking like a man is said as if it is the gravest insult there is for a woman. What these kinds of insults reveal is that femininity is aligned with heterosexual attractiveness and one is read as ugly when one's muscularity is close to that of a man's. The lack of difference renders one unattractive to the heterosexual gaze. By the same logic heterosexually attractive women should also not have facial hair, large genitalia, deep voices or breasts that are too small. Obviously all of these are degrees, and the too much or too little is defined in relation to men – as heterosexual attractiveness and desire is by definition difference to men.

Lesbians

The insults of ugliness and/or manliness directed at some female (accused or positively tested) dopers are remarkably similar to the now infamous remarks made by Martina Hingis about Amelie Mauresmo, who is openly lesbian. In German, Hingis was alleged to have said: '[S]he's here with her girlfriend. She's half a man' (*Slam! Sports* 1999), equating a woman who desires women with manliness. Hingis also makes her comment as if the worst insult she can make is to call Mauresmo 'half a man'. Being categorized as manly meant that she could not be an authentic woman. In other words, it is her lesbianism that brings into question her authenticity as a woman.

In a presumed female-friendly article promoting the lesser known women's Cambridge vs Oxford boat race in the UK, Cleary (1995) warns us: 'There is always the danger of pigeon-holing participants in women's sport as feminist crusaders or butch lesbians.' This speaks to the myth that women who do not stick to traditionally feminine sports are often accused of or presumed to be lesbian. Having indicated that there are no lesbians or feminists in the boat race, Cleary (1995) then describes the appearance of these said feminists and lesbians. 'There are no hairy moustaches to be seen, no bulging Popeye biceps, just a bunch of young women having a good time with their sport.' Embedded in this, then, is a conflation of lesbianism with a masculine appearance. Implicit in his description is that sexuality is visible in appearance.

In an ambiguous sentiment Martin (2000) begins his feature article on the women's professional surfing circuit with a comment that reveals the popular dislike of lesbians in sport. 'For years women were dismissed as useless or – worse – lesbians in the macho world of surfing'. Later he comments that there are 'perennial whispers about lesbianism (something that echoes many women's experience in sport)'. This presumes the popular conception that women who do activities that are traditionally thought of as masculine are lesbian.

Women who just don't fit

Of course there are those who are neither dopers, nor lesbians, who do not meet the criteria of heterosexual femininity. Since most sports require skills that are coherent with the norms of masculinity, a female sporting performance is one that is often interpreted as more suitable for men and better performed by men. These women do not fit the criteria of heterosexual femininity because from the outset they engage in a practice that is already coded as masculine. Unless they exhibit femininity in their bodily adornment, bodily shape and features, they are likely to be seen as too masculine. Zheng Haixia is a good example of this. Her bodily proportions do not show her to be sufficiently inferior in size to most men, thus her size is ridiculed with the nickname 'Baby Huey'. She is made out to be a freak and unattractive because she does not conform to heterosexual femininity.

One can surmise from the comment by Christy Martin that her rival, in boxing, Lucia Rijker, is not heterosexually feminine: 'I've heard maybe she's one of the women who use steroids or hormones, or may be more male than female. She must prove to me and the doctors that she's a woman' (Evans 1997). Implicated in this statement is the idea that this woman is too masculine and the only way to account for this is to claim that she is not really a woman. By relying on doctors or chromosome tests to verify that someone who claims to be is, really, a woman, is to assume that either through appearance, or superior athletic performance, a female athlete is not expressing the femininity that coheres with her sex. Rijker is attacked with the 'grave insult' of masculinity because she does not fit the heterosexually feminine norm of looking like a woman or athletically performing like a woman.

The sentiment that being too masculine means to not be an authentic woman is demonstrated in Myriam Bedard's rationale for suing Wrigley Canada. Wrigley altered Bedard's image in an advertisement to one that she described as hairless and androgynous. She objected to the image because it was humiliating; she said it 'infringed upon my integrity as a woman and the integrity of my image' (Ko 2001). According to this thinking, a real woman is one who appears to be so, and if one loses that image, as Bedard felt she did, the public recognition of being a real woman is in jeopardy. What is most disturbing about the idea of Bedard suing Wrigley Canada is that it demonstrated an anxiety about the repercussion this advertisement would have on Bedard's image, and therefore the aspect of her career that involves marketing. Suing in this instance is similar to suing for defamation of character in the sense that it is considered an unfair negative representation that may have employment implications and will tarnish Bedard's image. It is not only how good an athlete a woman is, but if you claim to be a woman it is important that you perform heterosexual femininity authentically to retain a desirable image.

Heterosexually feminine dopers

I consider Flo Jo an example of an accused doper who was not feminine enough (as described in the 'dopers' section), and as an accused doper who was feminine enough. For example, in a tribute article, Flo Jo was described in the following way:

> [H]er physical presence was startling: with her loose, flowing hair, her perfectly muscled body, her brightly-colored running outfits, her long, Technicolor fingernails. She was both the fastest and most glamorous female performer who had ever set foot on the track.
>
> (Cool Running 1999)

This description of Flo Jo's glamorous heterosexual femininity overshadowed her muscularity to leave her, overall, heterosexually feminine. This article acknowledges rather than disputes, that, even though she never failed a doping test, she was a doper. It also describes her death as fittingly mysterious and controversial. Interestingly, it is almost as if the accusations of doping added to her glamorous femininity, for it added to the intrigue, mystery and drama of her feminine and athletic performance. Thus she may have been a doper, but crucially she never stopped being heterosexually feminine.

Katrin Krabbe tested positive for Clenbuterol in 1992. Clenbuterol is a sensible choice for a female athlete who does not want to alert people to her doping. Clenbuterol has muscle-building effects, but does not have any of the so-called masculinizing effects of anabolic steroids. Krabbe was described as 'tall and willowy and fair and blue-eyed and fast, the 1991 world champion in both sprints at 21. The Grace Kelly of track and field, people were calling Katrin Krabbe' (Hersh 2000). This profile of Krabbe focuses far more on her appearance, and romanticizes it as one that is heterosexually feminine to an iconic level. She was more than a sprint champion, she was a champion of heterosexual femininity. This article does not reproach her or even call her a cheat, even though it refers to her manipulating tests and testing positive. Moreover, the article ends with comments about her picking up her children from school. Her heterosexual performance is so good that it trivializes her rule-breaking.

A striking commonality between these two heterosexually feminine dopers is that their use of banned substances is not described as having any moral significance or in negative tones. Moreover, they are both highly celebrated for their attractive appearances. As with the other categories described, appearance seems to be crucial to acceptability and authenticity as a female.

With the four categories of female athletes I have described, my objective has been to situate female dopers into a broader discourse of heterosexual femininity, which becomes visible when you consider the similarities between them and other women who are treated badly. Doping then is not the significant crime committed by female dopers; it is the failure to express heterosexual femininity. In popular sporting discourse, I suggest that the hegemonic notion of doping is doping that has masculinizing effects on female athletes. Coherent with this, women who have not doped, but are not heterosexually feminine, are criticized in the same way as female dopers who are considered to have become more masculine. The offence then is primarily one of appearance; it is women who do not visibly express heterosexual femininity who are disgusting. Masculinity is read as lesbianism in sport. Lesbianism is read as an aesthetic that matches the offensive aesthetic of masculinized female dopers.

Final thoughts

I see the structure of this article as having moved from the broad issue (the construction of sex, gender and sexuality) to a narrow one (the limitations of the sex/gender doping papers) to another broad matter (the aesthetic and athletic performances of women in sport). My suggestion, then, is that the doping ban is not only a sports-specific issue, but also an example of how dominant heterosexual values are implicated in why some people object to doping in sport. While doping is no doubt part of many other narratives and related to other values, in this narrative I situate it as one element in a pervasive objection to non-heterosexually feminine women. It is only by viewing doping in this broad way that we can begin to appreciate how it has parallels with and implications for how the appearances of some women are stigmatized and judged.

By bringing sexuality into the conversation with doping, sex and gender, my aim has been to develop the understanding of why doping continues to be highlighted as an unacceptable training technology. As König (1995) and Parry (1987) have argued, claims of doping's immoral essence have been little more than demonstrations in inconsistent argumentation. Contrary to these approaches, mine has been one of trying to establish relationships between doping and other things that are disliked for similar reasons. Beyond helping us see some of the complexity of the dislike of doping, it also enables us to see the fallacy of the essentialist approaches, and the political dimension or non-innocence of ethical positions.

This article has focused on women in sport because my purpose has been to show that the doping ban and its supporters cannot distinguish themselves from homophobic and heterosexual values and effects. My suggestion is that we should not exclude from the moral discussion of doping those who will suffer negative effects of the ban and anti-doping attitudes. Doping is a sporting issue, but it spills out of the stadium. This concern with the broader political, social and ethical implications of the doping ban is situated within a further critique of the ontological assumptions of the heterosexual matrix.

The newspaper articles I referred to demonstrate the dislike of doping. One of these dislikes is because doping is identified as creating non-heterosexually feminine athletes. But these non-heterosexually feminine athletes are also disliked because they are the *product* of doping. Doping poses a threat to the heterosexual matrix; doping enables one to cheat one's body and render it inauthentic. Moreover, this is a discourse where that which is aligned with natural is good, and that which is aligned with unnatural is bad. As characteristic of all tautologies, this position is non-reflective, self-perpetuating and neat enough to allow the assumption of an ontological foundation and distract from recognizing that perhaps the dislike of doping is without deeper foundation than circular arguments. Butler (1990) sees this as reason to be suspicious of presuming one's conviction is ontologically grounded. Instead, she suggests that we might recognize the two statements that make the tautology as having concealatory functions, of *constituting* one another by what they each *fabricate*. The dislike of doping is constituted by a dislike of what it produces – the non-heterosexually feminine woman, and the dislike of non-heterosexually feminine women is constituted by doping producing it. When such a tautology is set up the value claim of each statement can stand alone and have effects. One of these effects as I have mentioned is to reaffirm disliking someone on aesthetic grounds; for example, disliking females who do not dope but are not heterosexually feminine.

The construction of doping as bad and the construction of non-heterosexual femininity as ugly show the political and ethical implications of these essentialist discourses. If notions of ethics continue to be appealed to in legislation in sport and in people's attitudes, perhaps it is time the very idea of ethics embraced more self-critical and longer sighted analysis of the consequences of one's moral position. The ethical approach I advocate should consider not just those who are obviously related to the issue, but also those who will also be impacted by its implications.

Acknowledgement

Special thanks to Debra Shogan for her invaluable feedback, advice and editing throughout the writing of this article.

Notes

1 I write 'so-called side effects' because what is referred to as a side effect for some women can be a characteristic of a woman who has never doped. My ambivalent phrasing has the objective of problematizing the idea that these features are not only side effects even though dominant discourses of heterosexual femininity and anti-doping rhetoric try to suggest they are. Hereafter, I mark this ambivalence through quotation marks: 'masculinity' or 'masculinization'.

2 Testimony to the assumption of heterosexuality is the notion of 'coming out', if one is queer. One does not come out as heterosexual; instead it is a general or abstract assumption that people are heterosexual unless through performance they disrupt this assumption.

3 In Burke's (1998) paper male power refers to the administrative power that ensures that men define the criteria by which female bodies are judged.

4 Saltman (1998: 51) makes this very remark, '[T]he clitoris enlarges, likening itself to a penis'.

5 There is one way in which the heterosexually feminine body does not conflict with the sporting body, and this is if the female body can be read as dominantly feminine. For example, a woman could dress, wear make up, and speak of conformity with heterosexuality so that the woman comes across as first and fundamentally heterosexual, and her athleticism appears peripheral.

6 I am not sure exactly what counts as a female these day – genitalia, chromosome, sex cells. One effect of no clear definition is that any woman who is thought to not be feminine enough is open to attack because there is no grounds for defence.

7 For example, effeminate men are not acceptably feminine.

8 The position I take in this paper is an analysis of the dislike and accusation of women who are not conventionally heterosexually feminine. For this reason, I look at how they are read as too masculine, because this is how they tend to be talked about in the press. A more positive understanding of the physicality of these women is as people who diversify the meaning of feminine. These 'femininities' challenge and complicate the traditional idea of femininity as a narrow category, as they no longer adhere to a mutually exclusive binary of feminine/masculine; these femininities share traits and expression traditionally reserved for masculinity.

9 Just a few examples of this: Mackay (1999) reports that the most photographed female athlete in the US is not Marion Jones whose aspirations for 5 Olympic gold medals stand her 'on the edge of mortality' as an athlete, but the part-time model Amy Acuff, a high jumper who may not make the team who wears outrageous outfits. In terms of the attention of the media heterosexual femininity is taken to be more interesting than athletic achievement. In the same article Margaret Talbot claims that media portrayal of women athletes to be dependent on them looking like girls 'Women are expected to conform to a strong feminine stereotype'. However, it seems that this is not just the media who do this, but women are aware that femininity equates to popularity. Buckley (2000) reports that in the women's 75kg weight-lifting category 'Nearly all the contestants took the trouble to apply full make-up' which he interprets as a 'sexing up of sport'. Further, in discussing the current popularity of women's tennis, Dickson (1999) suggests 'Much of the game's growth has lain in the sex appeal and pop-star like attraction epitomised by Anna Kournikova and Martina Hingis'.

10 I say dominant social order to refer to what Burke and Roberts (1997) call the gender order and what I am arguing to be a heterosexual order.

11 All the dopers I have referred to in this section are not caucasian women. A reading of how the rhetoric around doping promotes aesthetic values of

heterosexual femininity and demonizes aesthetic values associated with stereo-typical notions of lesbianism would be appropriately complicated with values and assumptions made around race.

References

Alexander, J. and Curtain, C. (eds) (1994) 'Extra Time', *Guardian* (Sport Section) (10 Sept.) *The Guardian and the Observer on CD-ROM*: 17.

Black, T. (1996) 'Does the Ban on Drugs in Sport Improve Societal Welfare?', *International Review for the Sociology of Sport* 31(4): 367–81.

Black, T. and Pape, A. (1997) 'The Ban on Drugs in Sport: The Solution or the Problem', *Journal of Sport and Social Issues* 21(1): 83–92.

Buckley, W. (2000) 'Olympic Games: Sydney 2000: Maria Whistles to Glory', *Observer* (Sport Section) (24 Sept.) *The Guardian and the Observer on CD-ROM*: 8.

Burke, M. (1998) 'Drugs and Postmodern Female "Identities": A Response to Tara Magdalinski', *Bulletin of Sport and Culture* 15: 25–9.

Burke, M.D. and Roberts, T.J. (1997) 'Drugs in Sport: An Issue of Morality or Sentimentality?', *Journal of the Philosophy of Sport* 24: 99–113.

Burke, M. and Symons, C. (1999) 'Re-asserting Drugs as a Feminist Issue', *Bulletin of Sport and Culture* 17: 11–16.

Butler, J. (1990) *Gender Trouble: Feminism and the Subversion of Identity*. New York and London: Routledge.

Chaudhary, V. (1998) 'Were the Drug Whispers True', *Electronic Mail and Guardian* (Johannesburg). 25 September. http://www.mg.co.za/mg/news/98sep2/25sep-flojo.html.

Cleary, M. (1995) 'Bras Not for Burning on Banks of the Thames', *Observer* (Sport Section) (26 March) *The Guardian and the Observer on CD-ROM*: 8.

Cool Running (1999) 'The Top Runners of the 20th Century: Women', *Cool Running Marathon Training Online*. 5 July. http://www.coolrunning.com/20century/20th 02w.shtml.

Davis, L.R. and Delano, L.C. (1992) 'Fixing the Boundaries of Physical Gender: Side Effects of Anti Drugs Campaigns in Athletics', *Sociology of Sport Journal* 9: 1–19.

Dickson, M. (1999) 'Glamour's Good', *Daily Mail* (10 May): 67.

Dreger, A.D. (1998) *Hermaphrodites and the Medical Invention of Sex*. Cambridge, MA: Harvard University Press.

Epstein, J. (1990) 'Either/Or–Neither/Both: Sexual Ambiguity and the Ideology of Gender', *Genders* 7: 99–142.

Evans, G. (1997) 'Healthcheck: Gender Verification', *Guardian* (Sport Section) (12 Dec.) *The Guardian and the Observer on CD-ROM*: 15.

Fairchild, D.L. (1989) 'Sport Abjection: Steroids and the Uglification of the Athlete', *Journal of the Philosophy of Sport* 16: 74–88.

Fausto-Sterling, A. (2000) *Sexing the Body: Gender Politics and the Construction of Sexuality*. New York: Basic Books.

Hersh, P. (2000) 'Sprinter Katrin Krabbe Seemed Bound for Olympic Glory. Then a Doping Suspension Helped End Her . . .', *Chicago Tribune* (14 Sept.).

Ko, M. (2001) 'How to Play the Game: Women Athletes Prove their Femininity and Win Commercial Exposure by Doffing their Clothes', *Portfolio: Society and Culture* (23 Aug.). http://www.marnieko.com/playgame.htm.

König, E. (1995) 'Criticism of Doping: The Nihilistic Side of Technological Sport and the Antiquated View of Sport Ethics', *International Review for the Sociology of Sport* 34(3/4): 247–61.

Laqueur, T. (1990) *Making Sex: Body and Gender from the Greeks to Freud.* Cambridge, MA: Harvard University Press.

Mackay, D. (1999) 'The Gender Agenda: One for the Ladies', *Observer* (Sport Section) (4 July) *The Guardian and the Observer on CD-ROM*: 6.

Martin, A. (2000) 'Observer Sport Monthly: Zowie Waves and Wowie Mamas', *Observer* (3 Sept.) *The Guardian and the Observer on CD-ROM*: 52.

Parry, S.J. (1987) 'The Devil's Advocate', *Sport and Leisure* (Nov.–Dec.): 34–5.

Parvin, P. (2000) 'Lesbians Go to Market', *Houston Voice Online* (21 April). http://houstonvoice.com/houstonvoice/news/record.html?record=6726.

Saltman, K. (1998) 'Men with Breasts', *Journal of the Philosophy of Sport* 25: 48–60.

Slam! Sports. (1999) 'Mauresmo Speaks of Lesbian Relationship as Coach Rips Hingis', *SLAM! Tennis Online* (30 Jan.). http://www.canoe.ca/SlamTennis99 AustralianOpen/jan30_mau.html.

Spector, M. (2001) 'Positively Too Good to be True: Doping Scandals', *Edmonton Journal Online* (20 Aug.). http://www.canada.com/alberta/edmonton/worlds/story. html?f=/Stories/20010808/ 508014.html.

The Lesbian and Gay Staff Association (South Bank University) (2001) 'The Knitting Circle: Sports: Martina Navratilova', *Southbank University: World Wide Web Server* (5 July). http:www.sbu.ac.uk/~stafflag/martinanavratilova.html.

Chapter 9

Could a 'woman' win a gold medal in the 'men's' one hundred metres?

Female sport, drugs and the transgressive cyborg body*

Michael Burke

Introduction

It is widely argued in pro-feminist sport sociology that contemporary sport remains one of the primary sites of maintaining the historical pattern of male dominance and female subordination. Whilst there are several interrelated methods of maintaining this pattern in the contemporary sporting world, these methods may be collected together within two broad categories.

The first category of maintenance involves the acceptance of practices that lend support to the idea that almost all sports should only be played in single-sexed categories. The apparent motivations for this support may range from a well-meaning, though misplaced, concern for the safety and/or competitiveness of female athletes, to a chauvinistic desire to maintain the male homosociality of certain leisure endeavours. It is understandable, although highly paternalistic and misplaced, that medical, legal and scientific pronouncements against female participation in sport remain apparent in the contemporary sporting discourse when discussing women's participation in traditionally male sports such as boxing and football, given the long-standing association of men with these sports (McArdle 1999). It is, on the other hand, an abuse of certain principles underlying equal opportunities legislation, when this legislation is used by male-controlled sporting establishments to prevent women from participating on male sporting teams. In the last decade in Australia, sporting organisations have attempted to use biological justifications, about female deficiencies in strength and power, to exclude young female athletes who are excellent practitioners in sporting crafts as diverse as rodeo (Watt 1999), ice hockey (Sikora 1998) and lawn bowls.

* Originally published as 'Could a "woman" win a gold medal in the "men's" one hundred metres?: female sport, drugs and the transgressive cyborg body' in *Philosophy in the Contemporary World*, 2004, vol. 11, no. 1 (Spring), pp. 35–44. © Philosophy in the Contemporary World 2004.

It is when female sporting performance reveals the overlap between genders, that men most ferociously invoke this practice of segregation.[1] For example, the sport of skeet shooting was integrated at the Olympics until 1992 when a Chinese woman, Shan Zang, did so well that she won the gold medal and tied the world record. The IOC responded by segregating the event (Kane 1995: 214: n. 7). Segregation serves to protect the male gender from the recognition that there is an overlap between male and female performance. Integration exposes the overlapping continuums of male and female performance where a perceived biological/genetic reason for the differences between these continuums of performance is undermined by the apparent overlap of the continuums.

The second dimension for the maintenance of the hierarchy of sex in sporting discourse is to compare quantifiable results of exemplary male and female sporting performances in their separated competitions, and deduce that *no* woman can compete in male sporting competitions. Excellence in sports has been narrowly defined in terms that generally suit male athletes. Within the current set of sports there are few in which elite women outperform elite men in terms of the quantifiable criteria of measurement that dominate the contemporary sporting discourse. Hence, sport is a practice that makes public the apparent sexed differences in performance between exemplary men and women, and this ideology supports the concept of separate competitions as a biological necessity. These differences help to underpin the dominant conceptualization of human bodies as members of one or the other of two natural, dichotomous and hierarchically organized categories of sex in modern society.

The effect of these two dimensions of demarcation is that the male athlete and male sport is maintained as the standard, with the female athlete treated as an 'add-on' (Fairchild 1994: 67, 68). The strength of this belief is evidenced by the ways that different female sporting communities accept these acts of demarcation as beneficial, profitable and pleasurable for female athletes. Some institutions which govern female sports such as ice dancing, synchronised swimming or women's bodybuilding, oppose the 'masculinization' (or athleticism) of their athletes by legislating/adjudicating against certain practices such as excessive muscle bulk, and requiring other practices such as make-up, which maintain the trivialisation and stigmatisation of females as second-class athletes (but first-class females). Other sports, such as netball, basketball, cricket, athletics and hockey, promote the use of body-tight clothing to highlight the sexuality (heterosexuality) and eroticism of their female athletes.

Hence, Iris Young's suggestion that "sport and females are mutually exclusive categories" (1988: 336) is validated by some women, and some female sporting organizations, at the level of bodywork. It involves women accepting practices in order to be included in the community of appropriately sexed humans, even when such practices make them marginal members of the smaller community of athletes. Controlled by the desire to remain appropriately sexed, the female athlete may accept laws and aesthetic judgements that limit the development of her body, and maintain the "essential" inadequacies of her body when compared to male athletes on male terms.

The starting point for this paper is that sport offers females a practice in which they can challenge the way that their bodies are discursively inscribed as female and subordinate. But it is an extension of that contention that females would be well served to become more creative in thinking about their bodies and their activities in ways that do not perpetuate the idea that either is fixed. Females could become decidedly political about the hegemonic exclusions that have been imposed on them by the sporting discourse. If female sporting competition is separated from male competition through a variety of subtle interlocking mechanisms, then this separation permits a position of creative playfulness with the rules and practices that govern male sport. Whilst such playfulness has traditionally resulted in the reinforcement of traditional gender categories in female sport (e.g. make-up, uniforms), it may be more fruitful to investigate how this playfulness can challenge these categories. In other words, if men don't want women to play with them, then women can use this separation to challenge the rules of men's sport. In the particular case of investigating drug laws, women athletes could consider drug laws and the discourses that support these laws as mechanisms imposed on them to limit their quantifiable performances. And female resistance may take the form of rejecting such impositions. The use of performance-enhancing drugs could open the door to quantifiably excellent performance for some women who *choose* to pursue this way of gaining authority in sport.

This paper will use the image of the cyborg, and cyborg politics generally, to suggest that female athletes should consider a refusal of the ban on drugs in sport in order to produce 'new' and transgressive ways of females engaging in sport, and in the gender politics of sport. In this paper, the male notion of sporting excellence will be left untouched, and the political intervention will deal with changing the athletic bodies of females so as to better fit with this male notion. This paper will suggest that the female athlete consider the use of drugs as a facilitator to the production of a transgressive female athletic subjectivity. That is, it will not simply be in the use of the drugs that the refusal of the female athlete can be characterized, but also that the effects of drugs, both on the body and the performance of the female athlete, results also in the refusal of the gender order of sport, and society.

Cyborg politics, gender and sport

According to Donna Haraway (1985: 502), the cyborg is produced in/by late modernity's "informatics of domination", which is characterized by the control and flow of information [power] being deployed to privatize work, to instrumentalize sexuality, and to maintain disparities in wealth and power caused by technological literacy. This control is exercised over these processes in order to make all these processes more functional. Bodies become resources, able to be manipulated socially and technologically to become something different to, and more useful than, what they originally were (Pronger 1998: 289).

Sport is a ubiquitous example of the infiltration of the cybernetic person/body into the practices of modern life. The contemporary athlete has become a construction of the sport science community guided by the desire for maximizing efficiency. The athlete's body is tested, manipulated and perfected by sports science, their equipment is moulded to the shape of their body, and their performance is monitored by a set of prosthetic and surveillant devices. In contemporary sport, "[t]he body becomes a means of production that can be sacrificed for the product" of performance (Rail 1998: 149).[2]

One example will suffice. A television programme about scientific interventions and innovations in sport, shown in Australia in 1992, explained the following intervention in the batting technique for a Major League baseballer. The athlete would have copper wires injected into the muscles of their body, and electrodes would be attached to their body. The athlete would then repeat a number of 'hits' off a batting tee that was located in a laboratory. The scientists would investigate a computer analysis of the order of muscle contraction through the swings, and train the batter to commence their movement with leg rotation through the use of a set of stimulating devices. This intervention was described as a "natural" alternative to the scourge of drugs (Worner 1990).

Cyborg politics emanates from dissatisfaction with this deployment of the body in the technologically resourced condition. Cyborg political intervention involves the production of counter-discourses of subversion and transformation from a variety of dissatisfied subject positions. So the cyborg is both a creature produced by the social reality of late modernity's resourcing of the "natural" body, and a creature that fictions that same social reality and provides opportunities for new makings of the world and bodies/selves that are more satisfying.

The subversive discourse of the cyborg suggests "some very fruitful couplings" of objects that were once considered separate (Haraway 1985: 503). The recognition of the cyborg's disruption of the boundary between human and machine also calls into question a number of other boundaries (man/woman, culture/nature, reality/appearance, truth/illusion, theory/politics, self/other) that sustain the dualisms that help to contribute to the domination of certain groups in society. These dualisms, and the political effects that emanate from their use, may be disrupted in novel ways (Haraway 1985: 515). In this way, the transgressing cyborg both reveals the dominations that people are embedded in and created by in the modern condition, and, at the same time, allows for the vision of a better possibility. The cyborg cannot escape boundary projects, but it can confound boundary lines, and allow the person to take greater control over the effects the boundaries have on their lives, and hence, permit the possibility of a freer existence for groups of people that have not experienced large amounts of freedom within the modern condition (Pronger 1998: 285).

The female body is the locus of social control over the female (Bailey 1993: 102). The idea that we have biological categories of male and female is constructed and sustained by particular discursive practices in medicine, law, religion and other areas within culture, including sporting discourse. These discursive practices not only produce official knowledge about gender, but also institutionalize social relations and reproduce the knowledge through the education of professionals about gender (Bailey 1993: 107; Balsamo 1996: 34).[3]

But these discursive practices also produce resistance. It is at the site of bodies that the naturalistic fiction (of sex, and sexuality) can be disrupted through such bodies/subjectivities as the doubly sexed body, lesbian sex, transsexual dressing, the hairy woman, the surgically "enhanced" body, and the bodybuilder (Bailey 1993: 107). All these subjectivities denaturalize the perceived unity between sex, gender and heterosexuality by means of a non-disciplined performance that avows the distinctiveness of the three dimensions whilst also displaying how the unity is culturally fabricated. This displacement demonstrates the fluidity of gender identities that suggests "an openness to resignification and recontextualization" in a non-hegemonic way (Butler 1999: 418). Browning explains the political cyborg's guiding philosophy as the propensity to "manipulate my body in the world, like a prosthesis", a resourceful addition to myself which may increase the opportunities for my freedom (1997: 3).

The machines of late twentieth century sport have made "thoroughly ambiguous" the boundaries between natural and artificial, mind and body, human/animal and machines, male and female that ordered much understanding in the sporting world. Rather than dismissing these technologies as a deepening of the dualisms that order life, the cyborg embraces technology as potential mechanisms for the disruption of such dualisms (Haraway 1985: 505, 506, 515). The female can see technological machines as "prosthetic devices" (Haraway 1985: 523) that can aid in the positioning of women in social life.

This cyborg feminist intervention in sport may be particularly effective for two reasons. Firstly, as previously stated, sport is a discursive site where the technological "reconstruction" of bodies is already present and admired (Pronger 1998: 289). And secondly, there is a particular need for feminist political action in sport in order for females to appropriate positions of discursive authority because, as Cole argues, sport is "most usefully understood as . . . an ensemble of knowledges and practices that disciplines, conditions, reshapes and inscribes the body through the terms and needs of a *patriarchal, racist capitalism*" (1993: 86, my emphasis).

Female athletic resistance to sporting discourse could take the form of a playful cybernetic creativity about drug laws in the separated realm of female sport. The female athlete may recognize that the demands to push her performance to the limit may result in requirements to engage in a number of unhealthy practices and relationships. Hence, a recognition of the already existing unhealthy demands on her body could result in the athlete rejecting those rules that purport to limit other opportunities to improve her performance on the basis of health. For the transgression of such rules to be politically effective, the transgressive athlete must explicitly reject such rules, in order to produce the new subjective position. A deceptive refusal would not problematize the current rule.

The female athlete may also recognize that the demands of femininity may come into conflict with the demands of her sport. Recognition of this conflict may result in a questioning, and perhaps refusal, of one of the two sets of demands. The female athlete may either reject athleticism, or reject contemporary notions of emphasized femininity. The position taken in this paper is that a politically viable position for female sport is to consider the rejection of emphasized femininity and the embrace of the cyborg drug-taker in their separated world of female sport.

Athletes rejecting (?) emphasized femininity

In Western societies, the female body has been perceived most usually as either a passive site for medical intervention or a site of sexual spectacle. However, the technologies of power that attempt to produce docile bodies, either objectified by medicine or sexualized by patriarchy, also create pockets of resistance and opposition towards official knowledges. Miller and Penz (1991) argue that bodybuilding offers one such disparity in discourse, which has allowed females to claim some sense of power in a previously male-dominated sport. The built body has the potential to reframe female bodywork in a way that captures its liberating potentials, and so, also challenges dominant beliefs about females. Hence 'bodywork is not necessarily (that is, naturally) in the service of male interests' (Miller and Penz 1991: 152), it can provide areas for female freedom, mastery and control. The bodybuilders reclaim power by the use of their bodies in new and transgressive ways.

In contrast, Obel (1996) argues that if bodybuilding does transgress, it only transgresses emphasized forms of femininity, rather than dichotomous categories of gender. Female bodybuilders are forced by methods of adjudication to take up the docile subjectivities that are presented as desirable for them, that make their cybernetic bodies safe for social, cultural and economic consumption (Mansfield and McGinn 1993: 54). Whilst the bodies and performances of female bodybuilders present a contradictory notion of femininity to the dominant one, this contradiction and ambiguity is often negotiated by the athletes themselves within the existing gender order through the sexualization and objectification of their potentially resistant body (Markula 1995: 427). The bodybuilders do their gender in an exaggerated way; the threat posed by their bodies requires an even greater effort of docility and a "louder" expression of gender through other mechanisms such as dress, make-up, postures and sexuality (Coles 1999: 447; Mansfield and McGinn 1993: 64).

A most obvious example of how natural categories of gender are maintained by the institutions that control bodybuilding is that the female breast implant is the only type of implant that is allowable in competitive bodybuilding (Obel 1996: 194; Coles 1999: 447). This allowance satisfies two criteria simultaneously. It allows the female competitor to present herself as attractive to men. The rigors of training have not destroyed her 'natural' femininity. Secondly, it also permits the sport to present itself as more naturally suited to the male competitor. The male athlete's body is presented as the standard for the sport, and a standard that no woman could ever approach without technological artifice. Likewise, steroid use by female bodybuilders is criticized in the bodybuilding literature, not for health reasons, but for the side effects that confuse the gender of the taker (Coles 1999: 450; Mansfield and McGinn, 1993: 60; Balsamo 1996: 43–45), and so make her muscles dangerously big.

Fen Coles (1999: 445, 446) suggests a transgressive reading of bodybuilder that denies the need for a transgressive agent. She argues that the attempts made by female bodybuilders and bodybuilding organizations to dress female muscles up as feminine, demonstrates the ways that gender is performative and unstable. Coles agrees with Obel that individual female bodybuilders, and the bodybuilding media, conflate gender, heterosexuality and muscles through a variety of techniques. The bodybuilder engages in repetitious acts and practices of beauty, dress, cosmetic surgery, storytelling and parading that are all designed to dress up the bodybuilder and dress down her musculature. All these practices are designed to demonstrate that "these muscles are a difference that won't make a difference" to either femininity or heterosexual attractiveness (Schulze 1990 cited by Coles 1999: 446).

However, resistance still appears, regardless of the intentions of the actor, in the ambiguity that the built body produces. The mechanisms of containment merely expose the cultural work that is done to maintain femininity and heterosexuality as naturally produced embodiments. As Saltman explains, "The cosmetics that all female bodybuilders wear and the silicone breasts that many implant chafe against the intense masculinization they have undergone" (1998: 53). It is the exaggeration of the effects produced in her containment that demonstrates fully the artifice of gender. Even the breast implants that sexualize the female bodybuilder, allow for the recognition of the prosthetic nature of women's lives. The "necessity" of implants, prosthetics for women who have not lost any limbs, reveals the habitual need for all women to address their bodies as surfaces that require add-ons (Browning 1997: 8).

Recognizing the amount of technological augmentation that takes place in demonstrating the emphasized femininity of the female bodybuilder, allows for the suggestion of more politically fruitful couplings of athlete and technology that would displace gender and sporting performance. In the next section of this paper, the drugged athlete will be investigated as a site of possible resistance to the mechanisms of gender that have limited the female's appropriation of authoritative sites in sport.[4]

Drugs and cyborg feminists

Modern sport is a symbolic system where the meaning of the symbols, including the symbol of athletic bodies, is "derived from their position in a system of differentiation" (De Wachter 1988 cited by Rail 1998: 149). That is, modern sport allows for the boundaries of man and woman, heterosexual and homosexual, healthy and ill, able-bodied and disabled, white and "other" and several other oppositions to be expressed and maintained in a symbolic system of performance that is ubiquitous and powerful (Pronger 1998: 277, 278). The athletic body is the site of boundary control. But, as previously argued in this paper, the athletic body can also be the site for transgression of these same boundaries.

Traditionally a web of interlocking beliefs about health, fairness and naturalness, justifications which can all be considered gender-neutral, have been used to defend the ban on drugs. Yet the pervasive dislike of athletes using drugs is not explained entirely by the "good" practice of sport, health and fairness. It also has something to do with the fear of transgressing socially constructed, gender boundaries. That is, the drug ban can be viewed as symbolic of a practice, sport, that maintains a rigid control over the gendering of male and female bodies.

For example, Cole (2000) explains that drug-testing has replaced sex-testing as the mechanism for policing the boundary crossing of muscular female athletes. She suggests that the recent elimination of gender verification testing by the IOC and the IAAF is probably the result of feminist activism against the perceived discriminatory nature of the test. Yet the IAAF has been able to use the gender-bending existence of "excessive" musculature on female athletes to permit the visual inspection of genitals under the guise of drug testing. And the IOC made clear that a team of medical experts will be present at the 2000 Sydney Olympics to inspect any "suspicious" female athlete. The testing of male and female athletes for drug use permits the suggestion that such testing is non-discriminatory, whilst also maintaining the suspicion associated with excessive female musculature and/or exemplary female sporting performance. Hence, feminist opposition is nullified, whilst the natural and hierarchical categories of gender are strictly policed.

The cyborg athletic body offers the possibility to manipulate differentiating notions of female biology that limit the authoritative position of females in sport. Females who wish to participate in sports, and at levels, which have previously been denied to them because of "limitations" (on a male sporting scale) within their genetic bodies, may now see the drug ban as another way of reinforcing such limitations and the power differentials, which go with them. Hence, drug usage becomes a cyborg feminist issue; an issue of revealing the oppression caused by a strict adherence to the rules that reinforce these dichotomous sex categories and the subjectivities that are produced by them, by limiting the use of certain technologies that might confound these boundaries. Some might refute this by suggesting that the ban on drugs applies to both sexes. But cyborg feminists would respond by suggesting that applying the ban to both sexes makes it easier to convince females that the ban is a "rational" limitation, rather than a patriarchal one. The current ban on drugs can be viewed as one of the many discourses maintained by male-dominated sporting communities that collectively position males as dominant over females in the sporting community. The drug ban precludes one form of reconstruction for all athletes, but the effects of the drug ban are more extreme for women, who are sexed as weaker than men, and placed accordingly in inferior positions.

Such transgression may permit the appropriation of politically powerful positions for females within the practice of modern sport. Following from Haraway (1985), this form of transgression, which manipulates the boundary lines of gender, allows for the female athlete to take greater control over how the sporting discourses (and the sporting technology of drugs) affects her experiences and understandings of herself as an athlete, and as a woman. For female athletes utilizing performance-enhancing drugs, this could mean wresting control and responsibility from the patriarchal discourses which seek to limit female performances and embodiments to ones that are athletically inferior to those of males. And if this resistance helps to break down the dominance of male authority in these sports, females may experience new freedom, authority and occupations that have previously not been available to them.[5]

Conclusions

The starting point to this paper has been to work within the narrow, modern and phallocentric definitions of sporting excellence. Within this bounded area, the purpose has been to devise an innovative strategy for female athletes to appropriate authoritative spaces via the utilization of ideas about cyborg feminism.

The cyborg view of "boundary pollution" allowed for the idea that current relations of force between the genders in sport are fluid and reversible. Hence, even the apparently docile athletic female body, containing a happily docile "agent", may be resistant to official discourses of feminine subjectification. The female athlete dressed up and made up to exemplify her "otherness" to the male athlete, and happy in her display of that otherness, may still exemplify resistance to discourses about female passivity and weakness. In many contemporary sports, participation for females may break down the discourses that suggest a "biological" incapacity to play certain sports, even when the female athlete agrees to some sense of a biological incapacity to play these sports as well as men.

But moreover, the dressing up and making up of the "other" demonstrates the continuous performativity that is needed to produce gender. The athletic body, even when apparently contained and docile, leaks. The description of the acts of containment reveals the political/discursive work that is done to produce the gendered body. And this revelation allows for a different and strategic construction of gendered bodies, which will, in all likelihood, prompt a coincidental production of new discourses of containment.

The final section of this paper used these ideas to produce a counter-discourse about drug laws in sport. Drug laws were viewed as one of the mechanisms of containment of bodies to hierarchical gender categories. It was suggested that the cyborg feminist athlete could investigate the possibility of refusing this containment, and in so doing, appropriate possibly authoritative spaces through the production of excellent sporting performances on a male standard.

As with Haraway's (1991 cited by Brook 1999: 139) claim for the appropriation of cyborg bodies for females, the use of these mechanisms "may be a necessity rather than a choice" for future female athletes wishing to undermine male authority in sport. The transgressive, female athletic body offers the opportunity to deconstruct categorizations of the body that have left the female athlete in a position of powerlessness relative to the male. In a commentary about the cyborg body, drugs and sport, Pronger suggests:

> The transgressive politics of athletic cyborgs does not engage in nostalgia for a pre-technological, pure human body in "Just Say No" campaigns against drugs, but gives control over the taking of drugs to the athlete who plays with the cybernetic boundary pollution of the body . . . [A]s Haraway says, "Cyborg myth is about transgressed boundaries, potent fusions, and dangerous possibilities which progressive people might explore as one part of needed political work".
>
> (1985: 71 cited by Pronger 1998: 286)

Progressive female athletes may need to explore the opportunities offered by the cybernetic embrace of performance-enhancing drugs in their separated realm of women's sports. This embrace may lead to the appropriation of greater authority both within the sporting world, and outside of it.

Notes

1   This practice was vividly exemplified in the 1978 cliff diving championships, a competition which is held annually at Acapulco. A Texan woman qualified for the finals. However the Mexican men threatened to withdraw from the finals if she did not. The organizing committee subsequently disqualified her. As one of the Mexican competitors explained: "This is a death-defying activity – the men are taking a great gamble to prove their courage. What would be the point if everyone saw that a woman could do the same?" (Bryson, 1983: 422).

2   There could be a gendering of the resource that is produced in sport. For example, performance may only be a part of the resource that is usefully produced in women's sport, with aesthetic attractiveness being another aspect of the resources produced via female sporting performance.

3   Birrell and Cole's (1994: 207–237) study of the male to female transsexual tennis player, Renee Richards, demonstrates the work that is done, both by society and some transsexuals, to maintain the two-sex paradigm. It also shows how experts of the sex-role system produce the normalizing discourses and reinforce the subjectivities that are taken up by people. As Birrell and Cole remark, there is "male-dominated transsexual empire of surgeons, lawyers, and psychologists whose technological and discursive practices make it legally and . . . morally possible to change one's 'body/sex'" (1994: 213). This male-dominated empire has the power to monitor, regulate and control the body and sex of individual people. A person would not feel gender dysphoria unless they felt a need to satisfy the sex-role demands of the opposite gender, a subject position that is produced by the attachment to a model of two, and only two, natural, dichotomous and absolute sex categories (1994: 210, 211). Before sex-reassignment surgery, itself a discursive production imposed by the two-sex model, the transsexual "must live as a member of the opposite sex as proof of his or her ability to accomplish appropriately gendered behaviour" (1994: 211). Hence, gender, sex and heterosexuality are re-naturalized, and the ambiguity produced by the transsexual is redescribed as individual malfunction.

   The case of Richards reveals the ways that the individual monitors and regulates their behaviours in terms of the subjectivities that are produced through official discourses about sex. At the same time, the revelation of the work done by the media, by the transsexual empire and by Richards herself, to mould her story into the paradigm of the two-sex model, is resistant in that it reveals how this model is as constructed as any other.

4   I fully acknowledge that the "drugged" speaker is presently not an authoritative body. This does not mean that they will not be in the future.

5   Sharpe suggests that the exception to the New South Wales' anti-discrimination against transgendered persons Act (1996) that allows for discrimination in sport, suggests that sport is one site where unambiguous and biological gender hierarchies are established (1997: 40). If the postoperative transgendered female cannot produce ambiguity over dichotomous gender categories, I am not sure that the drugged female athlete will have any greater success.

References

Bailey, M.E. (1993). "Foucauldian Feminism: Contesting Bodies, Sexuality and Identity." In *Up Against Foucault: Explorations of Some Tensions Between Foucault and Feminism*. Edited by Caroline Ramazanoglu. London: Routledge, pp. 99–122.

Balsamo, Anne. (1996). *Technologies of the Gendered Body: Reading Cyborg Women*. Durham: Duke University Press.

Birrell, Susan and Cole, Cheryl L. (1994). "Double Fault: Renee Richards and the Construction and Naturalization of Difference." In *Women, Media and Sport: Challenging Gender Values*. Edited by Pamela J. Creedon. California: Sage Publications Inc., pp. 207–236.

Brook, Barbara. (1999). *Feminist Perspectives on the Body*. London: Longman Publishers.

Browning, Barbara. (1997). "When Snow Isn't White." *Women and Performance*, Issue 17 (Sexuality and Cyberspace), pp. 1–16 (accessed at www.echonyc.com/~women/Issue17.html).

Bryson, Lois. (1983)."Sport and the Oppression of Women." *Australian and New Zealand Journal of Sociology*, 19/3, pp. 413–426.

Butler, Judith. (1999). "Bodily Inscriptions, Performative Subversions." In *Feminist Theory and the Body*. Edited by Janet Price and Margrit Shildrick. Edinburgh: Edinburgh University Press, pp. 416–422.

Cole, Cheryl. (2000). "Testing for Sex or Drugs." *Journal of Sport and Social Issues*, 24/4, November, pp. 331–333.

Cole, Cheryl. (1993). "Resisting the Canon: Feminist Cultural Studies, Sport, and Technologies of the Body." *Journal of Sport and Social Issues*, 17/2, pp. 77–97.

Coles, Fen. (1999). "Feminine Charms and Outrageous Arms." In *Feminist Theory and the Body*. Edited by Janet Price and Margrit Shildrick. Edinburgh: Edinburgh University Press, pp. 445–453.

Fairchild, David L. (1994). "From the Mountains to the Valleys: Theorizing Gender in Sport through McIntosh's Phases." *Discourse on Sport: Proceedings of the 21st Annual Conference of PSSS*, CASPER: Bedford, pp. 66–74.

Haraway, Donna. (1985). "A Manifesto for Cyborgs: Science, Technology, and Socialist-Feminism in the 1980s". In *Feminist Social Thought: A Reader*. Edited by Diana Tietjens Meyer (1997). New York: Routledge, pp. 501–531.

Kane, Mary Jo. (1995). "Resistance/Transformation of the Oppositional Binary: Exposing Sport as a Continuum." *Journal of Sport and Social Issues*, 19/2, pp. 191–218.

Mansfield, Alan and McGinn, Barbara. (1993). "Pumping Irony: The Muscular and the Feminine." In *Body Matters: Essays on the Sociology of the Body*. Edited by Sue Scott and David Morgan. London and Washington: The Falmer Press, pp. 49–68.

Markula, Pirkko. (1995). "Firm but Shapely, Fit but Sexy, Strong but Thin: The Postmodern Aerobicizing Female Bodies." *Sociology of Sport Journal*, 12, pp. 424–453.

McArdle, David. (1999). "Can Legislation Stop me from Playing? The Distinction Between Sport Competitors and Sport Workers under the United Kingdom's Sex Discrimination Laws." *Culture, Sport, Society*, 2/2, Summer, pp. 44–57.

Miller, Leslie and Penz, Otto. (1991). "Talking Bodies: Female Bodybuilders Colonize a Male Preserve." *Quest*, 43, pp. 148–163.

Obel, Camilla. (1996). "Collapsing Gender in Competitive Bodybuilding: Researching Contradictions and Ambiguity in Sport." *International Review for the Sociology of Sport*, 31/2, pp. 185–201.

Pronger, Brian. (1998). "Post-Sport: Transgressing Boundaries in Physical Culture." In *Sport and Postmodern Times*. Edited by Genevieve Rail. Albany, NJ: SUNY Press, pp. 277–298.

Rail, Genevieve. (1998). "Seismography of the Postmodern Condition: Three Theses on the Implosion of Sport." In *Sport and Postmodern Times*. Edited by Genevieve Rail. Albany, NJ: SUNY Press, pp.143–161.

Saltman, Ken. (1998). "Men with Breasts." *Journal of the Philosophy of Sport*, XXV, pp. 48–60.

Sharpe, Andrew. (1997). "Naturalising Sex Differences through Sport: An Examination of the New South Wales Transgender Legislation." *Alternative Law Journal*, 22/1, February 1997, pp. 40, 41.

Sikora, Natalie. (1998). "Girl Goalie Frozen out of Sport." *The Herald-Sun Newspaper* (Melbourne, Australia), February 26, 1998, p. 13.

Theberge, Nancy. (1998). ""Same Sport, Different Gender": A Consideration of Binary Gender Logic and the Sport Continuum in the Case of Ice-Hockey." *Journal of Sport and Social Issues,* 22/2, May, pp. 183–198 (accessed from EBSCO host online display: pp. 1–11).

Watt, Amanda. (1999). "Ban Spurs Young Steer Rider." *The Courier Mail Newspaper* (Queensland, Australia), August 30, 1999, p. 7.

Worner, Tim (Producer) (1990). *Far Beyond Limited*. Television Broadcast directed by David Summons, 1990. Broadcast as *Zenith–Beyond 2000*. Channel 7, Melbourne, Australia, February 27, 1992.

Young, Iris Marion. (1988). "The Exclusion of Women from Sport: Conceptual and Existential Dimensions." In *Philosophic Inquiry in Sport*. Edited by William J. Morgan and Klaus V. Meier. Champaign, Illinois: Human Kinetics Publishers, pp. 335–341.

Part 4

Homophobia

Chapter 10

From the "muscle moll" to the "butch" ballplayer

Mannishness, lesbianism, and homophobia in U.S. women's sports*

Susan K. Cahn

In 1934, *Literary Digest* subtitled an article on women's sports, "Will the Playing Fields One Day Be Ruled by Amazons?" The author, Fred Wittner, answered the question affirmatively and concluded that as an "inevitable consequence" of sport's masculinizing effect, "girls trained in physical education today may find it more difficult to attract the most worthy fathers for their children" (1934: 43). The image of women athletes as mannish, failed heterosexuals represents a thinly veiled reference to lesbianism in sport. At times, the homosexual allusion has been indisputable, as in a journalist's description (Murray n.d.) of the great athlete Babe Didrikson as a "Sapphic, Broddingnagian woman" or in television comedian Arsenio Hall's more recent (1988) witticism, "If we can put a man on the moon, why can't we put one on Martina Navratilova?" More frequently, however, popular commentary on lesbians in sport has taken the form of indirect references, surfacing through denials and refutations rather than open acknowledgment. When in 1955 an *Ebony* magazine article on African American track stars insisted that "off track, girls are entirely feminine. Most of them like boys, dances, club affairs," the reporter answered the implicit but unspoken charge that athletes, especially Black women in a "manly" sport, were masculine manhaters, or lesbians.

The figure of the mannish lesbian athlete has acted as a powerful but unarticulated "bogey woman" of sport, forming a silent foil for more positive, corrective images that attempt to rehabilitate the image of women athletes and resolve the cultural contradiction between athletic prowess and femininity. As a stereotyped figure in U.S. society, the lesbian athlete forms part of everyday cultural knowledge. Yet historians have paid scant attention to the connection between female sexuality and sport.[1] This essay explores the historical relationship between lesbianism and sport by

* Originally published as 'From the "muscle moll" to the "butch" ballplayer: mannishness, lesbianism, and homophobia in U.S. women's sports' in *Feminist Studies*, 1993, vol. 19, no. 2 (Summer), pp. 343–368.

tracing the development of the stereotyped "mannish lesbian athlete" and examining its relation to the lived experience of mid-twentieth-century lesbian athletes.

I argue that fears of mannish female sexuality in sport initially centered on the prospect of unbridled heterosexual desire. By the 1930s, however, female athletic mannishness began to connote heterosexual failure, usually couched in terms of unattractiveness to men, but also suggesting the possible absence of heterosexual interest. In the years following World War II, the stereotype of the lesbian athlete emerged full blown. The extreme homophobia and the gender conservatism of the postwar era created a context in which longstanding linkages among mannishness, female homosexuality, and athletes cohered around the figure of the mannish lesbian athlete.

Amazons, muscle molls, and the question of sexual (im)mortality

The athletic woman sparked interest and controversy in the early decades of the twentieth century. In the United States and other Western societies, sport functioned as a male preserve, an all-male domain in which men not only played games together but also demonstrated and affirmed their manhood (Dunning 1986; Kimmel 1987; Mangan and Park 1987; Mrozek 1983). The "maleness" of sport derived from a gender ideology which labeled aggression, physicality, competitive spirit, and athletic skill as masculine attributes necessary for achieving true manliness. This notion found unquestioned support in the dualistic, polarized concepts of gender which prevailed in Victorian America. However, by the turn of the century, women had begun to challenge Victorian gender arrangements, breaking down barriers to female participation in previously male arenas of public work, politics, and urban nightlife. Some of these "New Women" sought entry into the world of athletics as well. On college campuses students enjoyed a wide range of intramural sports through newly formed Women's Athletic Associations. Off-campus women took up games like golf, tennis, basketball, swimming, and occasionally even wrestling, car racing, or boxing. As challengers to one of the defining arenas of manhood, skilled female athletes became symbols of the broader march of womanhood out of the Victorian domestic sphere into once prohibited male realms.

The woman athlete represented both the appealing and threatening aspects of modern womanhood. In a positive light, she captured the exuberant spirit, physical vigor, and brazenness of the New Woman. The University of Minnesota student newspaper proclaimed in 1904 that the athletic girl was the "truest type of All-American coed" (1904–5 Scrapbooks of Anne Maude Butner, Butner Papers, University of Minnesota Archives, Minneapolis). Several years later, *Harper's Bazaar* labeled the unsportive girl as "not strictly up to date," (Mange 1910, 246), and *Good Housekeeping* noted that the "tomboy" had come to symbolize "a new type of American girl, new not only physically, but mentally and morally" (de Koven 1912, 150).

Yet, women athletes invoked condemnation as often as praise. Critics ranged from physicians and physical educators to sportswriters, male athletic officials, and casual observers. In their view, strenuous athletic pursuits endangered women and threatened the stability of society. They maintained that women athletes would become manlike, adopting masculine dress, talk, and mannerisms. In addition, they contended, too much exercise would damage female reproductive capacity. And worse yet, the excitement of sport would cause women to lose control, conjuring up images of frenzied, distraught co-eds on the verge of moral, physical, and emotional breakdown. These fears collapsed into an all-encompassing concept of "mannishness," a term signifying female masculinity.

The public debate over the merits of women's athletic participation remained lively throughout the 1910s and 1920s. Implicit in the dispute over "mannishness" was a longstanding disagreement over the effect of women's athletic activities on their sexuality. Controversy centered around two issues, damage to female reproductive capacity and the unleashing of heterosexual passion. Medical experts and exercise specialists disagreed among themselves about the effects of athletic activity on women's reproductive cycles and organs. Some claimed that athletic training interfered with menstruation and caused reproductive organs to harden or atrophy; others insisted that rigorous exercise endowed women with strength and energy which would make them more fit for bearing and rearing children. Similarly, experts vehemently debated whether competition unleashed nonprocreative, erotic desires identified with male sexuality and unrespectable women, or, conversely, whether invigorating sport enhanced a woman's feminine charm and sexual appeal, channeling sexual energy into wholesome activity.

Conflicting opinion on sexual matters followed closely along the lines of a larger dispute which divided the world of women's sport into warring camps. Beginning in the 1910s, female physical educators and male sport promoters squared off in a decades-long struggle over the appropriate nature of female competition and the right to govern women's athletics (Gerber 1975; Himes 1986; Hult 1985). The conflict was a complicated one, involving competing class and gender interests played out in organizational as well as philosophical battles. It was extremely important in shaping women's sports for more than fifty years. Although historians of sport have examined the broad parameters of the conflict, they have paid less attention to the competing sexual perspectives advanced by each side.

Physical educators took a cautious approach on all matters of sexuality, one designed to safeguard vulnerable young athletes and to secure their own professional status as respectable women in the male-dominated worlds of academia and sport. Heeding dire warnings about menstrual dysfunction, sterility, and inferior offspring, educators created policies to curtail strenuous competition and prohibit play during menstruation. They worried equally about the impact of sport on sexual morality. Alleging that competition would induce "powerful impulses" leading girls into a "temptation to excess" and the "pitfall of overindulgence," educators and their allies pressured popular sport promoters to reduce the competitive stimulation, publicity, and physical strain thought to endanger the sexuality of their female charges (Inglis 1910; Paret 1900: 1567; Sargent 1913).

Popular sport organizations like the Amateur Athletic Union agreed that unregulated female competition posed physiological and moral dangers. But AAU officials countered protectionist physical education policies with a nationalist, eugenic stance which argued that strenuous activity under proper guidance would actually strengthen reproductive organs, creating a vigorous cadre of mothers to produce a generation of stalwart American sons (e.g., MacFadden 1929; Steers 1932). Although making some concessions to demands for modesty and female supervision, in the long run AAU leaders and commercial sport promoters also rejected educators' emphasis on sexual control. Sponsors of popular sport found that sexual hype, much more than caution, helped to attract customers and mute charges of mannishness. In working-class settings and in more elite sports like swimming, an ideal of the "athlete as beauty queen" emerged. Efforts to present the female athlete as sexually attractive and available mirrored the playful, erotic sensibility present in the broader commercial leisure culture of the early twentieth century (Erenberg 1981; Freedman and D'Emilio 1988; Peiss 1986).

The class and gender lines in this dispute were complicated by overlapping constituencies. Female educators adhered closely to middle-class, even Victorian, notions of respectability and modesty. But their influence spread beyond elite private and middle-class schools into working-class public schools and industrial recreation programs. And male promoters, often themselves of the middle class, continued to control some school sport and, outside the schools, influenced both working-class and elite sports. Moreover, Black physical educators advanced a third point of view. Although few in number, early twentieth-century African-American physical education instructors generally aligned themselves with popular promoters in favor of competition and interscholastic sports. Yet their strong concern with maintaining respectability created some sympathy for the positions advanced by white leaders of women's physical education (Arnett 1921; Dunham 1924; Ellis 1939; Roberts 1927).

On all sides of the debate, however, the controversy about sport and female sexuality presumed heterosexuality. Neither critics nor supporters suggested that "masculine" athleticism might indicate or induce same-sex love. When experts warned of the amazonian athlete's possible sexual transgressions, they linked the physical release of sport with a loss of heterosexual *control*, not of *inclination*. The most frequently used derogatory term for women athletes was "Muscle Moll." In its only other usages, the word "moll" referred to either the female lovers of male gangsters or to prostitutes. Both represented disreputable, heterosexually deviant womanhood.

By contrast, medical studies of sexual "deviance" from the late nineteenth and early twentieth centuries quite clearly linked "mannishness" to lesbianism, and in at least two cases explicitly connected female homosexuality with boyish athleticism (Chauncey 1989: 90–91; Ellis 1915: 250; Wise 1883: 88). It is curious then that in answering charges against the mannish Muscle Moll, educators and sport promoters of this period did not refer to or deny lesbianism. However, the "mannish lesbian" made little sense in the heterosocial milieu of popular sports. Promoters encouraged mixed audiences for women's athletic events, often combining them with men's games, postgame dances and musical entertainment, or even beauty contests. The image of the athlete as beauty queen and the commercial atmosphere that characterized much of working-class sport ensured that the sexual debate surrounding the modern female athlete would focus on her heterosexual charm, daring, or disrepute. The homosocial environment of women's physical education left educators more vulnerable to insinuations that their profession was populated by "mannish" types who preferred the love of women. However, the feminine respectability and decorum cultivated by the profession provided an initial shield from associations with either the mannish lesbian or her more familiar counterpart, the heterosexual Muscle Moll.

The Muscle Moll as heterosexual failure: emerging lesbian stereotypes

In the 1930s, however, the heterosexual understanding of the mannish "amazon" began to give way to a new interpretation which educators and promoters could not long ignore. To the familiar charge that female athletes resembled men, critics added the newer accusation that sport-induced mannishness disqualified them as candidates for heterosexual romance. In 1930, an *American Mercury* medical reporter decried the decline of romantic love, pinning the blame on women who entered sport, business, and politics. He chimed that such women "act like men, talk like men, and think like men." The author explained that "women have come closer and closer to men's level," and, consequently, "the purple allure of distance has vamoosed" (Nathan 1930). Four years later, the *Ladies Home Journal* printed a "Manual on the More or Less Subtle Art of Getting a Man" which listed vitality, gaiety, vivacity, and good sportsmanship—qualities typically associated with women athletes and formerly linked to the athletic flapper's heterosexual appeal— as "the very qualities that are likely to make him consider anything but marriage" (Moats 1934). Although the charges didn't exclusively focus on athletes, they implied that female athleticism was contrary to heterosexual appeal, which appeared to rest on women's difference from and deference to men.

The concern with heterosexual appeal reflected broader sexual transformations in U.S. society. Historians of sexuality have examined the multiple forces which reshaped gender and sexual relations in the first few decades of the twentieth century. Victorian sexual codes crumbled under pressure from an assertive, boldly sexual working-class youth culture, a women's movement which defied prohibitions against public female activism, and the growth of a new pleasure-oriented consumer economy. In the wake of these changes, modern ideals of womanhood embraced an overtly erotic heterosexual sensibility. At the same time, medical fascination with sexual "deviance" created a growing awareness of lesbianism, now understood as a form of congenital or psychological pathology. The medicalization of homosexuality in combination with an antifeminist backlash in the 1920s against female autonomy and power contributed to a more fully articulated taboo against lesbianism. The modern heterosexual woman stood in stark opposition to her threatening sexual counterpart, the "mannish" lesbian (Freedman and De'Emilio 1988; Simmons 1989).

By the late 1920s and early 1930s, with a modern lesbian taboo and an eroticized definition of heterosexual femininity in place, the assertive, muscular female competitor roused increasing suspicion. It was at this moment that both subtle and direct references to the lesbian athlete emerged in physical education and popular sport. Uncensored discussions of intimate female companionship and harmless athletic "crushes" disappear from the record, pushed underground by the increasingly hostile tone of public discourse about female sexuality and athleticism. Fueled by the gender antagonisms and anxieties of the Depression, the public began scrutinizing women athletes—known for their appropriation of masculine games and styles—for signs of deviance.

Where earlier references to "amazons" had signaled heterosexual ardor, journalists now used the term to mean unattractive, failed heterosexuals. Occasionally, the media made direct mention of athletes' presumed lesbian tendencies. A 1933 *Redbook* article, for example, casually mentioned that track and golf star Babe Didrikson liked men just to horse around with her and not "make love," adding that Babe's fondness for her best girlfriends far surpassed her affection for any man (Marston 1933: 60). The direct reference was unusual; the lesbian connotation of mannishness was forged primarily through indirect links of association. The preponderance of evidence appears in public exchanges between opponents and advocates of women's sport.

After two decades of celebrating the female collegiate athlete, yearbooks at co-ed colleges began to ridicule physical education majors and Women's Athletic Association (WAA) members, portraying them as hefty, disheveled, and ugly. A 1937 Minnesota *Gopher* yearbook sarcastically titled its presentation on the WAA "Over in No Man's Land." Finding themselves cast as unattractive prudes or mannish misfits, physical educators struggled to revise their image. They declared the muscle-bound, manhating athlete a relic of the past, supplanted by "lovely, feminine charming girls" whose fitness, suppleness, and grace merely made them "more beautiful on the dance floor that evening" (Mooney 1937; Sefton 1937).

Similar exchanges appeared in popular magazines. After *Literary Digest* published Fred Wittner's assertion (1934: 42) that "worthy fathers" would not find trained women athletes attractive mates, AAU official Ada Taylor Sackett issued a rebuttal which reassured readers that because athletic muscles resembled "those of women who dance all night," women in sport could no doubt "still attract a worthy mate" (1934: 43). When critics maligned athletic femininity, they suggested that athletes were literally un-becoming women: unattractive females who abdicated their womanhood and fell under sexual suspicion. When defenders responded with ardent assertions that women athletes did indeed exhibit interest in men, marriage, and motherhood, it suggested that they understood "mannish" to mean "not-heterosexual."

The butch ballplayer: mid-century stereotypes of the lesbian athlete

Tentatively voiced in the 1930s, these accusations became harsher and more explicit under the impact of wartime changes in gender and sexuality and the subsequent panic over the "homosexual menace." In a post-World War II climate markedly hostile to nontraditional women and lesbians, women in physical education and in working-class popular sports became convenient targets of homophobic indictment.

World War II opened up significant economic and social possibilities for gay men and women. Embryonic prewar homosexual subcultures blossomed during the war and spread across the mid-century urban landscape. Bars, nightclubs, public cruising spots, and informal social networks facilitated the development of gay and lesbian enclaves. But the permissive atmosphere did not survive the war's end. Waving the banner of Cold War political and social conservatism, government leaders acted at the federal, state, and local levels to purge gays and lesbians from government and military posts, to initiate legal investigations and prosecutions of gay individuals and institutions, and to encourage local police crackdowns on gay bars and street life. The perceived need to safeguard national security and to reestablish social order in the wake of wartime disruption sparked a "homosexual panic" which promoted the fear, loathing, and persecution of homosexuals (Bérubé 1990; D'Emilio 1983; Freedman and D'Emilio 1988).

Lesbians suffered condemnation for their violation of gender as well as sexual codes. The tremendous emphasis on family, domesticity, and "traditional" femininity in the late 1940s and 1950s reflected postwar anxieties about the reconsolidation of a gender order shaken by two decades of depression and war. As symbols of women's refusal to conform, lesbians endured intense scrutiny by experts who regularly focused on their subjects' presumed masculinity. Sexologists attributed lesbianism to masculine tendencies and freedoms encouraged by the war, linking it to a general collapsing of gender distinctions which, in their view, destabilized marital and family relations (Breines 1986; Penn 1991).

Lesbians remained shadowy figures to most Americans, but women athletes—noted for their masculine bodies, interests, and attributes—were visible representatives of the gender inversion often associated with homosexuality. Physical education majors, formerly accused of being unappealing to men, were increasingly charged with being uninterested in them as well. The 1952 University of Minnesota *Gopher* yearbook snidely reported: "Believe it or not, members of the Women's Athletic Association are normal" and found conclusive evidence in the fact that "at least one ... of WAA's 300 members is engaged" (257). And on May 10, 1956, a newspaper account of the University of Texas Sports Association (UTSA) women's sports banquet led off with the headline, "UTSA Gives Awards," followed by a subheading "Gayness Necessary." The second headline referred to a guest speaker's talk on positive attitudes, entitled "The Importance of Being Debonair," but the lesbian allusion was unmistakable and I believe fully intentional.[2]

The lesbian stigma began to plague popular athletes too, especially working-class sports noted for their masculine toughness. The pall of suspicion did not completely override older associations with heterosexual deviance. When *Collier's* 1947 article (Lagemann) on the Red Heads, a barnstorming women's basketball team, exclaimed "It's basketball—not a striptease!" the author alluded to both the heterosexual appeal and the hint of disrepute long associated with working-class women athletes. But the dominant postwar voice intimated a different type of disrepute. Journalists continued to attack the mannish athlete as ugly and sexually unappealing, implying that this image could only be altered through proof of heterosexual "success."

The career of Babe Didrikson, which spanned the 1920s to the 1950s, illustrates the shift. In the early 1930s the press had ridiculed the tomboyish track star for her "hatchet face," "door-stop jaw," and "button-breasted" chest. After quitting track, Didrikson dropped out of the national limelight, married professional wrestler George Zaharias in 1938, and then staged a spectacular athletic comeback as a golfer in the late 1940s and 1950s. Fascinated by her personal transformation and then, in the 1950s, moved by her battle with cancer, journalists gave Didrikson's comeback extensive coverage and helped make her a much-loved popular figure. In reflecting on her success, however, sportswriters spent at least as much time on Didrikson's love life as her golf stroke. Headlines blared, "Babe Is a Lady Now: The world's most amazing athlete has learned to wear nylons and cook for her huge husband," and reporters gleefully described how "along came a great big he-man wrestler and the Babe forgot all her man-hating chatter" (Andersen 1945; Gallico 1960; Farmer 1947; Marin 1947).

Postwar sport discourse consistently focused on women's sexual as well as their athletic achievements. As late as 1960, a *New York Times Magazine* headline asked, "Do men make passes at athletic lasses?" Columnist William B. Furlong answered no for most activities, concluding that except for a few "yes" sports like swimming, women athletes "surrendered" their sex. The challenge for women athletes was not to conquer new athletic feats, which would only further reduce their sexual appeal, but to regain their womanhood through sexual surrender to men.

Media coverage in national magazines and metropolitan newspapers typically focused on the sexual accomplishments of white female athletes, but postwar observers and promoters of African American women's sport also confronted the issue of sexual normalcy. In earlier decades, neither Black nor white commentary on African American athletes expressed a concern with "mannish" lesbianism. The white media generally ignored Black athletes. Implicitly, however, stereotypes of Black females as highly sexual, promiscuous, and unrestrained in their heterosexual passions discouraged the linkage between mannishness and lesbianism. Racist gender ideologies further complicated the meaning of mannishness. Historically, European American racial thought characterized African-American women as aggressive, coarse, passionate, and physical—the same qualities assigned to manliness and sport (Carby 1987; Collins 1990; Giddings 1984). Excluded from dominant ideals of womanhood, Black women's success in sport could be interpreted not as an unnatural deviation but, rather, as the natural result of their reputed closeness to nature, animals, and masculinity.[3]

Within Black communities, strong local support for women's sport may also have weakened the association between sport and lesbianism. Athletes from Tuskegee Institute's national championship track teams of the late 1930s and 1940s described an atmosphere of campus-wide enthusiastic support. They noted that although a male student might accuse an athlete of being "funny" if she turned him down for a date, in general lesbianism was not a subject of concern in Black sport circles (personal interviews, Alice Coachman Davis, Lula Hymes Glenn, and Leila Perry Glover, 1992). Similarly, Gloria Wilson (pseudonym, personal interview) found that she encountered far less uneasiness about lesbianism on her Black semipro softball team in the late 1950s and 1960s than she did in the predominantly white college physical education departments she joined later. She explained that the expectation of heterosexuality was ingrained in Black women to the point that "anything outside of that realm is just out of the question." While recalling that her teammates "had no time or patience for 'funnies,'" Wilson noted that the issue rarely came up, in large part because most team members were married and therefore "didn't have to prove it because then too, their men were always at those games. They were very supportive."

Although Black athletes may have encountered few lesbian stereotypes at the local level, circumstances in the broader society eventually pressed African American sport promoters and journalists to address the issue of mannish sexuality. The strong association of sports with lesbianism developed at the same time as Black athletes became a dominant presence in American sport culture. Midcentury images of sport, Blackness, masculinity, and lesbianism circulated in the same orbit in various combinations. There was no particular correlation between Black women and lesbianism; however, the association of each with mannishness and sexual aggression potentially linked the two. In the late 1950s, Black sport promoters and journalists joined others in taking up the question of sexual "normalcy." One Black newspaper (*Baltimore Afro-American*) in 1957 described tennis star Althea Gibson as a childhood "tomboy" who "in later life ... finds herself victimized by complexes." The article did not elaborate on the nature of Gibson's "complex," but lesbianism is inferred in the linkage between "tomboys" and psychological illness. This connotation becomes clearer by looking at the defense of Black women's sport. Echoing *Ebony*'s avowal (1955: 28, 32) that "entirely feminine" Black female track stars "like boys, dances, club affairs," in 1962 Tennessee State University track coach Ed Temple asserted in the *Detroit News*, "None of my girls have any trouble getting boy friends . . . We don't want amazons."

Constant attempts to shore up the heterosexual reputation of athletes can be read as evidence that the longstanding reputation of female athletes as mannish women had become a covert reference to lesbianism. By midcentury, a fundamental reorientation of sexual meanings fused notions of femininity, female eroticism, and heterosexual attractiveness into a single ideal. Mannishness, once primarily a sign of gender crossing, assumed a specifically lesbian–sexual connotation. In the wake of this change, the strong cultural association between sport and masculinity made women's athletics ripe for emerging lesbian stereotypes. This meaning of athletic mannishness raises the further question. What impact did the stereotype have on women's sport?

Sport and the heterosexual imperative

The image of the mannish lesbian athlete had a direct effect on women competitors, on strategies of athletic organizations, and on the overall popularity of women's sport. The lesbian stereotype exerted pressure on athletes to demonstrate their femininity and heterosexuality, viewed as one and the same. Many women adopted an apologetic stance toward their athletic skill. Even as they competed to win, they made sure to display outward signs of femininity in dress and demeanor. They took special care in contact with the media to reveal "feminine" hobbies like cooking and sewing, to mention current boyfriends, and to discuss future marriage plans (Del Rey 1978).

Leaders of women's sport took the same approach at the institutional level. In answer to portrayals of physical education majors and teachers as social rejects and prudes, physical educators revised their philosophy to place heterosexuality at the center of professional objectives. In the late 1930s, they invited psychologists to speak at national professional meetings about problems of sexual adjustment. Such experts described the "types of people who are unadjusted to heterosexual cooperative activity" and warned women in physical education to "develop a prejudice against segregation of the sexes" (National Amateur Athletic Federation—Women's Division 1938). Told that exclusively female environments caused failed heterosexual development, physical educators who had long advocated female separatism in sport were pressed to promote mixed-sex groups and heterosexual "adjustment."

Curricular changes implemented between the mid-1930s and mid-1950s institutionalized the new philosophy. In a paper on postwar objectives, Mildred A. Schaeffer (1945) explained that physical education classes should help women "develop an interest in school dances and mixers and a desire to voluntarily attend them." To this end, administrators revised coursework to emphasize beauty and social charm over rigorous exercise and health. They exchanged old rationales of fitness and fun for promises of trimmer waistlines, slimmer hips, and prettier complexions. At Radcliffe, for example, faculty redesigned health classes to include "advice on dress, carriage, hair, skin, voice, or any factor that would tend to improve personal appearance and thus contribute to social and economic success" (Physical Education Director, no date). Intramural programs replaced interclass basketball tournaments and weekend campouts for women with mixed-sex "co-recreational" activities like bowling, volleyball, and "fun nights" of ping-pong and shuffleboard. Some departments also added co-educational classes to foster "broader, keener, more sympathetic understanding of the opposite sex" (Department of Physical Education, 1955).[4] Department heads cracked down on "mannish" students and faculty, issuing warnings against "casual styles" which might "lead us back into some dangerous channels" (Ashton 1957). They implemented dress codes which forbade slacks and men's shirts or socks, adding as well a ban on "boyish hair cuts" and unshaven legs. For example, the 1949–50 Physical Training Staff Handbook at the University of Texas stated (16), "Legs should be kept shaved," while restrictions on hair and dress are spelled out in the staff minutes and physical education handbooks for majors at the universities of Wisconsin, Texas and Minnesota . . .

Popular sport promoters adopted similar tactics. Marshalling sexual data like they were athletic statistics, a 1954 AAU poll sought to sway a skeptical public with numerical proof of heterosexuality—the fact that 91 percent of former female athletes surveyed had married (Andersen 1954). Publicity for the Midwestern All-American Girls Baseball League (AAGBL) included statistics on the number of married players in the league. In the same vein, the women's golf tour announced that one-third of the pros were married, and the rest were keeping an eye peeled for prospects who might "lure them from the circuit to the altar" (All-American Girls Baseball League Records, Pennsylvania State University Libraries; *Saturday Evening* Post 1954).

The fear of lesbianism was greatest where a sport had a particularly masculine image and where promoters needed to attract a paying audience. Professional and semipro basketball and softball fit the bill on both accounts. Athletic leaders tried to resolve the problem by "proving" the attractive femininity of athletes. Softball and basketball tournaments continued to feature beauty pageants. Although in earlier times such events celebrated the "sexiness" of the emancipated modern woman, in later decades they seemed to serve a more defensive function. The AAU's magazine, the *Amateur Athlete*, made sure that at least one photograph of the national basketball tournament's beauty "queen and her court" accompanied the photo of each year's championship team. Behind the scenes, teams passed dress and conduct codes. For example, the All-American Girls Baseball League's 1951 constitution prohibited players from wearing men's clothing or getting "severe" haircuts. That this was an attempt to secure the heterosexual image of athletes was made even clearer when league officials announced that AAGBL policy prohibited the recruitment of "freaks" and "Amazons" (Markey n.d.; Feminine Sluggers 1952).

In the end, the strategic emphasis on heterosexuality and the suppression of "mannishness" did little to alter the image of women in sport. The stereotype of the mannish lesbian athlete grew out of the persistent common-sense equation of sport with masculinity. Opponents of women's sport reinforced this belief when they denigrated women's athletic efforts and ridiculed skilled athletes as "grotesque," "mannish," or "unnatural." Leaders of women's sport unwittingly contributed to the same set of ideas when they began to orient their programs around the new feminine heterosexual ideal. As physical education policies and media campaigns worked to suppress lesbianism and marginalize athletes who didn't conform to dominant standards of femininity, sport officials embedded heterosexism into the institutional and ideological framework of sport. The effect extended beyond sport to the wider culture, where the figure of the mannish lesbian athlete announced that competitiveness, strength, independence, aggression, and physical intimacy among women fell outside the bounds of womanhood. As a symbol of female deviance, she served as a powerful reminder to all women to toe the line of heterosexuality and femininity or risk falling into a despised category of mannish (not-women) women.

Notes

1 Among the works that do consider the issue of homosexuality are Lenskyj (1986), Zipter (1988), and Bennett (1982). On the relationship between male homosexuality and sport, see Pronger (1990).
2 Although the term "gay" as a reference to homosexuals occurred only sporadically in the mass media before the 1960s, it was in use as a slang term among some homosexual men and lesbians as early as the 1920s and quite commonly by the 1940s.
3 Elizabeth Lunebeck (1987) notes a similar pattern in her discussion of medical theories of the "hypersexual" white female. Because psychiatrists assumed that Black women were naturally "oversexed," when defining the medical condition of hypersexuality, they included only young white working-class women whose sexual ardor struck physicians and social workers as unnaturally excessive.
4 For curricular changes, I examined physical education records at the universities of Wisconsin, Texas, and Minnesota, Radcliffe College, Smith College, Tennessee State University, and Hampton University.

References

Andersen, Roxy (1945). "Fashions in feminine sport." *Amateur Athlete*, March.
—— (1954). "Statistical survey of former women athletes." *Amateur Athletes*, September.
Arnett, Ruth (1921). Girls need physical education. *Chicago Defender*, 10 December.
Baltimore Afro-American (1957). 29 June, Magazine Section, 1.
Bennett, Roberta (1982). "Sexual labeling as social control: Some political effects of being female in the gym." *Perspectives* 4: 40–50.
Bérubé, Alan (1990). *Coming Out Under Fire: The History of Gay Men and Women in World War Two*. New York: Free Press.
Breines, Wini (1986). "The 1950s: Gender and some social science." *Sociological Inquiry* 56 (Winter): 69–92.
Carby, Hazel (1987). *Reconstructing Womanhood: The Emergence of the Afro-American Woman Novelist*. New York: Oxford University Press.
Chauncey, George Jr. (1989). "From sexual inversion to homosexuality: Medicine and the changing conceptualizing of female deviance." In *Passion and Power: Sexuality in History*, edited by Kathy Peiss and Christina Simmons. Philadelphia: Temple University Press.
Collins, Patricia Hill (1990). *Black Feminist Thought: Knowledge, Consciousness, and the Politics of Empowerment*. Boston: Unwin Hyman.
D'Emilio, John (1983). *Sexual Politics, Sexual Communities: The Making of Homosexual Minority in the United Sates, 1940–1970*. Chicago: University of Chicago Press.
de Koven, Anna (1912). "The athletic woman." *Good Housekeeping*, August.
Del Rey, Patricia (1978). "The apologetic and women in sport." In *Women and Sport*, Carole Oglesby (ed). Philadelphia: Lea & Febiger.
Department of Physical Education, University of California, Los Angeles (1955). "Coeducation classes." *Journal of Health, Physical Education, and Recreation* 26 February: 18.
Detroit News (1962) 31 July, sec 6, p. 1.

Dunham, Elizabeth (1924). "Physical education for women at Hampton Institute." *Southern Workman* 53 (April): 167.

Dunning, Eric (1986). "Sport as a male preserve: Notes on the social source of masculine identity and its transformation." In *Quest for Excitement: Sport and Leisure in the Civilizing Process*, Eric Dunning and Norbert Elias (eds). New York: Basil Blackwell.

Ebony (1955). *Fastest women in the world*. June: 28.

Ellis, A.W. (1939). "The status of health and physical education for women in negro colleges and universities." *Journal of Negro Education* 8 (January): 58–63.

Ellis, Havelock (1915). *Sexual Inversion*. Vol 2 of *Studies in the Psychology of Sex*. 3rd rev. ed. Philadelphia: F.A. Davis.

Erenberg, Lewis (1981). *Steppin' Out: New York Nightlife and the Transformation of American Culture, 1890–1930*. Westport: Greenwood Press.

Farmer, Gene (1947). "What a Babe!" *Life*, June.

Feminine Sluggers (1952). *People and Places* 8(12), reproduced in AAGBL Records.

Freedman, Estelle and John D'Emilio (1988). *Intimate Matters: A History of Sexuality in America*. New York: Harper & Row.

Furlong, William (1960). "Venus wasn't a shotputter." *New York Times Magazine*, 28 August.

Gallico, Pual (1960). *Houston Post*, 22 March.

Gerber, Ellen (1975). "The controlled development of collegiate sport for women, 1923–36." *Journal of Sport History* 2 (Spring): 1–28.

Giddings, Paula (1984). *When and Where I enter: The Impact of Black Women on Race and Sex in America*. New York: William and Morrow.

Himes, Cindy (1986). *The Female Athlete in American Society, 1860–1940*, Ph.D. Dissertation. University of Pennsylvania.

Hult, Joan (1985). The governance of athletics for girls and women. *Research Quarterly for Exercise and Sport*. April: 64–77.

Inglis, William (1910). "Exercise for girls." *Harper's Bazaar*, March.

Kimmel, Michael (1987). "The contemporary 'crisis' of masculinity in historical perspective." In *The Making of Masculinities: The New Men's Studies*, Harry Brod (ed). Boston: Allen & Unwin.

Lagemann, John (1947). "Red heads you kill me!" *Collier's*, 8 February, 64.

Lenskyj, Helen (1986) *Out of Bounds: Women, Sport and Sexuality*. Toronto: Women's Press.

Lunebeck, Elizabeth (1987). "'A new generation of women': Progressive psychiatrists and the hypersexual female." *Feminists Studies* 13 (Fall): 513–43.

MacFadden, Bernard (1929). "Athletics for women will help save the nation." *Amateur Athlete* 4 (February–July): 7.

Mangan, J.S. and Roberta J. Park (eds) (1987). *From "Fair Sex" to Feminism: Sport and the Sexualization of Women in the Industrial and Post-Industrial Era*. London: Frank Cass.

Mange, Biolet (1910). "Field hockey for women." *Harper's Bazaar*, April.

Markey, Morris (no date). "Hey Ma, you're out!" 1951 Records of the AAGBL.

Marston, William (1933). "How can a woman do it?" *Redbook*, September.

Martin, Pete (1947). "Babe Didrikson takes off her mask." *Saturday Evening Post*, 20 September.

Moats, A. (1934). "He hasn't a chance." *Ladies Home Journal*, December.

Mooney, Gertrude (1937). "The benefits and dangers of athletics for the high school girl." Department of Physical Training for Women Records (Health Ed. Folder), box 3R251. Barker Texas History Center, University of Texas Austin.

Mrozek, Donald (1983). *Sport and the American Mentality, 1880–1910*. Knoxville; University of Tennessee Press.

Murray, Jim (no date). 1970s column in *Austin American Statesman*, Zaharis scrapbook, Barker Texas History Center, University of Texas, Austin.

Nathan, George (1930). "Once there was a princess." *American Mercury*, February.

National Amateur Athletic Federation—Women's Division (1938). Newsletter no. 79 (1 June 1938), from Department of Women's Physical Education, University of Wisconsin Archives.

Paret, J. Parmeley (1900) "Basket-ball for young women." *Harper's Bazaar*, October.

Peiss, Kathy (1986). *Cheap Amusements. Working Women and Leisure in Turn-of-the-Century New York*. Philadelphia: Temple University Press.

Penn, Donna (1991). "The meanings of lesbianism in post-war America." *Gender and History* 3: 190–203.

Physical Education Director (no date) Official Reports, Kristin Powell's collected materials on Radcliffe Athletics, Radcliffe College Archives, acc. No. R87.

Pronger, Brian (1990). *The Arena of Masculinity: Sport, Homosexuality, and the Meaning of Sex*. New York: St. Martin's Press.

Roberts, Amelia (1927). Letter to *Chicago Defender*, 12 March, sec 2, p. 7.

Sackett, Ada (1934). "Beauty survives sport." *Literary Digest* 117: 43.

Sargent, Dudley A. (1913). "Are athletics making girls masculine?" *Ladies Home Journal*, March.

Saturday Evening Post (1954). "Next to marriage, we'll take golf." 23 January.

Schaeffer, Mildred (1945). "Desirable objectives in post-war physical education." *Journal of Health and Physical Education* 16: 446–47.

Sefton, Alice Allene (1937). "Must women in sports look beautiful?" *Journal of Health and Physical Education* 8: 481.

Simmons, Christina (1989). "Modern sexuality and the myth of the Victorian Repression." In Passion *and Power: Sexuality in History*, Kathy Peiss and Christina Simmons (eds). Philadelphia: Temple University Press.

Steers, Fred (1932). Spirit. *Amateur Athlete*. October: 7.

Wise, P. M. (1883). "Case of sexual perversion." *Alienist and Neurologists* 4: 88.

Wittner, Fred (1934). "Shall the ladies join us?" *Literary Digest*, 19 May.

Zipter, Yvonne (1988). *Diamonds are a Dyke's Best Friend*. Ithaca: Firebrand Books.

Chapter 11

Outta my endzone

Sport and the territorial anus*

Brian Pronger

Desire and competitive sport—a nexus that is usually ignored. It is seldom a focus of the sport media, except where there are sex scandals, such as the recently publicized homosexual subculture in Canadian boys' and men's ice hockey: National Hockey League player Sheldon Kennedy, for example, has revealed that when he was a young man playing in the Canadian Hockey League, he submitted more than 300 times to the sexual demands of his coach, Graham James, who subsequently has been jailed for the offense. It has been widely reported in the media that numerous boys exchanged sexual favors for hockey tickets and other perks with employees of Toronto's Maple Leaf Gardens. It has also been revealed that there is widespread sexual violence in hockey club initiations. And the regular sexual exploitation of women who follow professional and semiprofessional male athletes in many competitive sports—in hockey, they are called puck-bunnies—is now frequently cited (Robinson, 1998).

Of course, athletes, both female and male, are often seen, indeed marked, as sexy. Their sexual desirability, however, is a by-product of their sport, not inherent in the activity itself. Athletic training builds taut muscular bodies that fit contemporary molds of the desirable body in consumer culture (Balsamo, 1998; Bordo, 1993b; Crawford, 1984; Featherstone, 1991; Goldstein, 1997; Harvey & Sparks, 1991; Hoberman, 1994). Because the culture of Euro-American competitive sport is popularly understood to confer orthodox masculinity on the men who engage in it; or are even simply fans of it (Connell, 1990; Kidd, 1987; Messner, 1992; Messner & Sabo, 1994; Pronger, 1990; Whitson, 1994), it is often considered by men, and some women, to confer an especially potent heterosexual aura—its amplification of masculinity stresses the participants' difference from femininity, dressing up the culturally produced difference men and women, which is the very pulse of heterosexuality. The youthful masculinity of the athlete has been a

---

* Originally published as 'Outa my endzone: sport and the territorial anus' in *Journal of Sport and Social Issues*, 1999, vol. 23, no. 4, 373–389.

feature of gay male erotic culture for at least the last 50 years (Pronger, 1990); it also had an important niche in the homosexual pedophilic culture of ancient Greece (Dover, 1978). Somewhat similarly, the physical power of the athletic female body has held an important place in Euro-American lesbian culture (Burton-Nelson, 1994; Cahn, 1994; Griffin, 1998; Jay, 1995; Rogers, 1994; Roxxie, 1998; Sykes, 1998). The aura of competitive sport, the sporting arena, the erotic power it confers on the bodies of athletes, then, is aphrodisia to sexual commerce outside the arena.

Almost all competitive sports are segregated along the lines of gender. This means that the practice of competitive sport itself can have homoerotic dimensions: the contact of the playing field, the spectacle of the partially clad body, the steamy environment of the showers and locker room. I have previously written positively about the covert homoeroticism of men's sport, suggesting that it affords opportunities for homoerotic vision and contact that are desirable not only for gay-identified boys and men but also for those whose homoerotic imaginations have not become explicit, integrated aspects of their lives. In *The Arena of Masculinity* (Pronger, 1990), I argued that men's sport allows men and boys to exclude women and girls from their all-male environments, permits them to play with each other's bodies, to surround themselves with naked men in the showers and locker rooms, to enjoy that all-male contact, without suffering the vilification that usually comes from the open acknowledgment and pursuit of masculine erotic contact, the stigma of "being homosexual." I also argued that the well-known homophobia of competitive sports serves an important structural socio-cultural function. It prevents the implicit homoeroticism of competitive sport, the pleasures of male bodies playing with each other, from proceeding to explicit sexual expression. That is to say, it maintains the panoptic line that must not be crossed if the orthodox masculine—which is to say the patriarchal heterosexual—credentials of competitive sport are to be maintained. In other words, the homophobia of competitive sport allows men to play with each other's bodies and still preserve their patriarchal heterosexist hegemony; they can have their (beef) cake and eat it, too.

The homoerotic/homophobic dynamics of women's competitive sport operates in a similar though not perfectly parallel way. Whereas men's competitive sport, especially the rougher team versions, is widely assumed to confer on men the mantle of respectable heterosexual masculinity, similar women's competitive sport is routinely suspected to undermine traditional heterosexual femininity. The homophobia of women's competitive sport finds its expression in the repeated renunciation by athletes, coaches, and sport administration that there is significant lesbian presence in women's sport. That homophobic culture of denial often ends in public purges of lesbian athletes and coaches and functions to prevent the implicit homoeroticism of women's sport from becoming an explicit, indeed celebrated practice.

The Euro-American globalized lesbian and gay "community" has attempted to address the homophobia of mainstream competitive sport by developing lesbian and gay community sports. In most major European and American cities, lesbian and gay sports groups are the largest community organizations. The Gay Games, which have been held quadrennially since 1982, are major commercial, cultural, and athletic events that attempt to combat the stigma of being homosexual by highlighting the fact that lesbians and gay men engage in "normal, healthy" activities such as sport. The competitive sports themselves are practiced in the same way that they are in mainstream competitive sport; indeed, they are often sanctioned by main-stream sport-governing bodies. Gay community competitive sports are essentially the same as masters sports, or ethnic and other community sports, where participation is a high priority. Depending on the individual athletes and the priorities of particular leagues, interpersonal competition may or may not be an important part of the phenomenon. The lesbian and gay communities' appropriation of competitive sport, more than any other cultural production of sport, has attempted to address the problematic homophobic organization of sexual desire in the athletic milieu. As I have argued elsewhere, however, that embrace of sport has not changed the principal structure of desire in competitive sport; it has only made it less brutally exclusionary of lesbians and gay men (Pronger, 1999).

During the past 20 years, competitive sport has been criticized on a number of fronts, mostly in the emerging academic discipline of the sociology of sport.[1] A survey here of the various critical paths that have been developed in the sociology of sport neither would be appropriate nor could it do the field justice. Suffice it to say that while there have been important critiques of sport along the lines of class, nationality, race, ethnicity, and gender, there has been little attention given to the construction of desire in competitive sport.[2] Feminist and pro-feminist critiques have come the closest by problematizing issues of sexual discrimination in sport, pointing out the ways in which lesbians and gay men are harmed by hegemonic masculinities, femininities, heterosexism, and homophobia.[3] The sociocultural organization of desire, the libidinal economies of bodily interactions required by the competitive structure of sport, however, have not been examined.

I propose an analytical framework for the construction of desire in competitive sport that emerges from the interplay of elements of feminists, postmodern, gay and queer theories. I am confining my argument to competitive sport, which is to say bodily games where the economy and logic of winning and losing are truly important. This means my analysis focuses on the formal structure of the competitive relationship. That relationship is more important in some settings and for some people than it is in others.

There are informal pickup games where there is no score keeping and where each event of scoring is of little or no significance. There are recrea-tional sport leagues that downplay the significance of scoring and being scored on, of winning and losing. My argument, on the other hand, is aimed primarily at spectators, governments, leagues, schools, teams, and individuals for whom competition is important, where the desire to win and not to lose is very strong, where winning is deeply satisfying and losing is genuinely disappointing. Indeed, there are many individuals and sports organizations who are willing to put enormous effort and expense into the project of winning and not losing. They are ready, for instance, to exclude people from their sporting organization who they think will undermine their efforts to win. There are many whose desire to win is so great they will break the rules of the game, or injure their opponents during a game, and even injure themselves in abusive training regimes. There are people who, in the most casual game, take personal satisfaction in beating others and feel somehow undermined when they themselves lose.

Of course, there is more to sport than competition. For instance, the individualized striving for existential expression in the swimming pool and on the playing field, track, or ice; the disciplinary process of physical and mental training in the Foucaultian dynamic of docility and productivity (Foucault, 1979); in team sports, the interpersonal dynamics of working together; the subordination of individual will to that of coaches and sports governing bodies; the different aesthetics of various sports in their varied cultural millieux; the complex class imperatives that compel different actors into the sports arena; and so on. These and many other sociocultural dynamics frame the discursive construction of desire that I will attempt to analyze here. The extent to which the discourse I am describing is operative in various cultural contexts is an empirical question beyond the scope of this theoretical analysis. It would be interesting to take the analytical framework that I am proposing and consider specific empirical instances of competitive sport and see how this discourse of desire affects and is affected by the different cultures of women's, masters', workers', lesbian and gay, and non-Western sports, for instance.

Drawing selectively on aspects of Gilles Deleuze and Felix Guattari (1983, 1987), I will suggest that modern competitive sport constructs desire by systematically limiting its expression to a libidinal economy of territorial domination. I question what Drucilla Cornell (1992) has called the philosophy of the limit as it is operative in competitive sport. I will argue that competitive sport demands a libidinal economy and emotional formation that is embedded in the masculine colonizing will to conquer the space of an "other" while simultaneously protectively enclosing the space of the self, in an attempt to establish ever greater sovereignty of self and consequent otherness of the other. This construction of desire is not unique to competitive sport: It is common to most masculine business, academic, and asexual practices. In competitive business, it shows in the desire to accumulate and safeguard wealth by taking it from others, keeping it for oneself and one's family, class, or nation. In academe, it shows in the desire to take intellectual pleasure and credit by discrediting the work of others while constructing an impenetrable edifice/orifice out of one's "own" work; this is the standard way to build an academic career. In sex, it shows in the desire to penetrate the holes of others and the desire to resist having the same happen to oneself. In competitive sport, it shows in the offensive desire to get points for oneself by taking them from an opponent and to defensively prevent the challenger from doing it to oneself, or one's team. I will critique competitive sport as a problematic construction of desire by showing how it parallels phallocentric, homophobic sexual desire. But I must emphasize that I am not suggesting in Freudian fashion that sexual desire is some sort of primordial drive that finds its repressed expression in competitive sport. On the contrary: I argue that the masculine construction of desire in competitive sport, commerce, academe, and sex formulates particular sociocultural economies of desire in more or less parallel ways, all of which reproduce oppressive modes of being in the world. The phallocentric formulation of desire that I will describe in competitive sport constitutes an essential element of what Foucault (1980), if he had concerned himself with sport, might have called the "biopolitics" of competitive sport.

First of all, competitive sport as a system of desire. Reworking Derrida's method of deconstruction, the feminist legal philosopher Drucilla Cornell (1992) says that systems (be they linguistic, judicial, musical, visual, sexual, economic, or athletic) impose limits on the power to appreciate, experience, and indeed create realities. Deconstruction, by the seeming negativity of the word itself, is sometimes confused with a kind of cynical, nihilistic reductionism: Take apart the constructs, and you are left with nothing. Some sociologists, philosophers, and political activists think that because deconstruction reduces everything to cynical and unreconstructable litter, political action is rendered impossible (Dews, 1987; Ebert, 1996; Habermas, 1983). To counteract such a misunderstanding, Drucilla Cornell has suggested renaming the project "the philosophy of the limit." Questioning limits has been the source of many politically active liberation movements: feminists questioning the limits of gender, anti-racists the limits of race, postmodernists the limits of modernity (Game, 1991: Gray, 1995; Hutcheon, 1989, Jameson, 1984, Lyotard, 1984; Miller, 1993), the handicapped the limits of ablism, gays the limits of homophobia, queers the limits of gay culture (Champagne, 1995; Kipnis, 1993; Warne, 1993), and post-queers the limits of queer (Simpson, 1996). All of these have engaged in some philosophy of the limit, questioning the ways in which social, economic, cultural, and bodily systems construct the limits of human possibilities. Clearly, there are activist political agendas in them all. Simply put: what limits are operative? How can they be justified? and, where and how might it be wise to dismantle them? The questions of limits are often most poignant for those who find themselves outside of them; that's why deconstruction is so popular with deviants, such as homosexual academics who are drawn to physical culture but alienated by competitive sport. The philosophy of the limit seeks to reveal what is left out of systems and show how such exclusions prohibit just, ethical relations. A philosophy of the limit of competitive sporting desire, therefore, will seek to expose the limits of that configuration of desire, and to question the ethics of those limits.

For the purpose of this short article, I will briefly call attention to three important and related elements that Cornell explores in *The Philosophy of the Limit* and which I think are particularly apt for the questions of desire in competitive sport: the logics of parergonality, secondness, and alterity. The logics of parergonality names the way in which the establishment of any system as a system suggests a beyond to it: that which the system excludes, by virtue of what the system cannot comprehend, or by what it prohibits to accomplish its systematic objectives. The philosophy of the limit asks: What lies beyond a particular system by virtue of its existence as a system? What are the system's limits? In the context of this article: What kinds of desire does competitive sport exclude? Why?

Cornell (1992) also draws on what Charles Pierce in his critique of Hegelian idealism has called secondness, which is "the materiality that persists beyond any attempt to conceptualize it. Secondness, in other words, is what resists" (p. 1). The philosophy of the limit, then, asks about what realities resists and persist beyond the systems that produce and interpret those realities. Where the system happens to be a dominating force, such as the formal and informal rules for the conduct of desire in competitive sport, the realities that either succumb or resist inside and outside a given system are extremely important. What material realities in sport, for instance, resists the system of competitive sport? Even more significantly, how do those systems either foster the potentialities of secondness, or attempt to control or erase them?

By alterity, Cornell refers to an ethical philosophy that remains open, indeed committed, to appreciating the ways in which the other is differentiated from and inaccessible to systems of interpretation and social organization. Cornell (1992) grounds the philosophy of the limit in the ambitious ethical quest to engage the other and otherness nonviolently:

> The entire project of the philosophy of the limit is driven by the ethical desire to enact the ethical relation . . . the aspiration to a nonviolent relationship to the Other and to otherness more generally, that assumes responsibility to guard the other.
>
> (p. 62)

Thus, the ethical question of the limit in competitive sport is: to what degree does competitive sport as a system of desire foster nonviolence, guarding that which is other to it as a system?

With the philosophy of the limit as an ethical framework, I will now suggest that competitive sport is a sociocultural system that limits the body, by ordering modalities of desire. To do so, I call selectively on Gilles Deleuze and Felix Guattari, who say that the body is a form of energy that is produced in historical discourses. It is the power of desire, which Deleuze and Guattari understand not as lack (the desire for that which one does not have) but as the fundamental flow of productive energy, the power of human being/becoming/actuality. Desire extends well beyond what is known generically as sex (love making, casual genital encounters, sadomasochistic scenes, and the like). Desire is the life force by which we move, by which we are being or becoming at all.

At the risk of oversimplifying their work, I suggest that Deleuze and Guattari say that desire (the body) is produced historically in the tension between two forms of power: *puissance* and *pouvoir*. The puissance of the body is its power to connect, to be connected, to make connection. Pouvoir is a form of power that "territorializes" puissance, our capacity for making connections, thus governing the connective potential of life. There are so many forms of pouvoir. Gender, race, class, ethnicity, and so on are all forms of pouvoir, powers that govern the possibilities for making connections precisely by their logics of parergonality. Similarly, I suggest, desire is governed by the configuration of competitive sport. Competitive sport, clearly, is a social form that orders the capacity of bodies to connect. There are many rules, both written and unwritten, that govern not only where and when bodies can move, and the ways in which they connect, but also conventions that govern the libidinal economy of bodies. Competitive sporting conventions govern how energy should be expressed, what its texture should be in sport, and how various kinds of space should be created, distributed, occupied.

Our free capacity to exist, to connect, to affect and be affected, which is to say our puissance, is channeled by the pouvoir of competitive sport. How does the pouvoir of competitive sport establish a logic of parergonality for the exercise of desire? I suggest that competitive sport renders desire selectively concrete, which is to say simulates desire, within the libidinal economy of territorial domination. Puissance is ordered by the pouvoir of a socially constructed territorial imperative, if you will. In the context of the philosophy of the limit, the question becomes: how does this ordering of desire construct a logic of parergonality? What is included? What is excluded? What is rendered second?

Considering the logic of parergonality: What does the competitive sport system of desire fail to comprehend or simply prohibit? I will answer that question of what competitive sport excludes by first suggesting what it definitely includes. Competitive sport, like warfare, is historically a masculine phenomenon. Women can, and indeed do, participate in this historical expression of masculinity, just as some have embraced other masculine forms in business and politics—Margaret Thatcher is often cited as a prime example of the ways in which women are more than capable of engaging in domineering, indeed blatantly aggressive, masculine practices. Participation in a cultural form such as masculinity clearly is not dependent on cultural identities such as manliness or physiological sex. Masculinity is a form of pouvoir that territorializes puissance, organizes the life force, the capacity to connect, to affect and be effected, in the economics of spatial domination. Some feminists have criticized that masculine organization of desire under the sign of the phallus. Phallocentrism could be defined as the despotic imperative to take up more space and yield less of it, be it physical, cultural, emotional, fiscal, hierarchical, or other kinds of space. Phallocentrism, like sexism and racism, territorializes the body, organizing its parts, its organs, as concrete simulations of the phallic enterprise.

I am referring here to Deleuze's concept of the simulacrum (Massumi, 1997). For Deleuze, the simulacrum is not the ethereal copy for which there is no original, which is Baudrillard's well-known formulation of the simulacrum.

> A common definition of the simulacrum is a copy of a copy whose relation to the model has becomes so attenuated that it can no longer be properly said to be a copy. It stands on its own as a copy without a model. Frederic Jameson cites the example of photorealism. The painting is a copy not of reality but of a photography which is already a copy of the original.
>
> (Massumi, 1997: 2)

Baudrillard says that the process has gone so far that there is no longer a real referent for signs, but only signs of signs. Deleuze has a much more materialist understanding. The simulacrum is a partial concretization of potential in a form that serves political or ideological ends, which I am arguing in the case of the phallus is the biopolitical quest for spatial domination. "Simulation does not replace reality ... it appropriates reality in the operation of a despotic overcoding" (Massumi, 1997: 3). By codifying desire, the simulacrum insinuates a reality that replaces desire's puissant capacity to create free connections. The simulacrum, thus understood, abstracts from bodies a "transcendental plane of ideal identities [e.g., the phallic ideal] ... and then folds that ideal dimension back on to bodies in order to force them to conform to the distribution it lays out for them [e.g., the traditional masculine desire to take space]" (Massumi, 1997: 2). The preeminent site for this stimulation, this "despotic overcoding," is the penis.[4] The phallus is simulated in the penis by the act of taking up space: it goes without saying that a limp, shriveled penis is not effective in simulating the domineering masculine organization of desire. Given that no penis can live up to its phallic boast, no matter how swollen it gets, phallocentrism finds other ways to territorialize the body: innocuously, possibly, in body building, and more despotically in the territorial violence of warfare and competitive sport, for instance.

Less boastful than the phallus, perhaps because of its embarrassing vulnerability or even more terrifying potential openness, is the phallus's companion,
the protective side of phallic desire, the side that can repel or admit others
into the space carved out by phallic aggression. The simulacrum of this other
side of phallic desire, I suggest is the asshole. It is the tightly closed orifice of
the phallic conqueror, as well as the (perhaps) reluctantly opened orifice
of the phallically conquered. Masculine desire is thus produced in the play
of the phallus and asshole. It stimulates desire as both homoerotic and homophobic: homoerotic in its preoccupation with phallic intent, homophobic in
its resistance to penetration. Masculine desire protects its own phallic
production by closing openings, preeminently the anus and the mouth; but
just as important by closing eyes, ears, touch, smell, mind, spirit—in short,
any vulnerability to the phallic expansion of others. Rendered impenetrable,
masculine desire attempts to differentiate itself, to produce itself as distinct
and unconnected. Its quest is to be conquering and inviolable, sovereign. The
pouvoir of masculinity territorializes puissances by simultaneously channeling
it and damming it up.

I should caution that I am not suggesting here that the symbolic power of
bodies and their parts is constructed in any essential way to convey particular
meanings or accomplish particular ends. In more emancipated libidinal
economies than sport (with its patriarchal and homophobic cultural origin),
the different parts of the body can mean very different things and accomplish
very different programs (Delueze & Guattari, 1987: 151). Bodies need not
be culturally constructed in only one way. In more open libidinal economies,
the asshole may well be as "gate endow'd with many properties," as Phineas
Fletcher suggested in 1633 (cited in Masten, 1997: 138). Jeffrey Masten
(1997), ironically paraphrasing St. Paul in I *Corinthians* 2: 9–10, says
"imagine a body in parts set loose from their customary meanings and
functions: hearing eyes, seeing ears, tasting hands, conceiving tongues,
reporting hearts. What is fundament [an asshole] in this context? What does
a bottom do?" (p. 140). Similarly, Deleuze and Guattari (1987) say, "Why
not walk on your head, sing with your sinuses, see through your skin, breathe
with your belly" (p. 151).

Although masculine desire is not restricted to men and boys, it is expected
of them, and women and girls are largely discouraged from producing their
desire so assertively and protectively. Since, on their own, no penis and anus
as mere body parts could ever produce the incessant territorial aspirations
of their phallocentric master and society, a host of strategies and practices
are promoted to encourage men and boys to take and enclose more space
beyond the limited purview of their "private parts." The point of this
conquering and enclosure of space is to make bodies differentiate themselves
from the vortex of unbounded free-flowing desire (which Deleuze and
Guattari call the deterritorialized body-without-organs) and thereby establish
territorial, sovereign, masculine selfhood. Men traditionally cherish such

sovereignty among themselves and resent it in women. Not all men and boys are equally territorial, or sovereign, of course. Consequently, there are vast systems that aid in the simulation of masculine desire and many rewards for its success. One of the most influential training grounds for masculine spatialization is competitive sport (Kidd, 1987; Messner & Sabo, 1994; Sabo & Gordon, 1995; Whitson, 1990, 1994). Sovereignty need not, of course, be a purely individual pursuit; adversarial team building is a well-known phallic extension.

Competitive sport is masculinizing, which is why women in patriarchal societies have been mostly discouraged from participating. (Of course, women and girls have participated, but usually against great odds and seldom with the same legitimacy as boys and men, a legitimacy that, I argue, the philosophy of the limit will reveal to be profoundly unethical.) Boys raised on competitive sport learn to desire, learn to make connections according to the imperative to take space away from others and jealously guard it for themselves. Competitive sport trains desire to conquer and protect space, which is to say it simulates phallic and anal desire on the playing field. The most masculine competitive sports are those that are the most explicitly spatially dominating: boxing, football, soccer, hockey. In these sports, players invade the space of others and vigorously guard the same from happening to themselves. The only honorable form of desire in these competitive sports is domineering and protective; it is anathema to welcome other men into one's space. The team whose desire produces the most invasive phallus, which is called offensive strategy, and tightest asshole, known as defensive strategy, wins the game.

The masculine desire to conquer and enclose is constructed similarly in other domains. The accumulation of capital and property, for example, depends on an equivalent desire for acquisition and retention. Certainly, much of academic debate is phallically aggressive and anally closed. The problem, of course, with masculine desire, is that it is essentially dominating, seeking to dominate others in ever-expanding phallic spaces and to domi-nate the self by tightening the holes that could be the undoing of the masculine self. Turned out in phallic prominence, masculine desire dominates surrounding space by appropriating it as its own. Turned inward as anal closure, it remains impervious to external probing influences, thus dominating internal space with the insistence of self-centered phallic/anal integrity. The closed orifices of masculine desire territorialize the freedom of desire by enclosing the masculine differentiating individual; this is the partial concretization of potential that marks the simulacrum in action. This phallic/anal ideal is "folded back on to bodies in order to force them to conform to the distribution it lays out for them" (Massumi, 1997: 2). This simulation of desire in the parergonal logic of phallic conquest is the essence of competitive desire.

This simulacrum is most obvious in those sports where the quest to forcefully take and maintain physical territory by bodily invasion is central to the game: football, hockey, basketball, lacrosse, and so on. Other sports are similarly territorial but invade only with projectiles (flying phalluses, as it were), racquet sports and curling, for example. Because the body itself does not enter the space of the other, these sports are typically seen to be less violent and thus less masculine than the former. Less masculine still are sports in which spatial domination is more abstract, such as various forms of racing, where the space is only temporal; or in jumping and throwing sports, where the space is marked by height and distances. In these sports, the competitors invade the abstract space of each other's yearning. The territories of bodies and their surrounding remain unviolated. The relative abstraction of such competitive sports makes them less brutally violating. But in all cases, hierarchical space is taken and violated in the differentiation of winners and loser, tops and bottoms, triumphant phallus and routed asshole.

Since one's participation in competition indicates one's commitment to phallic potency and one's defeat shows one's anal vulnerability and therefore phallic impotence, there is humiliation in defeat, in being penetrated by one's competitor. In his novel, *Ancient Evenings*, the infatuated student and lover of masculinity, Norman Mailer (1983), describes the humiliation of penetration, when the character Meni is penetrated by a male god: "The last of my pride was gone. . . . For I have never known more shame in the days that followed. . . . I was not like other men, although I felt more of a woman" (pp. 288–289). Being opened to the penetrations of phallic desire is feminizing, which in patriarchal culture is humiliating.

Because the "insult" of penetration is part and parcel of every competitive game, there are psychological strategies that help participants weather the denigration. It is called "being a good sport." Which is to say that one acknowledges defeat in the game, while refusing to acknowledge one's manifest feminization in the same. The expression, "take defeat like a man," means: maintain emotional closure; don't let it show that your phallic esteem, your phallic self-worth, has been penetrated, that your emotional vulnerabilities have been probed; there's always another game, another chance to show your phallic and anal power. Indeed, the ultimate defeat, which is to say the ultimate feminization, is to be seen crying at one's defeat—the only sport where such emotion if tolerated is the most feminine sports, figure skating. Another sportsmanlike strategy is to deflect attention from one's defeat, from one's diminution, by admiring the phallic skill of the victor. This valorizes the phallic project by de-emphasizing the anal violation.

The logic of parergonality in competitive sport simulates sovereign, masculine selfhood in the desire of phallic conquest and anal closure, which systematically excludes the desire of deference, openness, and vulnerability. The philosophy of the limit shows what kind of desire is excluded or rendered second in competitive sport; the desire to give oneself to the other, which is the desire to deconstruct the sovereign boundaries of phallic selfhood, the desire to open one's self. Simply put: competitive sport as a system of desire has no room for willing bottoms. The desire to open the body to the other, the desire to deterritorialize the limits of the self as a closed and sovereign subject, is rendered incomprehensible to the systematic objectives of playing competitive sport, which is a rude production of self by conquests and closure. The desire to open one's self to the other, the desire to deconstruct the limit of self and other by giving and sharing space in such a way that sovereignty disappears, is structurally prohibited in competitive sport.[5] The desire to be a welcoming and open space is unfathomable to the competitive logic of sport. The materiality that is rendered second and thus resists the libidinal economy and emotional logic of competitive sport is the desire to give up sovereignty, to open oneself to the other, so that sovereign other and sovereign self collapse, so that sovereignty itself loses its territory. This is not to say that such desire doesn't continue to exist: it is rendered second and finds its subordinate expression in the vast ironic, homoerotic subterfuge of body contact, team membership, and the spectacle of the locker room and showers, which I discussed in *The Arena of Masculinity*. Indeed, an important subversive reading of losing in competitive sport, is the secret pleasure of being penetrated against one's will. Such subversive pleasure transgresses the masculine point of competitive sport, which is the production of impenetrable sovereign selfhood. The philosophy of the limit of desire in competitive sport is fundamentally the productive parergonality of patriarchal homoerotic homophobia. In this still hegemonic moral system, the wrong kind of desire is the desire to be penetrated, the desire to be an open vessel for the pleasure of another, which in masculine terms would be the desire to undermine the phallic, space-enclosing, sovereign self. The humiliation of defeat is the revelation that one is not sovereign; that one has been shown to be more a gaping hole than a jutting phallus; that one is more like a woman than a man, as Mailer suggested; that one is permeable. Here, obviously, I am agreeing with Leo Bersani's (1987, 1995) much cited assertion that the rectum is indeed a grave, the grave of masculinity and the sovereign self. My justification, however, is not his Freudian one, but rather a more Deleuzian take on the territorialization of desire in the logic of the masculine construction of space. Homophobia is resistance to such penetration, resistance to the destruction of the enclosed masculine self. This is the conquest logic of competitive sport: to penetrate the other as an expression of the impenetrable self. It is an essentially homoerotic simulation of desire, however. There is no pleasure to be had in sport where one penetrates an asshole that has no phallic counterpart. In sport, there is no game where there is only one phallus; the structure of playful competitive desire demands the interplay of phallic wills. I am referring here, not to penises, but to the phallic simulacrum, which can be embodied by people with either penis or clitoris. That is the parergonal logic of competitive sport, regardless of the sex of the participants.

Competitive sport reproduces a set of binaries that emanate from traditional homophobic construction of desire: winner/loser, top/bottom, dominant/submissive, phallus/asshole. And these binaries have their fundamental logic in the patriarchal construction of masculine/feminine as the proper dispositions of men and women, respectively. Women's participation in competitive sport transgresses the "proper" place of women in patriarchy, as the nonphallic, willing and unresistant orifices for the phallic pleasure of men. Their successful participation in competitive sport shows that they can be just as phallically aggressive and anally closed as men. Women can be, indeed often are, masculine. To argue otherwise is to take an essentialist position: Women can take up masculine roles, but because they are women, they must do it differently, less aggressively, more kindly. Such a position suggests that when women enter traditionally aggressive masculine domains, they are incapable of doing the job in the same way as men. So, for instance, a business woman will be gentler with her competition. A woman soldier will kill in a kinder manner. A female athlete is not as competitive as a male. In these patriarchally constructed domains, which are by definition phallic, such an essentialist position would assert that women are not as capable as men. I suggest that while certainly many women are discouraged from such "capabilities," and that while there are women who prefer to modify the masculinist cultures they enter, women can and sometimes do perform the same jobs as men in accordance with established phallic structures. Highly competitive sport is such structure. It is a profoundly sexist position to suggest that women cannot do it.

Sporting women can simulate the same problematic desire as men; they can reproduce the logic of the same nasty binaries. It is a logic that purports to articulate and produce authentic human subjectivity, the adequately constructed human in the dialectics of domination and submission. A sport competition is illegitimate without the clear differentiation of the dominant and submissive. This is why important championships games cannot end in a tie.

Of course, there are homosexual scenes that repeat these same binaries of top and bottom. These are variations of patriarchal heterosexuality, in which the stakes are greater than in "ideal" heterosexuality, wherein the submissive identity of the feminine participant is known in advance. In such homosexual reformations of heterosexual scenes, there is competition to see who ends up "losing": one might call it sporting homosexuality. It is a popular homosexual pornographic trope: A competition is held to see who gets to fuck and who gets fucked. The homosexual irony, of course, is that the loser is the winner. In homosexual sex, unlike competitive sport, being the penetrated loser is not without its intrinsic pleasures.

As I said earlier, the territorial imperative is not the only dimension of desire in competitive sport. In the physical education literature of the 1970s, especially that with an existential or phenomenological orientation, for instance, much was made of the experience of flow, which is a kind of transcendental ecstasy that comes from a high level of focus on the experience of movement. There are also aesthetic dimensions, for instance. But I would maintain that such other dimensions are not featured in performance-oriented competitive sports education or in the entertainment business of competitive sport spectacles, the content of the sports pages beings proof. Andrew Cooper (1998) has argued that although competitive sport can offer its participants a powerful awareness of themselves in the experience of "playing in the zone" and feeling the flow of the game, the competitive structure of sport precludes any true spiritual awareness, which at least from a Buddhist perspective, requires not a conquest logic but the spirit of openness and compassion.

Competitive sport, far from breaking the bonds that seal the body and desire in forms of domination and submission, simulates desire in the ugly patriarchal economy of marauding phallus and plundered hole. Which brings me to the final ethical question in my analysis of the philosophy of the limit of competitive sport: What of alterity in competitive sport?

Competitive sport, I suggest, is structurally the ethical opposite of alterity, which you will recall Cornell (1992) described as "the aspiration to a nonviolent relationship to the Other . . . that assumes responsibility to guard the other" (p. 62). Competitive sport constructs desire within a libidinal economy whose very engine of desiring production is violation: the violation of the vulnerability of another to simulate the strength of the self. An ethic of alterity would construct desire as mutual; it would do no violence to the other; it would guard the other; where penetrating, it would construct penetration for the gratification of the desire of the other; it would not subtract from the other fulfillment of the other's desire, as does competitive sport; and certainly, it would take not pleasure in doing so. Sport simulates puissance, the capacity to connect and make connections, as a form of subtraction by which the victor pleasurably adds to him- or herself by taking space from another. The triumphant pleasure of competitive sport is the violent phallocentric pleasure of adding to oneself by subtracting from another. By its very construction as a system for the simulation of desire, it is an essentially brutal economy. One takes one's delight in the vulnerability of one's competitor, in one's phallic ability to pry open their otherwise closed openings against their will, and specifically because it is against their will. Indeed, the game is no fun at all if the opening is freely given. The more it resists, the more fun it is, and tellingly enough, the more "legitimate" the victory. The pleasure of penetration in competitive sport (i.e., of penetrating territory, be it the space of the opponent's endzone, net, or hoop; or the abstract space of fastest time in races; or the highest score in judged competitions) depends on withholding the same pleasure from one's opponents and violently taking it against their will for oneself.

The pleasure of adding to oneself by subtracting from another is also the pleasure of rape. In rape, the human capacity to open oneself to the other, the puissant mode of making connections, is violently abused. The rapist takes the vulnerable space of another, adds to himself precisely by going against the other's desire, in the profoundly transgressive act of violating the human capacity to connect. It produces in the rapist, in the victor, the pleasure of enforced hierarchy, dominance, and submission. The phallic simulacrum is instantiated most horribly in the practices of rape and murder. There are, however, social conventions that purport to make those instances of the simulacrum legitimate, the social conventions of warfare, for instance.

Similarly, the conventions of various competitive sports legitimize the phallic simulacrum in their various manifestations. In some sports, the pleasures of penetration and subtraction are strictly limited to the abstractions of time and distances: For example, it is socially unacceptable for a swimmer to physically assault his or her opponent in the quest for dominance, whereas in boxing, it is an essential part of the game. It is conventionally acceptable to show great joy in scoring against one's opponent—the stadium cheers at the moment of phallic penetration, at the pleasurable sight of conquest, at the frisson that comes from taking something away from someone else. The convention of most players consenting to play also serves to legitimate sport's brutal libidinal economy. Most participants in competitive sport do consent to playing the game; but once that consent is established, the pleasures of victory and distaste of failure are distributed as a direct result of the refusal of consent by the vanquished.

When, in the context of the philosophy of the limit, we consider the conventional pleasures of sport—the cries of victory when one puts the puck in the net of one's opponent, and the visible disappointment and dejection of the loser—we see the simulation of desire in the territorial project that transforms the puissances of human connection into the pouvoir of dominance and submission. Competitive sport, therefore, is a profoundly unethical way to organize desire. Significantly, it is a dominant feature of Euro-American popular entertainment culture and basic to the physical education of many children and young people. Increasingly, girls and women are lauded for joining in and doing it just like men and boys.

Competitive sort is frequently constructed as a public festival: the World Cup, the Super Bowl, the Commonwealth Games, the Olympic Games. The competitive sport festival offers the world an opportunity to enjoy the mean libidinal economy in which destruction (pouvoir) is given the value of creation (puissance). It is, as Nietzsche would say, a festival of cruelty.

Notes

1   A special 1997 edition of the *Sociology of Sport Journal*, 14(4) is devoted to the history of the sociology of sport.
2   Guttmann (1996) has written a little book of historical anecdotes on coitus and sports settings, from classical Greece to the present; but it does not analyze sport, sexuality, or desire.
3   See, for example, Burton-Nelson, 1994; Fusco, 1998; Griffin, 1998; Lenskyj, 1995; McKay, 1997; Messner & Sabo, 1994; Pronger, 1990; Whitson, 1994.

4   Susan Bordo (1993a) has done a wonderful job of demythologizing that phenomenon in "Reading the Male Body."
5   It could be said that in team sports, individuals give themselves over to their own team, thus opening and sharing space. There is some truth in this. However, I would counter that such sharing takes place only within the team, which constitutes itself as a phallic body relative to the other team. One's teammates, then, become phallic extensions of oneself, and vice versa.

References

Balsamo, A. (1998) *Technologies of the Gendered Body: Reading cyborg women.* Durham, NC: Duke University Press.

Bersani, L. (1987) Is the rectum a grave? *October, 43,* 197–222.

—— (1995) *Homos.* Cambridge, MA: Harvard University Press.

Bordo, S. (1993a) Reading the male body. *Michigan Quarterly Review,* 32: 696–737.

—— (1993b) *Unbearable Weight: Feminisms, Western Culture, and the Body.* Berkeley: University of California Press.

Burton-Nelson, M. (1994) *The Stronger Women Get, the More Men Love Football: Sexism and the American culture of sports.* New York: Harcourt Brace.

Cahn, S.K. (1994) *Coming on Strong: Gender and sexuality in twentieth-century women's sport.* Cambridge, MA: Harvard University Press.

Champagne, J. (1995) *The Ethics of Marginality.* Minneapolis: University of Minnesota Press.

Connell, R.W. (1990) An iron man: The body and some contradiction of hegemonic masculinity. In M. Messner & D. Dabo (Eds.), *Sport, Men, and the Gender Order* (pp. 83–96). Champaign IL: Human Kinetics.

Cooper, A. (1998) *Playing in the Zone: Exploring the spiritual dimensions of sports.* Boston: Shambhala.

Cornell, D. (1992) *The Philosophy of the Limit.* New York: Routledge.

Crawford, R. (1984) A cultural account of "health": Control, release, and the social body, in J.B. McKinlay (Ed.), *Issues in the Political Economy of Health Care* (pp. 60–106). New York: Tavistock.

Deleuze, G., & Guattari, F. (1983) *Anti-Oedipus: Capitalism and schizophrenia* (R. Hurley, M. Seem, & H. Lane, Trans.). Minneapolis: University of Minnesota Press.

—— (1987) *A Thousand Plateaus: Capitalism and schizophrenia* (B. Massumi, Trans.). Minneapolis: University of Minnesota Press.

Dews, P. (1987) *Logics of Disintegration: Post-structuralist thought and the claims of critical theory.* London: Verso.

Dover, K. (1978) *Greek Homosexuality.* Cambridge, MA: Harvard University Press.

Ebert, T. (1996) *Ludic Feminism and After: Postmodernism, desire, and labor in late capitalism* (Critical Perspectives on Women and Gender). Ann Arbor: University of Michigan Press.

Featherstone, M. (1991) The body in consumer culture. In M. Featherstone, M. Hepworth, & B.S. Turner (Eds.), *The Body: Social process and cultural theory* (pp. 170–197). London: Sage.

Foucault, M. (1979) *Discipline and Punish: The birth of the prison* (A. Sheridan, Trans.). New York: Vintage.

—— (1980) *The History of Sexuality: Vol. 1. An introduction* (R. Hurley, Trans.). New York: Vintage.

Fusco, C. (1998) Lesbians and locker rooms, in G. Rail (Ed.), *The Subjective Experiences of Lesbians in Sport* (pp. 87–116). Albany: SUNY Press.

Game, A. (1991) *Undoing the Social: Towards a deconstructive sociology.* Toronto: University of Toronto Press.

Goldstein, L. (1997) Signing the body electric: Buying into pop cult bodies. In P. Moore (Ed.), *Building Bodies.* New Brunswick, NJ: Rutgers University Press.

Gray, C.H. (Ed.) (1995) *The Cyborg Handbook.* New York: Routledge.

Griffin, P. (1998) *Strong Women, Deep Closets: Lesbians and homophobia in sport.* Champaign, IL: Human Kinetics.

Guttmann, A. (1996) *The Erotic in Sports.* New York: Columbia University Press.

Habermas, J. (1983) Modernity: An incomplete project. In H. Foster (Ed.), *The Anti-aesthetic: Essays on postmodern culture.* Port Townsend, WA: Pay Press.

Harvey, J., & Sparks, R. (1991) The politics of the body in the context of modernity. *Quest*, 43: 164–189.

Hoberman, J. (1994) The sportive-dynamic body as a symbol of productivity. In T. Sioebers (Ed.), *Heteropia: Postmodern utopia and the body politic* (pp. 1998–2228). Ann Arbor: University of Michigan Press.

Hutcheon, L. (1989) *The Politics of Postmodernism.* London: Routledge.

Jameson, F. (1984) Postmodernism or the cultural logic of late capitalism. *New Left Review*, 146: 52–92.

Jay, K. (Ed.) (1995) *Lesbian Erotics.* New York: New York University Press.

Kidd, B. (1987) Sports and masculinity. In M. Kauffman (Ed.), *Beyond Patriarchy: Essays by men on masculinity.* Toronto: Oxford University Press.

Kipnis, L. (1993) *Ecstasy Unlimited: On sex, capital, gender and aesthetics.* Minneapolis: University of Minnesota Press.

Lenskyj, H. (1995) Sport and the threat to gender boundaries. *Sporting Traditions*, 12(1): 47–60.

Lyotard, J.-F. (1984) *The Postmodern Condition: A report on knowledge* (G. Bennington & B. Massumi, Trans.). Minneapolis: University of Minnesota Press.

Mailer, N. (1983) *Ancient Evenings.* Boston: Little, Brown.

Massumi, B. (1997) *Realer Than Real: The simulacrum according to Deleuze and Guattari.* http://www.anu.edu.au/HRC/first_and_last/works/realer.htm.

Masten, J. (1997) Is the fundament a grave? In D. Hillman & C. Mazzio (Eds.), *The Body in Parts: Fantasies of corporeality in early modern Europe.* New York: Routledge.

McKay, J. (1997) *Managing Gender: Affirmative action and organizational power in Australian, Canadian, and New Zealand sport.* Albany: State University of New York Press.

Messner, M. (1992) *Power at Play.* Boston: Beacon.

Messner, M., & Sabo, D. (1994). *Sex, Violence, and Power in Sports: Rethinking masculinity.* Freedom, CA: Crossing Press.

Miller, T. (1993) *The Well-tempered Self: Citizenship, culture, and the postmodern subject.* Baltimore, MD: Johns Hopkins University Press.

Pronger, B. (1990) *The Arena of Masculinity: Sports, homosexuality, and the meaning of sex* (1st ed.). New York: St. Martin's.

—— (1999). Fear and trembling: Homophobia in men's sport. In P. White & K. Young (Eds.), *Sport and Gender in Canada* (pp. 197–214). Toronto: Oxford University Press.

—— (1999) Homosexuality and sport: Who's Winning? In J. McKay, M. Messner and D. Sabo (Eds.), *Masculinities and Sport*. London: Sage.

Robinson, L. (1998) *Crossing the Line: Violence and sexual assault in Canada's national sport*. Toronto: McClelland and Stewart.

Rogers, S.F. (1994) *Sportdykes: Stories from on and off the field*. New York: St. Martin's.

Roxxie. (1998) *Girljock: The book*. New York: St. Martin's.

Sabo, D., & Gordon, D. (Eds.) (1995) *Men's Health and Illness: Gender, power, and the body*. London: Sage.

Simpson, M. (Ed.) (1996) *Antigay*. London: Cassell.

Sykes, H. (1998) Turning the closets inside/out: Towards a queer-feminists theory in women's physical education. *Sociology of Sport Journal*, 15(2): 154–173.

Warner, M. (Ed.) (1993) *Fear of a Queer Planet: Queer politics and social theory*. Minneapolis: University of Minnesota Press.

Whiston, D (1990) Sport in the social construction of masculinity. In M. Messner & D. Sabo (Eds.), *Sport, Men, and the Gender Order: Critical feminist perspectives* (pp. 19–30). Champaign, IL: Human Kinetics.

—— (1994) The embodiment of gender: Discipline, domination, and empowerment. In S. Birrell & C.L. Cole (Eds.), *Women, Sport, and Culture* (pp. 353–372). Champaign, IL: Human Kinetics.

Chapter 12

Openly gay athletes

Contesting hegemonic masculinity in a homophobic environment*

Eric Anderson

Researchers who have examined the issue of gays in sports largely agree that organized sports are a highly homophobic institution (Bryant 2001; Clarke 1998; Griffin 1998; Hekma 1998; Messner 1992; Pronger 1990; Wolf Wendel, Toma, and Morphew 2001). Messner (1992: 34) said, "The extent of homophobia in the sports world is staggering. Boys (in sports) learn early that to be gay, to be suspected of being gay, or even to be unable to prove one's heterosexual status is not acceptable." Hekma (1998: 2) stated that "gay men who are seen as queer and effeminate are granted no space whatsoever in what is generally considered to be a masculine preserve and a macho enterprise." And Pronger (1990: 26) agreed, saying, "Many of the (gay) men I interviewed said they were uncomfortable with team sports. . . . Orthodox masculinity is usually an important subtext if not *the* leitmotif" in team sports.

Sports (particularly contact sports) have been described as a place in which hegemonic masculinity is reproduced and defined, as an athlete represents the ideal of what it means to be a man, a definition that contrasts what it means to be feminine and/or gay (Connell 1995; Messner 1992). And as women have increasingly gained access to once masculine-dominated institutions, sports have become contested terrain in which men try to validate masculine privilege through their ability to physically outperform women, thus symbolically dominating women (Burton-Nelson 1995).

However, as Griffin (1998) suggested, if gay male athletes, who are stigmatized as being feminine, can be as strong and competitive as heterosexual male athletes, they may threaten the perceived distinctions between gay men and straight men and thus the perceived differences between men and women as a whole. Bourdieu (2001) maintained that the gay man is uniquely situated to undermine masculine orthodoxy because of his unique ability to invisibly gain access to masculine privilege before coming out as

* Originally published as 'Openly gay athletes: contesting hegemonic masculinity in a homo-phobic environment' in *Gender & Society*, 2002, vol. 16, no. 6, 860–877. © Sage 2002.

gay. Because of this ability, the gay man may be uniquely positioned to align with feminists in a terrain of progressive coalition politics to symbolically attack male dominance. Thus, gay male athletes—who are seen as a paradox because they comply with the gendered script of being a man through the physicality involved in sports but violate another masculine script through the existence of same-sex desires—may threaten sport as a prime site of hegemonic masculinity and masculine privilege.

Homophobia, therefore, presents itself in the form of resistance against the intrusion of a gay subculture within sports and serves as a way of maintaining the rigidity of orthodox masculinity and patriarchy. Sports not only rejects homosexuality but also venerates hyperheterosexuality (Griffin 1998; Hekma 1998; Pronger 1990; Wolf Wendel, Toma, and Morphew 2001). Gay men are perceived "largely as deviant and dangerous participants on the sporting turf" in that they defy culturally defined structures of hegemonic masculinity (Clarke 1998: 145).

Drawing on Gramsci's (1971) notions of hegemony, in which a cultural group manages a dominant position, I examine two forms of hegemony in relation to gays in sports. First, I draw on Connell's (1995) notion of hegemonic masculinity, in which one form of masculinity (which includes being exclusively heterosexual and physically powerful) maintains its dominance by suppressing all others. Second, by using Butler's (1997) notions of heterosexual hegemony (in which heterosexuality is viewed as right and proper while homosexuality is stigmatized), I examine the gendering performance of sport and the queer contestation of it.

I look to sport as a site of contestation for the construction and reproduction of masculinity by qualitatively investigating how gay athletes challenge orthodox assumptions of masculinity by publicly coming out as gay within their high school or collegiate athletic teams. I examine how openly gay athletes are affected by homophobia, how they negotiate hegemonic masculinity, and how they operate within a heterosexist institution.

Despite the fact that they are both culturally silenced and are under constant threat of physical violence, gay male athletes define themselves as being treated well, perhaps because, as I show, there is a near absence of overt homophobia in the form of physical and verbal abuse. Sport only tolerates openly gay athletes as long as they are valuable to the mantra of athletics—winning. Otherwise, sport uses homophobic discourse, the threat of physical violence toward gay athletes, and the silencing of gay identities to maintain the virility of masculine hegemony and to prevent the acceptance of homosexuality in general, as well as to prevent the creation of a gay identity that shows homosexuality and athleticism as compatible. The same techniques are used regardless of whether the sport sits atop the masculine hierarchy (e.g., football) or is a marginalized sport (e.g., cross-country running).

Background

A significant use of sport in recent times has been to reproduce hegemonic masculinity by turning young boys away from qualities associated with femininity or homosexuality and (attempting) to teach them how to be masculine, heterosexual men (Adams 1993; Crosset 1990; Kidd 1987; Parks 1987). In the process, sport has become a leading definer of masculinity in a mass culture that has lost male initiation rituals (Connell 1995; Messner 1992). In fact, throughout the twentieth century, sport has served as a test of masculinity in Western societies. Sports remain a bastion of hegemonic masculinity, heterosexism, and homophobia today (Anderson 2000; Connell 1995; Griffin 1998; Hekma 1998; Messner 1992; Pronger 1990).

Although research on gay male athletes is generally limited (Bryant 2001; Hekma 1998; Pronger 1990; Wolf Wendel, Toma, and Morphew 2001), research on male athletes who are publicly out with their homosexuality to their ostensibly heterosexual teams has been nonexistent. Until now, our best understanding of the relationship between the gay male athlete and sport has come from researchers who have interviewed closeted gay male athletes (Hekma 1998), from athletes on all-gay teams (Price 2000), and from research on the attitudes held by heterosexual male athletes toward the possibility of openly gay athletes being on their teams (Wolf Wendel, Toma, and Morphew 2001). Indeed, studying openly gay athletes was not possible in what might be called a first wave of discrimination against gay athletes, because the social sanctions for coming out of the closet were simply too high. My research reflects a second wave of discrimination toward the gay athlete, characterized by a lessening of overt homophobia in recent years (Widmer, Treas, and Newcomb 1998).

While none of the previous studies illuminate the circumstances under which openly gay athletes play on heterosexual teams, they do draw attention to the fact that there appears to be more than one type of discrimination against gays in sport. While the most salient form of discrimination may be physical assault or verbal harassment, Pharr (1997) described another form of discrimination, heterosexism, as safeguarding the one form of sexuality (heterosexuality) deemed noble while marginalizing and stigmatizing homosexuality. The operations of heterosexism lead people to believe that the expression of heterosexuality is right, just, and natural, while all other forms of sexuality are immoral, unhealthy, or inferior. Butler (1997) described another component of discrimination in the use of repetitive homophobic discourse as a form of resistance toward the cultural acceptance of homosexuality. She suggested that this discourse changes the perceptual frameworks of gay identities, so that gay identity itself includes notions of deviance.

Despite the fact that American culture as a whole is rapidly moving away from both forms of homophobia (Loftus 2001), recent studies report that heterosexual athletes object to any notion of the desirability of gay male athletes (Hekma 1998; Price 2000; Wolf Wendel, Toma, and Morphew 2001). Wolf Wendel, Toma, and Morphew wrote, "Examining the overall message from these results, we found hostility to gay men and lesbians on nearly all teams and at all the case study sites. Clearly those in inter-collegiate athletics are generally unwilling to confront and accept homosexuality" (2001: 470). They attributed this attitude to the mandates of masculinity, which the informants believed stand in contrast to homosexuality, a hypothesis congruent with older research (Connell 1995; Messner 1992; Pronger 1990). Wolf Wendel, Toma, and Morphew believe that when compared to the liberalization of white attitudes regarding race, attitudes held by heterosexual athletes toward homosexuality have not progressed. They attribute this to the lack of experience with, or even knowledge of, openly gay male athletes.

Encouragingly, Price's (2000) ethnographic study of an English gay men's rugby team shows that when athletes do come out of the closet, the attitudes of their heterosexual opponents change. This is congruent with my own experience as an openly gay coach (Anderson 2000) in that the attitudes of other teams' athletes toward homosexuality slowly improved with each subsequent year I coached. However, Price found that the gay rugby team went through exhaustive measures to present an image of normality. Except for their sexual orientation, they attempted to present an image that they were just the same as the other rugby players. Price noted that players were required to conform to heterosexist structures and endure discriminatory practices to maintain acceptance in this setting. For example, players self-silenced by suppressing "camp" style (a gay form of verbal expression and body language) for a more orthodox masculine vernacular, and the club purposefully made little mention of the fact that the athletes were gay when talking to the press. The rugby athletes were also instructed by their coaches to be respectable in the locker rooms and not to engage in horseplay for fear that such play could be laced with camp-style behavior.

Research by Wolf Wendel, Toma, and Morphew (2001), Hekma (1998) and Price (2000) makes it evident that the transformative potential of gay athletes in sport is neutralized through potentially overt homophobia and also through covert mechanisms, such as the normalization of homophobic language and the silencing of gay discourse, identity, and behaviors.

Contrary to what many researchers might have predicted (Clarke 1998), and a noteworthy finding in its own right, none of the 26 openly gay athletes in my study were physically assaulted, and only 2 could recall being verbally harassed. This is not to say that homophobia did not present itself. Indeed, quite the opposite is true; sport was rife with homophobia, although openly gay athletes discounted its importance in assessing how they were treated. The data clearly show a persistent pattern of homophobia in all sports, regardless of whether the activity was a team sport, individual sport, contact sport, or noncontact sport.

Initially, this research set out to account for differences in contact sports (which are generally team sports) versus noncontact sports (which are generally individual sports) as Griffin (1998) has suggested that team sports might reproduce hegemonic masculinity while individual sports might reproduce a more subordinated masculinity. But surprisingly, these two categories did not seem to vary enough in their treatment of gay athletes to warrant further investigation. While I maintain that the type of sport influences how masculinity gets constructed—that graceful or individual sports do not reproduce hegemonic masculinity in the same way that football or hockey does—it seems that once an athlete does come out to a team, the manner in which he is treated is nearly the same, regardless of the sport played, at least in my small sample; so this finding may not be made more generally. While finding covert discrimination may not be surprising, finding a lack of physical and verbal aggression toward openly gay athletes suggests that the social production of orthodox masculinity in sport is not a perfectly integrated, self-reinforcing system. Quite the opposite, the mere existence of openly gay male athletes in sport suggests that hegemonic masculinity is not seamless and that it can and is already beginning to be contested.

Method

Finding participants for this research was difficult as few gay male athletes come out to the community and fewer still come out to their athletic teams. This scarcity is exacerbated by the fact that once an athlete does come out of the closet, he is more likely to drop out of sport because he may no longer feel that he needs the false representation of heterosexuality that being an athlete provides (Hekma 1998; Pronger 2000). I located 42 informants, of whom 26 were openly gay on their teams, through a variety of means. The majority came to me through the use of the Internet after I posted queries on gay Web sites and listservs. I also obtained informants by keeping e-mails that gay athletes sent to me after I published an article on gay athletes in the August 1999 issue of *XY Magazine*, a national magazine designed for gay youth.

I conducted this research from a grounded theory approach. Grounded theory is a way of generating theory from qualitative data (Corbin and Strauss 1990; Strauss and Corbin 1990). I attempted to understand the meanings that actors gave to their social experiences in sport, and grounded theory may be best suited for analyzing the relationship between hegemonic process and the social realities created by human actors in sport (Dilorio 1989). Based in masculinities research, and using Connell's (1995) concept of hegemonic masculinity as a heuristic tool, I use in-depth interviews to examine how gender is produced in sport and how openly gay athletes negotiate gender.

Athletes from the following sports were represented: bowling (1), cheerleading (1), crew (3), cross-country (8), diving (3), fencing (1), football (6), hockey (1), rodeo (1), rugby (1), soccer (6), speed skating (1), swimming (4), tennis (2), track (12), volleyball (2), waterpolo (3), and wrestling (3). Although 26 of the 42 informants were openly gay on their teams, openly gay athletes were represented in all of the sports mentioned with the exception of water polo. The number of teams represented above (59) is larger than the number of athletes in my sample (42) because some informants participated in more than one sport. Their ages ranged from 18 to 25 years.

An important characteristic of the sample is that almost all of the interviewees turned out to be exceptional athletes on their teams. In fact, the sample represented a number of state and national champions. This, of course, has serious theoretical implications regarding human capital and the acceptance of gay athletes (which falls outside the scope of this article), but it shows that the athletes had the chance to prove themselves before coming out, that they had essentially possessed enough of what I call masculinity insurance to be able to withstand the social sanctions of coming out publicly. Another proviso of the sample is that almost all of the athletes were on the team before coming out, so the results may not apply to a gay athlete who had not yet proven himself and had not already been accepted socially.

The sample included athletes from both contact and noncontact sports and from all regions of North America. Race could not be accounted for because there was not enough variation in the sample: informants identified as white. In addition, the sample may have been weighted toward cross-country and track athletes because of the respondents' interest in the fact that the researcher is an openly gay cross-country and track coach. The athletes' names have been changed to protect their identity, and the taped interviews are locked to restrict access to all but the principal investigator.

Criteria for inclusion in this study were that (1) athletes had participated on high school or college athletic team(s) during the past two years, (2) they had been aware of their homosexual orientation at the time they played, (3) they had competed in the sport for at least one full season, and (4) they were openly gay. Bisexual and heterosexual athletes were excluded, as were 16 athletes who considered themselves closeted on their teams and believed that their teammates were unaware of their homosexual orientation. To expand my sample of 26, I used data from eight in-depth interviews that were published in *Jocks: The Stories of America's Gay Male Athletes* by Dan Woog (1998). Although Woog is not an academic researcher, he is a respected and valuable contributor to the field through his journalistic interest in the subject.

Aside from using these published interviews, I conducted 26 in-depth interviews, mostly by phone. Although I came into the interviews with some preconceptions about what it would be like to be an openly gay athlete on a high school or college team, my intention was to hear the experiences of the athletes and to let the theory develop from the data. To facilitate this, the athletes were questioned in detail about their socialization into sport, why they chose their sport, what their experiences were as gay athletes, what those experiences meant to them, and how they dealt with homophobia in sport. The interviews were loosely structured, but I maintained a set of topics to use as a guideline. The taped interviews ranged from 40 to 90 minutes in length. Each tape was then transcribed, and the data were coded using an emerging set of themes.

While sport has been shown to be homophobic for both gay and lesbian athletes (Griffin 1998) there are important differences between the two. Women's athleticism in itself is a contradiction to femininity, so female athletes are frequently assumed to be lesbians. Because of these differences, I have chosen to examine the gay male athlete only; therefore, my findings cannot be generalized to women. Below, I review my findings in order of the major emergent themes in the data: coming out, segmented identities, and homophobic discourse.

Coming out

Given the homophobia of American society, one would hardly expect gay athletes to report positive experiences when coming out to their teams. Ryan contradicts this stereotype. A 19-year-old first-year student at a private university in California (a progressive state on gay issues), he came out to his crew team in a rather public manner. Ryan tried out for the team while wearing gay pride jewelry. His petite frame and leadership skills made him perfect for the position he occupies as a coxswain where his job is to order eight 200-pound athletes to row faster or harder. He yells at them, "Get your fucking oar in sync!" Yet Ryan reports never having once heard a negative comment from them.

"The whole school knows about me, so from the first day of practice the team also knew about me." His comment gives credence to Griffin's (1998) argument that athletes on teams in schools that already have a strong support structure for gays and lesbians will have an easier time than those who are not. "I thought the real test would be when we were out on the road, when we had to share a bed. That was when it would come down to it," he said. When the bedding situation worked out to where only three athletes needed to share a room, with two beds per room, one person could have their own bed. But the rowers did not want that bed to go to Ryan. They feared that not sharing a bed with him would send a message that they were homophobic. "We talked about it for a while, and we just pushed the two beds together and made one big one. That way nobody felt bad," Ryan said.

Ryan's experience was the notable exception for the 26 openly gay athletes. It may have been made better by the public manner in which he came out, the liberal attitudes of his coach and school, and the fact that the position he occupied in this sport is one that is often occupied by a woman so his team-mates were used to being ordered around by people who are further removed from the hegemonic form of masculinity. Still, Ryan's story helps illustrate that there is no one universal experience when coming out of the closet.

Most of the athletes I interviewed were unexpectedly pleased with their coming out experience. I asked, "If you could do it all over again, what, if anything, would you do differently?" Most of the participants reported that they would have come out earlier because it was not as difficult as they had thought it would be. One athlete said, "It was so much easier than I thought. Now I look back and wonder why the hell I didn't do it sooner." And another said, "I forgot what I was supposed to be so worried about after I came out."

But these informants may have over generalized how good things were. Further discussion with the informants, with the notable exception of Ryan, brought up less positive experiences. For example, one of the participants, Gabriel, initially spoke of his coming-out experience in glowing terms. He came out after two of his fellow teammates already had and said that his overall experience was "very good." He even praised his coach and teammates for their support:

> The first people I came out to were actually runners and my coach. I went to a private school, and one day we were sitting around talking . . . and a runner came out to us . . . so I did too. . . . From then, I was able to open up to other runners. . . . And no one really had a problem or an issue with the fact that we were gay.

Gabriel went on to tell me about his state finals 1,600-meter relay race:

> My friend (also openly gay) and I were approached by our other two (heterosexual) teammates right before the final race. They reached into their bag and pulled out two pairs of gay pride socks and said that they wanted us to wear them. We were really touched. And then they pulled out two more pairs and said that they were going to wear them in support of us.

Gabriel's experience seemed truly positive to him, especially in broad retrospect. But when I asked him for a more detailed account about his initial coming out, he recalled that all was not that blissful. Contradicting his earlier positive assessment, he indicated that he had actually lost a friend when word spread about his sexuality:

> We were at camp, and we had been around these guys for years, and someone had found out that we were gay and had a fit over it. I was kind of hurt by it. Certain things that were said were out of place. This individual completely left the camp and did not run that year because of

what his friends would think because he was running with us. . . . I'd say he was one of our good friends . . . he no longer spoke to me.

Gabriel typified how the athletes relayed their experiences to me. They began by speaking of their experience as a general positive, praising their teammates, and talking about how well accepted they felt. But when I began to inquire further as to just how they were treated, when I began asking questions about their overnight trips, the way their teams treated their lovers, or how their teams talked about their homosexuality, a different story emerged. I heard stories of extreme heterosexism, silencing, and the frequent use of homophobic discourse. But the pattern of athletes being in high spirits about their coming out was almost universal among the informants. They seemed unbothered and mostly unaware of the high degree of heterosexism and homophobic discourse that their stories often revealed.

What truly surprised me, however, was that even when I pointed out the inequality to the informants, they still did not seem to feel the impact of having been discriminated against. There was obviously something else occurring here. Something was preventing the athletes from feeling the substantial discrimination they encountered and from seeing it when I pointed it out to them.

While sociologists usually discuss people who compare themselves to others who have it better (Davies 1962; Tilly 1978), these athletes seemed to compare themselves to those who had it worse. It is often the fear of what might happen when gay athletes come out that enhances their sense of well-being, even if all was not well. In essence, I found a reverse relative deprivation occurring with the informants. Things seemed to go well for them in comparison to what might have been.

Before coming out, the athletes I interviewed generally saw their sport as being highly homophobic, as judged primarily through the unbridled use of homophobic discourse. But after coming out of the closet, the athletes were greeted by a much more hospitable team than they had imagined. Like most, Jason, a high school cross-country and track runner, feared that coming out to his teammates would be a difficult and possibly dangerous event:

> One of the things that was holding me back from coming out was, like, my own fear of locker room situations. Because in my mind I didn't want to make other people uncomfortable around me in the locker room, and I didn't want them to make it an issue. . . . I'd heard some horror stories from some of my friends. . . . One of my friend's friend was beaten to a bloody pulp because they thought he was gay.

Steve, another high school cross-country and track runner, also feared coming out: "I didn't know how they would react or what they would say. . . . It's like the fear of rejection, I guess." Charlie, a high school football player, who was outed to his teammates against his will, reports his outing as having been "positive," even "a relief," despite the fact that a few of his teammates decided they could no longer talk to him:

> Well, at first I didn't want to go to practice, 'cause I was scared about what was gonna happen. But my coaches came to me and said, "Don't worry it's gonna be OK; they (teammates) like you a lot." So I went out there, and I was kinda scared, but everyone kept being the same. You know, they kept being my friends, and there were like only two or three that stopped talking to me . . . and one of them, I used to be best friends with him . . . and as soon as he found out he stopped talking to me.

Charlie defined having only "two or three" players stop talking to him because of his sexual orientation as a good result because Charlie had expected to lose all his teammates' friendships.

The fear of violence or a negative response by athletes to one's homosexuality may partially come from the fact that athletes are often the unofficial rule enforcers of hegemonic masculinity in school settings (Bissinger 1990; Miracle and Rees 1994; Wilson 2002) and even gay nonathletes may fear homophobia from athletes. For example, Derek, who came out to his school before joining a team said, "I didn't have any problems at the school, *even* from the people on the sports teams," indicating that he had expected the athletes to be less accepting than the school population at large.

The fear of violence is justified. I once coached a heterosexual track athlete who was physically beaten by a member of the school's football team who assumed him to be gay. A 250-pound football player sat on him and beat him, fracturing four facial bones and trying to gouge his eyes out with his fingers as he yelled, "I'm going to kill you, you fucking cross-country faggot" simply because his coach was gay (Anderson 2000). And recall Jason describing how one of his friends was "beaten to a bloody pulp" because some athletes thought he too was gay.

Herek and Berrill (1992) described these types of events as hate crimes because they send a message to all in the gay community to "watch out, this can happen to you," effectively terrorizing an entire community. While my study had no such cases of physical abuse to report, the highly publicized story of Greg Congdon, a high school football player in a small Pennsylvania town, helps spread fear to all gay athletes.

Greg, an average football player, was outed against his will after a suicide attempt. The word soon got back to his teammates, and despite the fact that Greg had been their close friend, he was shunned and threatened with physical violence if he were to return to the team (Greg never competed on a team as an openly gay athlete). His story was covered by ESPN, and I interviewed him after seeing it. "I walked into the school and I started getting shoved around, and pushed around. My friends wouldn't talk to me, so that kind of made me really hate myself more. Like, I was told that if I played any sports, that they'd make my life living hell." Teammates drove by Greg's house at night shouting homophobic and threatening taunts, and his teammates, coaches, and even his best friends all ceased conversing with him, effectively marginalizing him from his community.

Greg's story and the story of the young men I coached highlight how severe the intolerance of gay athletes can be. But Greg's story is by far the worst of all the participants I interviewed. While my sample is too small and unrepresentative to make the claim that physical aggression and verbal harassment toward openly gay males in high school and college sports does not happen, it does show that sport is not always overtly homophobic. These results seem not only different from what researchers have predicted but also different than what many of the athletes had expected. I argued that it is these fears that inflated the sense of well-being among the informants, resulting in a reverse relative deprivation.

Segmented identities

I talked to Tim, an openly gay tennis player, and asked him if he was treated any differently after coming out. "No," he said. "They didn't really treat me as gay, if that's what you mean. In fact, they didn't even mention it really. They just treated me like one of the guys and stuff. Sorta like nothing had changed or anything." I then asked him if this included verbal sexualizing of women. "Yeah, they ask me like who I think is hot and stuff." But when I asked Tim if they ever asked him what guys he thought were hot he replied, "Hell no. They'd never do that. They don't want to hear that kind of stuff."

Tim's experience is one of a segmented identity. His teammates know he is gay but don't treat him as if he were. They are willing to recognize his athletic accomplishments but unwilling to talk of his social/sexual life as they do with the heterosexual athletes. Perhaps his teammates think they are doing what is best for Tim, and perhaps Tim thinks it is what is best too. The situation is one of "don't ask, don't tell," a compromise that allows gay athletes to reveal their true sexual orientation (at least once) but allows heterosexual athletes to pretend that nothing has changed—thus denying the gay athletes' true identity.

Ken, an NCAA champion track runner, illustrated the don't ask, don't tell policy well when he said,

> And even to this day, people know, but people just won't say it. . . . It's like they just can't talk about it. It makes me so uncomfortable knowing that some people know, but then they still ask me about girls . . . it's really frustrating. . . . Not one time on the team did anyone ask me, "Ken, are you gay?"

Most of the time, however, the gay athletes failed to recognize that their identities were being denied, and they often took part in their own oppression by self-silencing and partaking in heterosexual dialogue. Jeff, a college cross-country runner and soccer player, illustrated collusion in his own oppression when he informed me that he frequently engaged in conversations about women with them as if he were heterosexual. "The guys will be talking about girls and stuff, and they will ask me what I think of somebody, and I'll just say, yeah, she's hot, or something like that."

Victimized by a hegemony that resists discourse on homosexuality, gay athletes often view their silencing as acceptable and fall into a negotiated, segmented identity that contributes to their own culture of silence (Hekma 1998). One reason is that athletes, out of fear of either physical hostility or discrimination, are simply too afraid to talk much about their sexuality (Griffin 1998). The other reason is that athletes may not know why they don't discuss their sexuality; they just feel that it is not right for them to discuss their sexuality on par with heterosexual athletes. Gay athletes often excuse this by repeating what Frank said to me: "Sport is not the appropriate place for such discussions." He later added, "Well, it's none of their business." And, Rob, a crew athlete who came out implicitly to his team by snuggling with another guy in a cold boathouse, said that he never really talked about it after that. When I asked him why, he replied, "I just didn't feel it was necessary. It never really came up. I mean I didn't jump out of the closet at them, or force my homosexuality on them." A runner said, "The gay thing was never talked about because we ran together; we enjoyed running cross-country, and that was the extent of it."

Rob's use of the phrase "forcing my homosexuality" to describe a simple affirmation of his sexuality and the runner's phrase "the gay thing" take on tones of heterosexual hegemony in which any proclamation of hetero-sexuality is "just" and "right" and never scrutinized, but the mere mention of homosexuality is perceived as being "in your face" (Butler 1997; Connell 1995; Messner 1992; Pharr 1997; Pronger 1990, 2000). Presumably, it is perceived as being in your face because it opens up a door to the development of a gay culture within sport or because it legitimates homosexuality. Perhaps this is why the informants failed to see that their teams often followed a norm of not talking about their sexual identity, or social/sexual life, even when the team talked openly about the sexual identity or social/sexual lives of their heterosexual counterparts. Whatever the reason, the don't ask, don't tell policy not only existed between gay athletes and their straight teammates but surprisingly also existed between gay athletes themselves. One athlete described the sport of diving to me as "a gay Mecca," but with the unusual twist that "nobody talks about it." He said, "Everyone knows about everyone else, but no one talks about it. . . . It's not a big gay thing; you go, you dive, and you leave."

Homophobic discourse

Frank, an openly gay football player, told me that he was surprised at how well he was received on his team because his teammates had used such a high degree of homophobic discourse on this team before he came out:

> I couldn't believe how cool the guys were with me. I mean I expected them to be really unaccepting of me because they'd called me a fag for so long. I mean, they call everyone a fag, so it's not like they thought I was gay or anything, but still I thought that when they found out I really was, you know gay, that they'd hate me.

When I asked him if they still call him a fag now that he came out he responded, "No. Not really. I mean, every now and then they might say it, but they usually apologize and say that they didn't mean it that way."

Athletes in my study commonly heard one heterosexual teammate say to another, "knock it off, fag" as a form of venting frustration with another or in a supposed jocular manner. One football player told me, "Oh yeah, I hear 'fag' all the time." When I asked him if he used the word "fag" the way his teammates do he replied, "No. No. I did before I came out of the closet, but not now." And when I asked why, he responded, "I don't know. I guess it's just not cool."

Furthermore, none of the athletes in my sample reported being called a fag in a harassing or violent manner. (Greg was not part of my sample because he had not actually competed as an openly gay athlete). They may have heard "hurry up fag," but they did not hear "knock it off you faggot." In fact, most of the athletes reported that their heterosexual teammates tried not to use the word "fag" in association with them at all, even if they did continue to use it as an insult among each other.

Despite the attempts of some of their teammates to reduce homophobic discourse through use of the word "fag," most informants reported much less sensitivity toward their teammates' use of the word "gay." Frank said, "Oh yeah, they say everything is gay if they don't like it. I mean, if you're being dumb, they say, 'don't be gay,' and if your team was given a penalty unfairly they say, 'that's so gay.'" Ken said, "They say, 'this is gay,' and 'that's gay,' but they don't mean it like that," even though Ken reports not using the word in such manner himself. In fact, none of the informants strongly objected to the use of the word "gay" by their teammates to describe things distasteful, even though they did not use the word in such a manner themselves.

These findings are consistent with that of both Hekma (1998) and Price (2000), who each found that gay athletes frequently hear antigay language spoken by their heterosexual teammates and opponents, yet they report that the gay athletes themselves do not necessarily view this language as being homophobic. Price argued that homophobic language takes on a significantly different meaning, as it appears to be an accepted element of the game. And Hekma found that antigay verbal harassment was reported so frequently that gay athletes treated it casually, dismissing it by saying, "they didn't really mean anything by it."

Many of the openly gay athletes I interviewed did not seem to take offense to the use of the words "fag" or "gay," justifying their use in the same way that Hekma (1998) found by saying, "Oh, they didn't mean it that way." But unlike Hekma's respondents, not all athletes in my sample dismissed the hostile capacity of such discourse. Specifically, many of the closeted athletes felt that it created a hostile environment, and they used such discourse to gauge the level of comfort their teams maintained toward homosexuality. Indeed, most of the closeted athletes I interviewed reported that one of the reasons they had not come out was because they felt their teammates were highly homophobic, as evidenced by homophobic discourse. Jon, a closeted high school football player, described his sport as "the most homophobic" by saying that "everything was fag this and fag that." One openly gay informant said to me that before he came out he feared doing so because of the degree of homophobic discourse he heard on his team: "I was totally afraid to come out to my teammates; I mean they are always calling other people fags and stuff."

Highlighting the operation of this discourse in discrimination, Thorne (1998), McGuffey and Rich (1999), Davis (1990), and Adams (1993) have all shown that a primary way to maximize the influence of hegemonic masculinity is for one male to call another a "fag" or accuse him of being "gay." Even if one does not seriously think the other is gay, by stigmatizing another male, a male shows that he is meeting at least one mandate of hegemonic masculinity—that of being heterosexual—while raising his social status at the expense of another.

Interestingly, almost all of the athletes reported hearing frequent use of the word "fag," regardless of whether they played a contact or noncontact sport. Therefore, members of lower-status sports, such as cross-country or tennis, seem to borrow the same tools of orthodox masculinization and hegemony as members of higher-status sports such as football.

I believe that such behavior is rooted in the fact that it is truly impossible for one to prove that he is heterosexual, as it is commonly known that gay males frequently pass by having sexual and romantic liaisons with women. In the narrow field of sport, where heterosexuality is compulsory, and homosexuality is taboo, effeminacy and gayness are essentially considered the same. Thus, regardless of the true sexual orientation of the individual in question, the word "fag" serves to relegate one to the sphere of being "a lesser man," a position that brings much strife. In fact, Adams (1993) credited the stress of always being thought gay for the early retirement of several professional figure skaters.

What my research does not answer is just why some gay athletes felt that homophobic discourse created an air of hostility toward them, while others did not. Perhaps it is because athletes who come out, or were outed, discovered unexpected acceptance levels that blinded them to the homophobic discourse. Or perhaps it is because the openly gay athletes in my study were so good (they were almost exclusively the best on their teams) that they did not perceive the discourse of "fag" as pertaining to them because they approximated many of the mandates of hegemonic masculinity through their athleticism.

Conclusion

Male-dominated sports have been described as a mainstay for the reproduction of hegemonic masculinity. But openly gay athletes, even though they may conform to all other mandates of orthodox masculinity with the exception of their sexuality, threaten the ability of sports to reproduce the hegemonic form of masculinity. Rather, gay male athletes, especially those who prove to be as good as or better than heterosexual athletes, threaten to soften hegemonic masculinity. In doing so, they may help open the doors to increased acceptance of subjugated masculinities, such as gay identities, and perhaps even the acceptance of female athleticism.

In this research, the first to be conducted with openly gay high school and collegiate athletes, I examined how openly gay athletes negotiate hegemonic masculinity in a homophobic environment. I found that openly gay athletes were generally surprised by how well they were treated. They frequently credited their coaches and teammates as being open-minded and accepting. However, these athletes may have overstated this acceptance because they were treated better than they had expected to be. This reverse relative deprivation was largely influenced by the fact that they were not physically assaulted or verbally harassed—the opposite of what most expected before coming out.

However, to show that these athletes encountered little physical or verbal hostility is not to say that there was an absence of homophobia in sports. Indeed, homophobia appeared in many ways, including the presence of a don't ask, don't tell policy in which gay athletes' sexual identities were not treated on par with that of heterosexual athletes. In fact, heterosexual discourse is so pervasive in sport that it subtly leads gay athletes to feel that they have no right to discuss their sexuality, despite the overflowing discussions of heterosexuality around them.

In this manner, sport is not unlike the U.S. military, another highly masculinized institution, which bans openly gay and lesbian soldiers under the now famous 1994 U.S. military policy of don't ask, don't tell. Britton and Williams (1995) showed that the silencing of gays and lesbians in the U.S. armed services reflects institutional and cultural privileging of a heterosexual masculine ideal. Through the use of sanctions and conscious control, the U.S. military attempts to ensure the reproduction of soldiers as hegemonically masculine. Comparing the situation of openly gay athletes to that of the U.S. military's don't ask, don't tell policy highlights that what cannot be discussed is just as powerful a weapon of heterosexual hegemony as what can be discussed.

In the absence of an ability to ban openly gay athletes from sport, heterosexual athletes within both contact and noncontact team sports resisted the intrusion of openly gay athletes through the creation of a culture of silence around gay identities. Although publicly out, the informants in this study were victimized by heterosexual hegemony and largely maintained a heteronormative framework by self-silencing their speech and frequently engaged in heterosexual dialogue with their heterosexual teammates. The combined effect of the attempted silencing of gay identities within sport and the willful promotion of heterosexuality serves to venerate heterosexuality, while marginalizing homosexuality (Butler 1997; Connell 1995; Messner and Sabo 1990; Pronger 1990) and prevents homosexuality from being seen as compatible with athleticism.

The heteronormativity of sport was further maintained through the use of homophobic discourse geared to discredit homosexuality and treat it as something loathsome. Heterosexual athletes habitually ostracized other (assumed heterosexual) athletes by calling them "fags" and referred to unjust situations as being "gay"—an occurrence that happened so often that many of the gay athletes dismissed the harmful potential of such discourse. Homophobic discourse as an acceptable form of expression also perpetuates heterosexual hegemony and dominance and is powerful in preventing the softening of hegemonic masculinity.

I theorize that the normalization of homophobic dialogue in American sport serves to subjugate the gay male identity as an inferior form of masculinity and helps marginalize gay athletes so that they must maintain segmented identities. Their identities as athletes are accepted but their identities as gay are not. In contrast, heterosexual athletes more closely conform to hegemonic masculinity, so their identities as heterosexual and athletes are nearly synonymous.

Butler (1997) suggested that this antigay discourse is part of a larger heterosexist framework, which inhibits the acceptance of homosexuality. I add that by creating a hostile environment toward the acceptance of homosexuality, even before the team is made aware of the actual presences of a gay athlete on the team, such discourse helps protect the reproduction of hegemonic masculinity from the threat of gay athleticism. It sends a message that homosexuality is not welcomed. This homophobic discourse has proven to be almost as effective as an all-out ban on gay athletes from sport (Wolf Wendel, Toma, and Morphew 2001).

Taken together, the creation of a culture of silence combined with the normalization of antigay discourse makes it difficult for gay male athletes to establish social connections within the sport that are necessary for the production of a positive gay athletic identity, one that would view homosexuality and athleticism as compatible. So while I may have found a near lack of overt discrimination against openly gay athletes, sports, whether they are contact or noncontact, remain steadfast in their reproduction of heterosexual hegemony and hegemonic masculinity.

Still, heterosexual athletes do allow for some gay males to participate within sport, and one could argue that the mere presence of openly gay males in sport suggests that the antecedents are there for the development of a gay identity within. Just why these particular gay athletes have been permitted within sport is an important question. And the answer, I maintain, is that heterosexual athletes are willing to tolerate gay athletes if they comply with the overarching motif of sport—winning. The openly gay male athletes in this study were all the best on their teams, while the closeted gay male athletes represented more average athletic abilities. Thus, gay athletes essentially had enough "masculinity insurance" to withstand the blast of coming out of the closet, and their heterosexual teammates allowed them to exist without overt discrimination because they helped their teams win. Yet these openly gay athletes are really neither welcomed nor accepted; rather, they appear to be merely tolerated, and one would certainly wonder how an athlete would be treated who came out as an openly gay benchwarmer. As one athlete described to me, "you don't mess with the best." Of course, in this case I might add, "you don't mess with the best," as long as they comply with the masculine norms of dominance, competitiveness, and winning, and the other mandates of hegemonic masculinity including a form of don't ask, don't tell silence about their sexual identity.

Finally, the data suggest that while heterosexual athletes are not likely to accept the creation of a substantial gay subculture anytime soon, gay athletes are beginning to contest sport as a site of hegemonic masculine production. Perhaps most encouraging is the fact that I could conduct this research at all, that there is a new phenomenon of openly gay male athletes who come out in high school and collegiate sports. This suggests that hegemony in the athletic arena is not seamless, and sport will remain contested terrain for years to come.

References

Adams, M. L. (1993) To be an ordinary hero: Male figure skaters and the ideology of gender. In T. Haddad (ed.), *Men and masculinities*. Toronto: Canadian School Press.

Anderson, Eric (2000) *Trailblazing: The true story of America's first openly gay track coach*. Los Angeles: Alyson Books.

Bissinger, H. G. (1990) *Friday Night Lights: A town, a team, and a dream*. Reading, MA: Addison-Wesley.

Bourdieu, Pierre (2001) *Masculine Domination*. Translated by Richard Nice. Stanford, CA: Stanford University Press.

Britton, Dana M., and Christine L. Williams (1995) "Don't ask, don't tell, don't pursue": Military policy and the construction of heterosexual masculinity. *Journal of Homosexuality* 30 (1): 1–21.

Bryant, Michael (2001) *Gay Male Athletes and the Role of Organized Team and Contact Sports*. Unpublished master's thesis, Seattle Pacific University.

Burton-Nelson, Mariah (1995) *The Stronger Women get the More Men Love Football: Sexism and the American culture of sports*. New York: Avon Books.

Butler, Judith P. (1997) *Gender Trouble: Feminism and the subversion of identity*. New York: Routledge.

Clarke, G. (1998) Queering the pitch and coming out to play: Lesbians and physical education in sport. *Sport, Education, and Society* 3 (2): 145–60.

Connell, Robert W. (1995) *Masculinities*. Berkeley: University of California Press.

Corbin, J., and A. Strauss. (1990) Grounded theory research: Procedures, canon, and evaluative criteria. *Qualitative Sociology* 13 (1): 3–21.

Crosset, Todd (1990) Masculinity, sexuality, and the development of early modern sport. In Michael Messner and Don Sabo (eds.), *Sport, Men and the Gender Order: Critical feminist perspectives*. Champaign, IL: Human Kinetics.

Davies, James (1962) Toward a theory of revolution. *American Sociological Review* 27: 5–19.

Davis, Laurel (1990) Male cheerleaders and the naturalization of gender. In Michael Messner and Donald Sabo (eds.), *Sport, Men and the Gender Order*. Champaign, IL: Human Kinetics.

Dilorio, J. A. (1989) Feminism, gender, and the ethnographic study of sport. *Arena Review* 13 (1): 49–59.

Glaser, Barney, and Anselm Strauss (1967) *The Discovery of Grounded Theory: Strategies for qualitative research*. New York: Aldine De Gruyter.

Gramsci, Antonio (1971) *Selections from Prison Notebooks*. London: New Left Books.

Griffin, Pat (1998) *Strong Women, Deep Closets: Lesbians and homophobia in sport*. Champaign, IL: Human Kinetics.

Hekma, Gert (1998) As long as they don't make an issue of it . . .: Gay men and lesbians in organized sports in the Netherlands. *Journal of Homosexuality* 35 (1): 1–23.

Herek, Gregory M., and Kevin Berrill (1992) *Hate Crimes: Confronting violence against lesbians and gay men*. Newbury Park, CA: Sage.

Kidd, Bruce (1987) Sport and masculinity. In Michael Kaufman (ed.), *Beyond Patriarchy: Essays by men on pleasure, power, and change*. Toronto, Canada: Oxford University Press.

Loftus, Jeni (2001) America's liberalization in attitudes toward homosexuality, 1973 to 1998. *American Sociological Review* 66 (5): 762–82.

McGuffey, C. Shawn, and Lindsay B. Rich (1999) Playing in the gender transgression zone: Race, class, and hegemonic masculinity in middle childhood. *Gender & Society* 13 (5): 608–10.

Messner, Michael (1992) *Power at Play: Sports and the problem of masculinity*. Boston: Beacon.

Messner, Michael, and Donald F. Sabo. (1990) *Sport, Men and the Gender Order: Critical feminist perspectives*. Champaign, IL: Human Kinetics.

Miracle, Andrew W., and C. Roger Rees (1994) *Lessons of the Locker Room: The myth of school sports*. Amherst, NY: Prometheus Books.

Parks, Roberta (1987) Biological thought, athletics and the formation of a "man of character": 1830–1900. In J. A. Mangan and James Walvin (eds.), *Manliness and Morality*. Manchester, UK: Manchester University Press.

Pharr, Suzanne (1997) *Homophobia: A weapon of sexism*. Berkeley, CA: Chardon Press.

Price, Michael (2000) *Rugby as a Gay Men's Game*. Unpublished dissertation, University of Warwick.

Pronger, Brian (1990) *The Arena of Masculinity: Sports, homosexuality, and the meaning of sex*. New York: St. Martin's.

—— (2000) Homosexuality and sport: Who's winning? in, J. McKay, M. Messner, and D. Sabo (eds.), *Masculinities and Sport*. London: Sage.

Strauss, Anselm, and Juliet Corbin (1990) *Basics of Qualitative Research: Grounded theory procedures and techniques*. Newbury Park, CA: Sage.

Thorne, Barrie (1998) Girls and boys together . . . but mostly apart: Gender arrangements in elementary school. In Michael Kimmel and Michael Messner (eds.), *Men's Lives*, 4th ed. Boston: Allyn & Bacon.

Tilly, Charles (1978) *From Mobilization to Revolution*. Reading, MA: Addison-Wesley.

Widmer, Eric D., Judith Treas, and Robert Newcomb (1998) Attitudes toward nonmarital sex in 24 countries. *Journal of Sex Research* 35 (4): 349.

Wilson, Brian (2002) The "anti-jock" movement: Reconsidering youth resistance, masculinity, and sport culture in the age of the Internet. *Sociology of Sport Journal* 19 (2): 206–33.

Wolf Wendel, Lisa, Douglas Toma, and Christopher Morphew (2001) How much difference is too much difference? Perceptions of gay men and lesbians in intercollegiate athletics. *Journal of College Student Development* 42 (5): 465–79.

Woodward, Rachel (2000) Warrior heroes and little green men: Soldiers, military training, and the construction of rural masculinities. *Rural Sociology* 65 (4): 6–40.

Woog, Dan (1998) *Jocks: True stories of America's gay male athletes*. Los Angeles: Alyson Books.

Postscript

Paul Davis and Charlene Weaving

Iris Marion Young (1979) concludes the first essay of this anthology with the suggestion that 'the liberation of women and the liberation of sport . . . require . . . the invention of new sports and the inclusion in our concept of sport of physical activities presently outside or on the boundaries of sport.' To what extent, three decades later, have Young's prescriptions materialised?

There is a conspicuous emergence of new sports in the last two decades or so, the ethos of which ought to please feminist sports philosophers and activists opposed to the hypermasculinity of traditional sport. Loland (Tannsjo and Tamburrini 2000: 54) observes windsurfing, off-road biking, surfing, skateboarding, and snowboarding. Citing Humphreys (1997) approvingly, Loland suggests that sports such as these are 'expressions of youthful opposition, of rebellion against quantification and objectification in favour of playfulness' (54). (Sports such as these are now sometimes called – oddly – 'lifestyle' sports.)[1] Whitson (Birrell and Cole 1994: 363 and 365), writing several years earlier, argues persuasively that the recent interest in noncombative sports and physical activities, such as running, cross-country skiing, aerobics, dance and yoga, manifests alternative understandings of physical empowerment that are robustly emancipatory for both women and men.

However, neither Young nor Loland nor Whitson nor any other contributor was liable to believe that the emergence of sports such as those above is sufficient for the liberation of either sport or women. Germaine Greer (Greer 1999: 18) complained in 1999 that the world is less feminist than thirty years ago, and these downbeat words might yet apply to sport, despite the preceding interstices of opposition. At the elite level, commercial motivations are now monstrous. Sporting events, stadia, clubs, and tournaments vie unsettlingly to be the 'biggest' or 'biggest ever'. For instance, Manchester United's status as 'the biggest football club in the world' gets almost as much excited and admiring mileage as their now formidable record or the quality of their play. Similarly, the unprecedented 'bigness' of the Beijing 2008 Olympics was the flagship theme during a bloated 'countdown'. The phallic territorializing described in Chapter 11 by Pronger has rippled outwards from the contest to the realm of structural and institutional discourse. Elite performers are now, in terms of wealth and status, more remote than ever from followers more eager than ever to supplicate and to fund. The feminist distaste and suspicion of idolatry, grandstanding, and territorializing aggrandizement has much to busy itself with in the elite sport world of today.

Similarly, the sexualisation, heterosexism, 'emphasised femininity', hyper-masculinity, and homophobia of which contributors to this anthology complain continue to disfigure present-day sport. Was the exultation that characterised the Anglo-American reaction to Maria Sharapova's 2004 Wimbledon win over Serena Williams entirely a response to the flair of the former and the new name on the trophy? Or was it at all inscribed by the fact that the muscularity and greater power of Williams makes her signifi-cantly less 'heterosexually successful' than Sharapova? Does the poignant story of thoughtful, aesthetic, and heterosexual footballer Graeme Le Saux (http://www.timesonline.co.uk/tol/sport/football/premier_league/article2419 068.ece) betray something yet more parochial and defensive than mere homophobia, i.e. a panicky confusion about 'non-laddish' heterosexual men? Examples could no doubt be multiplied.

Patrick Grim posits an ideal, polyandrogynist society in which 'each person could choose any combination of morally acceptable behaviors and psychological traits, regardless of that person's sex' (Grim 1981: 65).[2] He subsequently observes that this ideal is obstructed by the social images of the sexes, images in turn perpetuated by the social structure of sports (67). Therefore, we have moral reason to change the social structure of sports (67). The reflections throughout this book suggest that approximately two decades of social evolution leave Grim's conclusions current, despite some genuinely upbeat developments. It is business as usual, though not business without hope. The trajectory and form of that business will continue to be a matter of intriguing contestation.

Notes

1   For discussion of lifestyle sports, see Wheaton (2004).
2   Grim acknowledges that the anti-androgynist might counter that 'just which behaviours are morally acceptable depends on one's sex' (ibid. 68). He opts to sidestep the question at this point. At any rate, it would be difficult to find any anti-androgynist who believes that all sex-indexed behavioural pressures, in sport and elsewhere, are moral requirements grounded in sex.

References

Birrell, S. and Cole, C.L. (1994) Women, Sport and Culture. Champaign, Il: Human Kinetics.
Greer, G. (1999) The Whole Woman, 2nd edn. London: Anchor.

Grim, P. (1981) 'Sport and two androgynisms', *Journal of the Philosophy of Sport*, 8(1): 64–68.

Humphreys, D. (1997) '"Skinheads go mainstream?" Snowboarding and alternative youth', *International Review for the Sociology of Sport*, 32: 2.

Tannsjo, T. and Tamburrini, C. (2000) *Values in Sport*. London: E & FN Spon.

The Times (2007) 'How gay slurs almost wrecked my career', 10 September. Available from: http://www.timesonline.co.uk/tol/sport/football/premier_league/article2419068.ece.

Wheaton, B. (ed.) (2004) *Understanding Lifestyle Sport: Consumption, Identity and Difference*. London: Routledge.

Recommendations for further reading

Mann, P.S. (1994) *Micro-Politics: Agency in a Postfeminist Era*. Minneapolis: University of Minnesota Press.

Prokhovnik, R. (1999) *Rational Woman: A Feminist Critique of Dichotomy*. London: Routledge.

Young, I.M. (1990) *Throwing Like a Girl and Other Essays in Feminist Philosophy and Social Theory*. Bloomington, Indiana: Indiana University Press.

Index

Routledge Sport

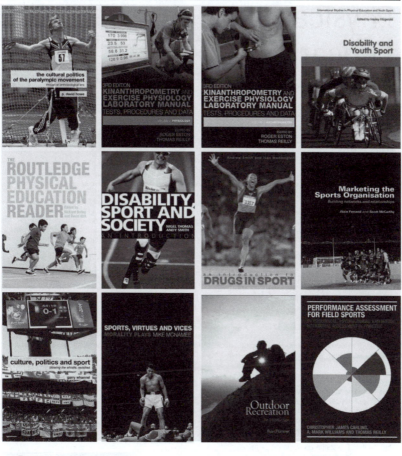

Physical Activity and Health
Second Edition
The Evidence
Explained

Adrianne Hardman, Loughborough University, UK
David Stensel, Loughborough University, UK

Now in a fully updated and revised edition, Physical Activity and Health explains clearly, systematically and in detail the relationships between physical activity, health and disease, and examines the benefits of exercise in the prevention and treatment of a wide range of important health conditions.

The book critically considers the evidence linking levels of physical activity with disease and mortality. It explores the causes of specific health conditions and syndromes prevalent in developed societies, such as cardiovascular disease, Type 2 diabtetes, obesity and cancer, and discusses the role of physical activity in their prevention or alleviation. Throughout, the book draws on cutting edge research literature and is designed help the student to evaluate the quality and significance of the scientific evidence. A concluding section explores broader themes in exercise and public health, including therapeutic uses of exericse; exercise and ageing; children's health and exercise, and physical activity and public health policy, and includes a critical appraisal of current recommendations for physical activity. Containing useful pedagogical features throughout, including chapter summaries, study activities, self evaluation tasks, guides to 'landmark' supplementary reading and definitions of key terms, and richly illustrated with supporting case-studies, tables, figures and plates, Physical Activity and Health is an essential course companion. It is vital reading for degree-level students of sport and exercise science, public health, physical therapy, medicine, nursing and nutrition.

R Routledge
Taylor & Francis Group

April 2009
PB: 978-0-415-42198-0: **£29.99**
HB: 978-0-415-45585-5: **£85.00**

www.routledge.com/sport